THE PERSISTENCE OF VIOLENCE

THE PERSISTENCE OF VIOLENCE

Colombian Popular Culture

TOBY MILLER

RUTGERS UNIVERSITY PRESS
New Brunswick, Camden, and Newark, New Jersey, and London

LCCN 2019045294

A British Cataloging-in-Publication record for this book is available from the British Library.

∞ The paper used in this publication meets the requirements of the American National Standard for Information Sciences—Permanence of Paper for Printed Library Materials, ANSI Z39.48-1992.

www.rutgersuniversitypress.org

Manufactured in the United States of America

CONTENTS

THE PERSISTENCE OF VIOLENCE

INTRODUCTION

The Persistence of Violence

This book emerged from my desire to understand the history and present moment of violence in Colombia, as incarnated in popular culture. It bears in mind the immediate and vital question of a putative end to the conflict involving the Fuerzas Armadas Revolucionarias de Colombia (the FARC) and other *guerrilla*[1]—a conflict that has gripped the nation during the lifetime of virtually all its citizens. But the book does not principally focus on that issue. Instead, it considers violence "beyond" the conflict, as simultaneously an ordinary and extraordinary part of Colombian life; something both normal and shocking, accepted and reviled—and contested.

My personal experience of Colombia dates from inaugurating the country's first doctoral program in communications, at the Universidad del Norte in Barranquilla in 2011. I subsequently worked for twelve weeks a year at UniNorte across three annual visits between 2014 and 2018, giving graduate classes when in Colombia, and advising doctoral students and researching and writing with faculty then and while away. I also taught for some months at the Universidad Tecnológica de Bolívar in Cartagena de Indias in 2019. Over my time spent on the Caribbean coast, I have addressed various topics related to the popular and violence, on my own and with colleagues. I learnt much from them and from students. *The Persistence of Violence* is the product of those efforts, and several chapters involve coauthors, from Barranquilla, Bogotá, and Medellín.

So unlike many scholars from the Global North who write about Colombia, I did not study the country in college or graduate school; nor did I go there to do fieldwork. My research may therefore suffer from a lack of formal training—but benefit from an immersion in learning and teaching, and a network of contacts of the kind that can become available to an established, and fortunate, professor.

The fundamental theme animating *The Persistence of Violence* is that Colombia's headline story, about the peace process with the FARC and attendant controversies, may not deal adequately with a fundamental contradiction of the nation, famously identified by Gabriel García Márquez in his pictorial essay *Por un país al alcance de los niños* (*A Country for Children*) (1998). Gabo, as he is known in the region, wrote evocatively about a common dualism within the population that spanned generosity and violence, warmth and hatred. He described a powerful bifurcation coursing through Colombia, the product of its particular pattern of invasion, dispossession, and enslavement. This resulted in a restless quest to identify the subject of violence—is it the nation, the right, the left, the landowners, the state? At one point in *La mala hora* (*The Hour of Evil*), Gabo says: "Es todo el pueblo y no es nadie" (It's the whole town and it's nobody) (García Márquez 1987: 89).

He spoke of a place that was two countries in one—the ideal and the real—with all the associated paradoxes of a semiotic encounter between *langue* and *parole*, the abstract and the everyday:

- A proclivity for making laws and ignoring them
- A cathexis onto paperwork amid contempt for bureaucratic norms
- A dedicated work ethic and love of get-rich-quick schemes
- A taste for creating icons, then ridiculing and bringing them down
- An obsession with sporting triumph and failure, greater than any identification with human suffering
- A love of life mixed with murderous tendencies
- An adoration of animals but neglect of the loss of species and the environment in general, alongside imperilment of one of the world's great rivers
- A loathing of negative international stereotypes of Colombia while failing to admit that the reality may be worse (García Márquez 1998: 10–11)

García Márquez deemed Colombians capable of both the noblest and the most abject acts imaginable, in a world where it seemed anyone might do anything, from the beautiful to the horrendous. Like many others, I have found this duality—bizarrely akin to Barthes's renowned binary list, "J'aime, je n'aime pas" (I like, I don't like) (1994: 116–117)—enormously suggestive.

Gabo's topics enumerated above inspired the themes covered in the chapters to follow. The book you hold in your hands examines violence in Colombia as reflected, refracted, generated, and criticized at specific sites:

- Football, *narcotraficantes*, and militarism
- Tourism, sexual exploitation, and imperialism
- Journalism, *narconovelas*, and gender
- The environment and emotion

Victor Hugo is reported to have satirized the 1863 Colombian Constitution as "faite des anges" (written for angels) (quoted in Blanquer and Gros 1996).[2] The nation labors under what the *Financial Times* calls "extreme legalism": a bewildering array of laws and courts of review, matched only by its bewildering array of lawbreakers (Rathbone and Long 2018). This collective irony is emblematized by Francisco José de Paula Santander Omaña, the man regarded as the country's founding parent of law following independence who was in fact a key figure in maintaining an intransigent political-economic elite (Calvino Ospina 2008: 13).

The apparent lawfulness of what has been a political democracy for six decades leads many outsiders to admire seemingly significant governmental initiatives. For example, the International Organization for Migration details well-codified Colombian legislation forbidding sexual violence (Organización Internacional para las Migraciones 2015); the world's most famous liberal philosopher praises it for policies protecting women (Rawls 1999: 110); and the state produces impressive-looking reports for the UN's Committee on the Elimination of All Forms of Discrimination against Women (2017). But anyone with material knowledge knows that this is one more case where policing, the courts, government, and everyday life are distant from such ideals and claims. Hence the Organisation for Economic Co-operation and Development (OECD) producing an *Integrity Review* as part of deciding on Colombia's accession to the group and to propose a way forward to genuine peace (2017). It continues to find major flaws in the country's claims that it is implementing the Organisation's Anti-Bribery Convention (OECD Working Group on Bribery 2019). For the long-standing and contemporary reality is that many citizens bribe public officials as a matter of course. They regard Colombia as a profoundly corrupt blend of collusive private and public interests, clientelism, fraudulent elections, and criminal-justice abuses (Transparency International and Chr. Michelson Institute 2013; Transparency International 2017).

The situation is summed up in the idiomatic expressions (not unique to Colombia, but particularly popular there) "Hecha la ley, hecha la trampa" (When you pass a law, you create a loophole) and "muy viva" (truly alive)—the notion that one must be slyly on the make to be fully "with it." For example, the mythic *vivo* (street sharp), makes his living from the *tonto* (fool) who actually bothers to work in the formal economy. This is a means of dealing with the duality of a supposedly open capitalist system governed by rules and open to competition, versus the reality of stubbornly immobile oligarchies and oligopolies.

That inevitably leads to stereotypes from foreign observers. It is a shock, even from this distance, to read Darwin referring to "the savages of Colombia" (2008: 307). A century and a half later, Eric Hobsbawm alarmingly described the country as "a naturally bloodthirsty culture" (1994: 52). Edgar Morin typifies Colombia as taking the underside to all societies and internationalizing it via drugs (Baudrillard and Morin 2004: 61). This puts such thinkers uncomfortably close to elites in Bogotá and Washington, who speak "as if Colombians had an innate propensity to shed one another's blood" (Hylton 2006: 8) and the common local discourse arguing that Colombia is a "sick" society (Woodward 2018). The head of the Instituto Colombiano de Medicina Legal (Colombian Institute of Legal Medicine) reflected on the 2016 peace accord by saying that the population had interiorized violence as ordinary conduct. Its form might alter with history, but a dark underlying reality still characterized the nation (Valdés 2017).

Alongside Gabo's imaginative cultural interpretations and others' Olympian generalizations, some basic definitions and data are necessary in order to comprehend the grisly phenomenon of Colombia's persistent violence. The statistics and stories make chilling reading:

- Millions killed over the life of the country
- The largest national displacement of a citizenry in history
- The ongoing kidnapping, murder, and "disappearance" of activists[3] and journalists
- Levels of domestic and street violence that both color and transcend the conflict

Mass killings in what is now Colombia began with the Spanish state's attacks on the Muisca people in 1595. The Catholic Church collaborated: it sought the destruction of alternative religious materials and customs, with information obtained through torture and punishment gladly meted out (González and González 2007: 60–61). Ever since, human devastation has taken so many forms, and in so many, often isolated, parts of the country, that even with the increasingly systematic collection of data, judicial and medical statisticians, the police, and peace activists all doubt the reliability of the numbers they come up with and compare, which tend to stress urban violence, neglecting rural realities (Rubio 2000; Cumbre Agraria et al. 2018).

Of the quarter-of-a-million people killed by firearms worldwide in 2016, half perished in the Americas, with Colombia a leading contributor (Global Burden of Disease 2016 Injury Collaborators 2018). The first official Colombian homicide figures, from 1938, counted sixteen murders per hundred thousand residents. The ratio diminished with the introduction of limited hours of alcohol availability, but was spurred on again by contests over cocaine production and distribution, increasing in the 1950s and hovering between twenty and thirty deaths per hundred thousand until a dramatic hike in the 1980s, from forty to eighty. (United Nations Office on Drugs and Crime 2014: 22–23, 26, 37, 75–76). By 2015, the ratio had fallen to seventeen, but that was still almost double the level considered to be endemic (Guerrero and Fandiño-Losada 2017).

Both Human Rights Watch (2015) and the Colombian government ("Colombia's Santos" 2015) estimate that well over two hundred thousand people have been killed and almost eight million displaced in "the conflict" since the 1960s—but the

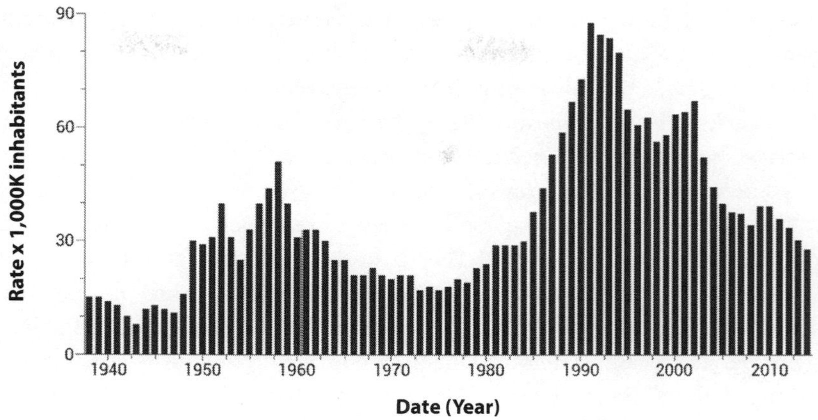

FIGURE 1. Colombian homicide rate per hundred thousand people, 1938–2014. (Source: Guerrero and Fandiño-Losada, 2017.)

state only began systematic collection of these data in 1985, and 85 percent of murders probably elude human-rights discourse (Human Rights Watch 2017: 152). They are often defined as "common crime" (W. Tate 2007: 4) but approach warlike figures, especially with three thousand people a year kidnapped at the turn of the century and an annual average between 1990 and 2010 of 1,800 (see figure 1) (Pécaut 2001; Bergman 2018: 64).

In 2018, the state announced that the conflict had claimed 262,197 lives—of whom just 46,813 were combatants (Romero 2018), with the *paramilitares* specializing in mass killings and disappearances, the *guerrilla* in kidnapping, and the military in falsifying the number of enemies killed by counting civilians they had murdered (Hunt 2009; Uribe Alarcón 2011; Aranguren Romero 2017: 2–3; Human Rights Watch 2017; Bergman 2018: 64). The Institute for Economics & Peace's *Global Terrorism Index* ranks the country in 27th place worldwide, 28 points above any other South American state (2018: 38). Improvised explosive devices killed 221 Colombians in 2018, up from 57 the year before (Oquendo 2019). Since the FARC came out of jungle hideouts in 2017, handed over their arms, and moved to supposedly safe areas, many have been assassinated: 31 in 2017, 65 in 2018, and 77 in 2019 (Torrado 2019; United Nations Verification Mission in Colombia 2019). Official figures for 2019 list over ten thousand homicides in the first eleven months, up more than 2 percent on 2018 ("Colombia cierra" 2019). One wonders how the nation could embark on "a new era of post-conflict when the paramilitary's surmounting debt with humanity is nowhere close to being paid" (Hristov 2014: xviii; see also Manrique Rueda and Tanner 2016; Centro Nacional de Memoria Histórica 2018b).

How to explain the persistent violence? Colombia's mythic nineteenth-century liberator, Simón José Antonio de la Santísima Trinidad Bolívar Palacios

Ponte y Blanco, thought of the "new" Americans as bicultural products of usurping Spaniards and resistant indigenous folk, and hence inheritors of both a rule-governed struggle to impose empire and a fiercely elemental refusal of invasion and conquest (Villota Galeano 2017). The reality was that the violence of the *conquista* (conquest) amplified following independence, as the new *criollo* rulers (direct descendants of the Spanish) sought to take over, govern, and exploit more and more territory in order to confirm their colonization, statehood, and economic future (Colmenares 1996). Bolívar's remarkable 1815 letter from Jamaica leaves no doubt as to his preferred identity. Even though he acknowledges Spanish "[a]trocities [that] transcend the limits of human perversity," refers to a "genocide," and regards slavery as "inherently corrupt," Bolívar says "natives [must] become civilized," and deems Columbus to be "the creator of our hemisphere" (2003: 13, 18, 26–27). That mythic version of the struggle for independence has been handed down over generations. It denies the role of Afro-descendant and indigenous Colombians in the movement (Cote 2019) and sidesteps Bolívar's own taste for violence (García Márquez 1998).

Local and foreign novelists, essayists, activists, survivors, fighters, and social scientists have endeavored to explain the long and disturbing history of Colombia's violence (Farnsworth-Alvear et al. 2017).[4] These *violentólogos* attribute the nation's violent characteristics to numerous causes in addition to those mentioned by Gabo and Bolívar (García Villegas 2015). They include the following:

- A topography that militates against the effective government of numerous regions (Cauca, Antioquia, the Andes, and the north coast) with people left to fight for terrain and power in the absence of a functioning state
- Machismo
- Systematic class inequality
- Discrimination against indigenous and Afro-descended Colombians
- Marxism
- The role of the United States, from the creation of the Panama Canal to Plan Colombia and Peace Colombia (today's military policies)
- The World Bank making Colombia a template for development via the exploitation of natural resources and antisocialist strategies
- The Janus face of neoliberalism, as a blend of economic deregulation and statist reformation of citizens
- Cross-generational oligarchy
- Media dominated by clientelist and familial ties to politics
- Paramilitary, *guerrilla*, and mafia forces
- Kidnapping, drug dealing, and the informal economy
- A state riddled with corruption
- Public distrust of the police, the judiciary, and politics

Since the 1960s, being in a "state of siege" has become routine in Colombia, enabling exponential growth in the size, reach, and violence of the military and its U.S. partners. Emergency is a daily condition; counterinsurgency, a norm of political organization (Aranguren Romero 2017: 13–14). No surprise, then, that the late 2019 nationwide protests against neoliberal authoritarianism saw 170,000 troops mobilized within moments ("Colombia Anti-Government" 2019).

The country "is synonymous with 'violence'" in a "global imagination . . . of kidnappings and assassinations" (Karl 2017: 1). In the eyes of "most international observers, violence remains the primary evidence of Colombian national failure" (W. Tate 2007: 31)—what Alfredo Molano has called its "diabólica inercia" (diabolical inertia) (2001: 13). No wonder Ana María Ochoa Gautier describes violence as the country's "foundational myth" (2014: 159) and Idelber Avelar avows that it "has come to represent Latin America's ultimate instance of violence as a constant, pervasive element in the nation's self-definition" (2004: 20).

For many Colombians, familial violence, from murder to sexual assault, is "a daily occurrence," generally associated with machismo, alcohol, narcotics, and unemployment. As a consequence, the streets often feel safer to children than their homes, leading to new forms of criminality and violence deriving from drug use and truancy (Moser and McIlwaine 2000: 3–4). Polling indicates that many Colombians endorse personal and systematic violence alike. Half the urban population believes in taking force into their own hands and killing to protect their families. A third favors eliminating criminality through *limpieza social* (social cleansing) and deploying corporal punishment against children (Guerrero and Fandiño-Losada 2017). It is estimated that 39 percent of children under the age of 4 have suffered such physical assaults at home (Cuartas 2018). And while Law 294 of 1996 only permits parents to "correct them and sanction them moderately," Civil Code 1883 allows "violent punishment in the home" (Global Initiative 2018).

Comparative social psychology proposes that authoritarian conservative ideology is close to Colombians' sense of a national self and may involve a certain admiration for violence when associated with success (Espinosa Pezzia et al. 2017). Public-opinion research suggests that just half the population favors democracy over other forms of government—a lower percentage than in most of the continent—and voter turnout is the lowest across Latin America (Hellinger 2015: 8, 397). Such attitudes, born of a history of intense malevolence, contrast with much of the Global North (Puig-i-Abril and Rojas 2018). True believers in biological roots of conduct throw their hands in the air when thinking about Colombia (Raine 2013: 125) or blame it on the "decivilizing" antics of "gangs of drugged or drunken hooligans" (Pinker 2011: 437).

Prior to explaining the history and contemporaneity of this violence and outlining the chapters to come, I want to spend some time working in more conceptual detail on two key themes: violence and the popular.

VIOLENCE

Across the globe, violence is one of the world's most pressing yet enduring issues. From time immemorial, it has been a key theme of religion, social organization, family dynamics, and politics—a central concern of public policy, social movements, academic research, journalism, drama, fiction, military strategy, god-bothering, and policing. In other words, violence is a universal problem. Whether we look at nuclear weaponry, civil war, or domestic assault, violence stalks both social and interpersonal relations. I cannot imagine newspapers, current-affairs programs, or congressional debates without it.

Colombians under the age of 75 have no experience of life beyond the conflict/civil war that began in the 1940s. For women around the world, both the street and the home can be places where violence must be avoided on a daily basis (Goel and Goodmark 2015). The World Health Organization (WHO) (2017) estimates that a third of women have suffered physically at the hands of lovers. For working-class U.S. youth, the military is a "poverty draft" (Mariscal 2006). Australians date their emergence as a nation from the bloody attempt to invade Turkey in 1915 (McKay 2018). French and U.S. citizens rise to national anthems celebrating weaponry and slaughter. Colombians sing along to words glorifying the fact that their land emerged from "surcos de dolores" (furrows of pain) and "se baña en sangre de héroes" (bathes in the blood of heroes).[5] Marginalized, low-income groups in Colombia came up with sixty different definitions of violence in the late 1990s, with most connected to economic deprivation (Moser and McIlwaine 2000: 2). Such linguistic distinctions may derive from profound experience: regression analysis correlates violence with income inequality across Colombia's regions like no other factor, while at the urban level key elements also include poverty, the labor market, and education (Cotte Poveda 2012, 2011). Bogotá's incapacity to keep its citizens safe and govern whole swaths of the country places under erasure its ability to govern.

Around the world, there are differences between state, group, and interpersonal violence; between planned and passional violence; and between fatal and nonfatal forms. And even free-speech absolutists worry that hateful language, whether interpersonal or demagogic, may index or provoke violence. The WHO favors this broad definition:

> The intentional use of physical force or power, threatened or actual, against oneself, another person, or against a group or community, that either results in or has a high likelihood of resulting in injury, death, psychological harm, maldevelopment or deprivation. It takes the forms of self-directed violence, interpersonal violence and collective violence. (2002)

That focus on intentionality, power, and threats has set the tone for many scholars, states, and activists (Lee 2019).

The OECD specifies political violence as

> the use of force towards a political end that is perpetrated to advance the position of a person or group defined by their political position in society. Governments, state militaries, rebels, terrorist organisations and militias engage in political violence, as well as actors who may adopt both political and criminal motives. (2016: 20)

It describes social violence like this:

> a broader manifestation of grievances, criminal behaviours and interpersonal violence in society. These include multiple types of crime, homicides, and interpersonal and self-directed violence. (2016: 20)

The United Nations defines violence against women as

> any act of gender-based violence that results in, or is likely to result in, physical, sexual, or mental harm or suffering to women, including threats of such acts, coercion or arbitrary deprivation of liberty, whether occurring in public or in private life. (1993)

Official pronouncements and statistics clearly don't cover the totality of violence. But they derive from scholarly and social-movement influences as well as governmental ones and affect the way we calculate the phenomenon's dimensions. They must be understood through the lens of theoretical reasoning, whether via philosophy or faith.

A lock on the legitimate use of force is foundational to the essence of the state. It is intimately bound up with the nation via mythic origins and obligations, through policing and war. Weber's classic definition of sovereignty is of a "human community that (successfully) claims the monopoly of the legitimate use of physical force within a given territory" (1946: 78). Achille Mbembe modifies Weber's account to argue that "necropolitics" is the state's way of life, "that the ultimate expression of sovereignty resides, to a large degree, in the power and capacity to dictate who may live and who must die" (2003: 11). Both are of course dependent on Tolstoy's provocation that "government is violence" (1990).

Wars are generally thought of as occurring between governments. Few theorists of war have been able to transcend von Clausewitz's capacious yet precise definition of it (Sharma 2015), even if his use of the first-person plural is troubling in its certitude about the allegedly universal desire for power: "War is . . . an act of force to compel our enemy to do our will" (von Clausewitz 1989: 75). Von Clausewitz avowed that it "is not merely an act of policy but a true political Instrument, a continuation of political intercourse, carried on with other means" (1989: 87).[6] Yet Michael Howard suggests that wars have long been understood as "an aberration in human affairs . . . an occurrence beyond rational control," and more recently as effects of masculinity, class greed, or evolutionary necessity (1984: 90). Those accounts still resonate, but we have some newer ones.

Institutionalist political science identifies "power theories, power transition theories, the relationship between economic interdependence and war, diversionary theories of conflict, domestic coalitional theories, and the nature of decision-making under risk and uncertainty" (Levy 1998: 139). Quantoid neoliberals advise the following:

> There are two prerequisites for a war between (rational) actors. One is that the costs of war cannot be overwhelmingly high . . . there must be some plausible situations in the eyes of the decision makers such that the anticipated gains from a war in terms of resources, power, glory, territory, and so forth exceed the expected costs of conflict. Second, . . . there has to be a failure in bargaining, so that for some reason there is an inability to reach a mutually advantageous and enforceable agreement. (Jackson and Morelli 2011)

This decontextualized game theory, founded on rational action as defined by a capitalist consumer mentality, dominates the deracinated world of mainstream political science—the reductive, selfish side of rationality (Altman 2015; Meadwell 2016). Psychological explanations have been diminished to such assumptions and their cozily artificial experiments (Böhm et al. 2015); cliometricians are also subject to the imposing spells of this warlockcraft (Eloranta 2016; Jenke and Gelpi 2017).

Such approaches form part of the warfare/welfare mentality that colors U.S. and northern European social science, alongside service to capital. In the case of war, we see such forms of life adopted and encouraged by technocrats and militarists alike (Roxborough 2015). In short, mainstream academia, diplomacy, and the military are wedded to the notion that "war between states is to be seen in terms of rationally decided aggression rather than in the internationalization of social conflict" (Halliday 1990: 207).

Contra those perspectives, we confront J. A. Hobson's (1902) ideas about imperial conquest being driven by the capitalist problem of domestic overproduction; Marxist theories of class war caused by unequal control of the means of production; Maoist arguments for the peasantry as motors of revolutionary change; feminist critiques of masculine violence; and postcolonial insights into wars that derive from decolonizing cartography (Gruffydd Jones 2006).

Keynes (1936: 381) provides a succinct political-economic explanation:

> War has several causes. Dictators and others such, to whom war offers, in expectation at least, a pleasurable excitement, find it easy to work on the natural bellicosity of their peoples. But, over and above this, facilitating their task of fanning the

> popular flame, are the economic causes of war, namely, the pressure of population and the competitive struggle for markets

The development economist Frances Stewart (2002) advises the following:

- The incidence of war has been rising since 1950, mostly within rather than between states.
- Wars may be prompted by race and religion, but with underlying economic causes.
- The principal stimuli are political, economic, and social inequality; poverty; economic stagnation; poor government; high unemployment; environmental degradation; and individual incentives.

The Royal Geographical Society nominates "land disputes, politics, religious and cultural differences and the distribution and use of resources" as causes of war, while the Heidelberg Institute for International Conflict Research database finds that ideological struggle is a source of most wars, generally nested with other factors.[7]

Like states, most religions take the codification and enactment of violence as fundamental to their very being, as any glance at doctrines of allegedly just war or putatively holy tracts will attest (Finlay 2019). For true believers, deities are intimately bound to crime and punishment, requiring them to "root . . . out heresy, natural impulses, and evil" (Fanon 2004: 176). Virtually all religions justify violence under defined circumstances, and a desire for their gods to rule humanity with unquestioned authority (Popovski et al. 2009; Jerryson et al. 2013). Prelates of righteous, omniscient deities ready to judge and mete out painful punishment are matched by political theorists and military commanders discerning when and how might is right in order to make the remaining life 'better.' Sometimes these groups overlap in their membership.

The Olympian idea of violence as purifying also relates to secular revolutionary fantasies about clearing away the past to free the future. Hence Engels (1968: 151, 154) and Rosa Luxemburg (2004: 64) saying acts of violence are ipso facto political, as private property only emerges from theft and assault, notably during primitive accumulation; Sorel (2004) and Michels (2001) viewing proletarian violence as a riposte to decadence that paradoxically revives the bourgeoisie; or Sartre naming it "the midwife of history" in his endorsement of "murderous rampage" as the "collective unconscious" of the colonized to their subjugation. One must destroy colonial authority in order to "erase the marks of violence: violence alone can eliminate them" (2004: 117, 127, 135). In Fanon's words, "decolonization reeks of red-hot cannonballs and bloody knives" (2004: 165). For her part, Emma Goldman saw political violence as a response to "accumulated forces in our social and economic life," akin to Nature's "storm and lightning"; it "may destroy life and cause great loss," but "also bring relief" (1917: 1). Nietzsche regarded it as crucial to modernity (2002: 78).

Sexuality and gender issues are crucial to comprehending violence. Wherever you look, from diplomats to bombardiers to correspondents, war is an implicitly male activity. This is rarely if ever recognized in mainstream media coverage and academic knowledge, or problematized as such (Ackerly et al. 2006; Hearn 2012; Sjoberg 2013). But the astonishing inequality between men and women, in socioeconomic power and cultural representation alike, relies on the threat and the actuality of violence to undergird it, as exemplified in the fact that so many more men than women bear arms, both inside and outside the military. Violence between men is also important in determining who among them obtains the spoils of this gendered dominance, and as an index of, and displacement from, other crises such as economic disadvantage (Connell 2005: 82–83).

Feminist international relations theory stresses the significance of gender in the causes of war, emphasizing these factors at structural and interpersonal levels, from across the world system to internal dynamics within nations, including the masculine priorities and personalities that drive conflicts. At the level of mythology, the "right" way of doing violence births ideas of male nobility, from protective dueling knights to endless military campaigns allegedly waged in the name of women, whose putative vulnerability is routinely invoked as a justification for conflicts, even as they suffer from the violence that ensues (Riley et al. 2008; Mackie 2012). Of course, the claim that women are naturally nurturing or pacific has not stood up to a multitude of counter-examples, from feminist *guerrilla* (in the FARC as elsewhere) to women who are violent to children (Enloe 1983; Feinman 2000; Rayas Velasco 2009). But this violence is in no way symmetrical with male militarism.

Recent, rather sanguine, analyses argue that war is, so to speak, dying out. They rely on the Uppsala Conflict Data Program, which emphasizes state participation and battlefield casualties. The Program privileges a form of warfare that has been partially superseded by violence done to civilians by non-state actors (Kaldor 2012: 10–11). That tendency underscores that fully-fledged, declared wars are only the most spectacular and all-encompassing form of violence.

POPULAR CULTURE

Unsurprisingly, violence is a common theme in popular culture. Much drama derives from interpersonal and international conflict, many sports are dedicated to physical brutalization, and numerous social anxieties derive from the fear that representing violence may encourage it.

The word *popular* generally denotes "of the people," "by the people," and "for the people." In other words, the popular both constitutes and is constituted by the following:

- Subjects, whom it incarnates via such genres as sports, information, and drama
- Workers, who produce performances and recordings
- Institutions, which industrialize, regulate, and sell their work
- Audiences, who interpret it

In Latin America, however, the word *popular* connotes the proletarian, the peasant, or the poor and their production of meaning: "prácticas culturales de las clases de bajos ingresos y/o de grupos racializados o subordinados que *no* se han domesticado al negociar su entrada en las esferas mediáticas nacionales o globales" (cultural practices of low-income classes and/or racialized or subordinated groups who have neither been disciplined, nor have they tailored their points of entry into national or global media spheres) (Yúdice 2016: 95). *The Persistence of Violence* moves easily and uneasily—as one can and must—between hegemonic Anglo understandings of the popular and its Latin American connotations, which are both similar and different from what one finds elsewhere.

The word *culture* derives from the Latin *colere*, which describes tending and developing agriculture (Benhabib 2002: 2; Adorno 2009: 146). With the advent of capitalism's division of labor, culture paradoxically came to *embody* instrumentalism and to *abjure* it, via the industrialization of farming, on the one hand, and the cultivation of individual taste, on the other. Eighteenth-century Spanish, French, and German dictionaries document this metaphorical shift from agricultural cultivation to spiritual elevation. As the spread of literacy and printing saw customs and laws passed on, governed, and adjudicated through the written word, cultural texts supplemented and supplanted physical force as guarantors of authority. With the Industrial Revolution, populations urbanized, food was imported, and textual forms were exchanged. An emergent consumer society produced such events as racing, opera, exhibits, and balls. The impact of this shift was indexed in cultural labor: *poligrafi* in fifteenth-century Venice and hacks in eighteenth-century London wrote popular and influential conduct books. These works of instruction on everyday life marked the textualization of custom and the development of new occupations. Anxieties about cultural imperialism also appeared, via Islamic debates over Western domination (Mowlana 2000; Briggs and Burke 2003).

Immanuel Kant ideologized these commercial and imperial changes, arguing that culture ensured "conformity to laws without the law." Aesthetics could generate "morally practical precepts," schooling people to transcend particular interests via the development of a "*public* sense, i.e., a faculty of judging which in its reflective act takes account (*a priori*) of the mode of representation of everyone else . . . to weigh its judgement with the collective reason of mankind" (2007: 123). Kant envisaged an "exit from . . . self-incurred immaturity," independent of religion, government, or commerce (1996: 62).

Culture's organic law and lore, and their textual manifestations, have come to represent each "epoch's consciousness of itself" (Althusser 1969: 108). As a consequence, audiences, creators, governments, and corporations make extraordinary investments in it. For imperial Britain, the study of culture formed "the core of the educational system." It was "believed to have peculiar virtues in producing politicians, civil servants, Imperial administrators and legislators," incarnating and indexing "the arcane wisdom of the Establishment" (Plumb 1964: 7) to reproduce and renovate what Matthew Arnold called "that powerful but at present somewhat narrow-toned organ, the modern Englishman" (1875: x).

Culture has usually been understood in two quasi-Kantian registers, via the social sciences and the humanities. They emerged as secular alternatives to deistic knowledge (Schelling 1914) focused on dual forms of "*self-realization*" (Weber 2000)—truth and beauty. This heuristic distinction grew substantive as time passed (Williams 1983: 38). Culture came to be understood as a marker of differences and similarities in taste and status within groups. It could be explored interpretatively or methodically.

So art is understood through iconography, quality, and representativeness, as framed by cultural criticism and history. The social is understood through language, religion, custom, time, space, and exchange, as framed by ethnography and statistics. Whereas art articulates differences within populations via symbolic norms (for example, providing some of us with the cultural capital to appreciate high culture) the social articulates such differences via social norms (such as legitimizing inequality through doctrines of human capital) (Bourdieu 1984; Wallerstein 1989). An aesthetic discourse about culture sees it elevating people above ordinary life, transcending body, time, and place. A folkloric discourse expects culture to settle us into society through the wellsprings of community, as part of daily existence. A populist discourse idealizes fun, offering secular transcendence through joy (Frith 1991: 106–07).

For some Anglo analysts, popular culture is the apex of modernity. It stands for the expansion of civil society—the moment in history when the state becomes receptive to, and part of, the general community. The general population is hence made part of the social rather than excluded from the means and politics of political calculation. This occurs along with diminished authority, augmented rights, and newly intense, large-scale human interactions that are necessitated by industrialization and aided by the media: the spread of advertising is taken as a model for the breakdown of social barriers, exemplifying the triumph of the popular (Shils 1966; Hartley 1992). "Administrative research" was named and valued in the 1940s and operates under this sanguine sign (Lazarsfeld 1941). It supports technological innovation, buoyant demand, audience measurement, marketing, regulation, enforcement of property relations, and so on, in the name of capitalist efficiency and governmental normativity—making capitalism function by ensuring a skillful, willing, and docile populace.

But popular culture also elicits critique. At the onset of European imperialism, Antonio de Nebrija wrote in his *Grammar of the Castilian Language*, published in the fateful year 1492, that one must systematize and promulgate an orthodox Spanish in order to elevate readers beyond "romances or stories" that consisted of "a thousand lies and errors" (2016: 203). And for centuries, the links between art as a form of market-based entertainment and a reflection and generator of social identities have produced very varied reactions: during Europe's Industrial Revolution, anxieties about a suddenly urbanized and educated population raised the prospect of a long-feared "ochlocracy" of "the worthless mob" (Pufendorf 2000: 144). Ever since, theorists from both right and left have argued that newly literate or minimally educated publics could be manipulated by demagogues. Bourgeois economics may assume that rational consumers determine what is popular culture, but even neoclassical/neoliberal chorines worry that ordinary people can be bamboozled by unscrupulously fluent ones. Marxism has often viewed popular culture as a route to false consciousness that diverts the working class from recognizing its economic oppression; feminist approaches have moved between condemning the popular as a similar distraction from gendered consciousness and celebrating it as a distinctive part of women's culture; and cultural studies has regarded it as a key location for the symbolic resistance of class, race, and gender oppression (Hall and Jefferson 1976; Mattelart 1980; Smith 1987).

There has been a cross-generational, cross-disciplinary emphasis on the number and conduct of audiences to popular culture: where they came from, how many there were, and what they did as a consequence. Such concerns are coupled with a focus on content: *what* were audiences watching when they. . . . Both audiences and texts are conceived of as empirical entities that can and must be known, via research instruments derived from sociology, the psy-function, criticism, demography, linguistics, communications, law, anthropology, accountancy, economics, and marketing.

Administrative research was originally juxtaposed with the anti-Nazi Frankfurt School's critiques of popular culture, which suggest that its commercial conditions "impress . . . the same stamp on everything." The principals of that School, Theodor Adorno and Max Horkheimer (1977), saw consumers and citizens as manipulated from the social order's economic apex, with "[d]omination" masquerading as choice in a "society alienated from itself." On this reading, culture becomes just one more industrial process, ruled by economic forces that diminish ideological or generic innovation in favor of standardization. That organizational form necessitates repetition rather than difference, because of the factory-like production of film, music, news, and radio.

The Frankfurt School and its adherents worry that popular culture commodifies and governmentalizes signification. As a consequence, while semiosis begins as a reflection of reality, commodity signs displace representations of the truth with false information. Then these two delineable phases of truth and lies become indistinct. Once underlying reality is lost, signs become self-referential, with no residual correspondence to the real: they have adopted the form of their own simulation (Baudrillard 1988). People are said to buy commodities to give meaning to their lives because societies no longer make them feel as though they belong. This concatenating simulation has implications for the aesthetic and social hierarchies that "regulate and structure . . . individual and collective lives" (Parekh 2000: 143) in competitive ways that harness popular culture for social and commercial purposes. For this reason, analysts discern close ties between ideological content and industrial impact.

More positive responses to popular culture also exist within critical thought. For example, Brecht admired, copied, and sought to transcend the popular, welcoming passionate crowds as potential sites of resistance to government and capital (1964). Even Adorno reflected that sports had "an anti-barbaric and anti-sadistic effect by means of fair play, a spirit of chivalry, and consideration for the weak" (2005: 196–197). Historical and contemporary analyses of slaves, crowds, pirates, bandits, minorities, women, and the working class have utilized archival, ethnographic, and statistical methods to emphasize day-to-day noncompliance with authority, via practices of popular-cultural consumption that frequently turn into practices of cultural production. For instance, U.K. research has lit upon Teddy Boys, Mods, bikers, skinheads, punks, school students, teen girls, Rastas, truants, dropouts, and magazine readers as magical agents of history—groups who deviated from the norms of schooling and the transition to work, thereby generating moral panics. Scholar-activists examine the structural underpinnings to collective style, investigating how bricolage subverts the achievement-oriented, materialistic values and appearance of the middle class. The working assumption has often been that subordinate groups adopt and adapt signs and objects from dominant culture, reorganizing them to manufacture new meanings. The oppressed become producers of new fashions, inscribing alienation, difference, and powerlessness on their bodies (Leong 1992).

A commitment to social and cultural justice as well as academic theorization and research has proven magnetic to many subordinate groups embarking on international academic exchange over the last fifty years. Hence the appeal of studying popular culture not only at the conventional scholarly metropoles of the United States and Britain, but in Colombia, Brazil, Turkey, India, and other important sites that are all too accustomed to being theorized and analyzed; and all too *un*familiar with being regarded as the *sources* of ideas, not merely places for their application.

Perhaps the foremost theorist of popular culture in critical thinking of the kind represented in *The Persistence of Violence* is Gramsci. He maintained that each social group creates "organically, one or more strata of intellectuals which give it homogeneity and an awareness of its own function not only in the economic but also in the social and political fields": the industrial technology, law, economy, and culture of each group. The "'organic' intellectuals that every new class creates alongside itself and elaborates in the course of its development" assist in the emergence of that class, for example via military expertise. Intellectuals operate in "[c]ivil society . . . the ensemble of organisms commonly called 'private,' that of 'political society' or 'the State.'" They represent the "'hegemony' which the dominant group exercises throughout society" as well as the "'direct domination' or command exercised through the State and 'juridical' government." Ordinary people give "spontaneous' consent" to the "general direction imposed on social life by the dominant fundamental group" (Gramsci 1978: 5–7, 12). In other words, popular culture legitimizes socioeconomic-political arrangements in the public mind and can be a site of struggle as well as domination. Gramsci also crucially noted that the words for "national" and "popular" were similar in several languages, such was their affinity, and called for a closer alignment between everyday concerns and intellectual practice to reflect that linguistic kinship and animate socialism (2000: 366). The process might take dialectical form: for example, cinema has been the property and design of elites seeking to recruit the population to their projects through film's carnivalesque expressivity and mythologies of upward mobility, but brokered through multinational taste cultures of a very different kind that bring status and rewards from a cosmopolitan cultural élite.

Raymond Williams (1977) drew on the idea of residual, dominant, and emergent hegemonies to describe the process whereby class formations compete over narratives that legitimize social control. Examples of these categories might be the remains of an empire, a modern mixed economy, and neoliberal transformation, respectively. Extensive use has been made of Gramsci's beyond the Global North, in South Asia and segments of the Arab and African worlds (Marks and Engels 1994; Patnaik 2004; Dabashi 2013). Across Latin America, his notion of the national popular harnessing class interests is common sense for both left and right (Massardo 1999); for example, music represented this incorporation of popular urges into officially-sanctioned and -enjoyed culture in many parts of the region from the 1920s to the 1940s (Yúdice 2016).

I well remember arriving late to a meeting in Guadalajara prior to the 2006 presidential elections in Mexico, when it seemed likely that the left would triumph. A group had been assembled to plan a new cultural policy. I entered quietly and remained so, in part due to my lateness and in part through lack of familiarity with the people present. Two middle-aged men were citing Gramsci and Benjamin. I thought "Good grief, here we go again—leftist academics droning on about Euro theorists. Pointless." Little did I know. For the speakers were both members of Congress, including a senator; one a survivor of the Tlatelolco massacre of 1968, the other a campaigner for media reform. Unlike my experience of the white-settler colonies and Britain, such embodied theorization was part of capital *P* political discourse. In Colombia, Gramsci's ideas have been adopted and adapted since the 1950s by academics, social movements, arts educators, writers, the teachers' union, and the Communist Party, which proceeded to endorse guerrilla resistance (Brands 2010: 17; Santofimio-Ortiz 2018).

Hegemonic cultural ideas have always mattered. They informed imperial expansion through the religious, civilizational fervor of Spain's *conquista de América* (conquest of America), Portugal's *missão civilizadora,* and France and Britain's *mission civilisatrice* (civilizing mission), as western Europe sought to remake the globe in its own phantasmatic image (Rojas 2002). The Spanish wrote self-aggrandizing tracts to celebrate killing native peoples (Braudel 1984: 393; Colmenares 1996). And from the first days of her empire, Queen Isabella's functionaries established Castilian as a mode of conquest and management. Indeed, the imperial grammarian de Nebrija argued that "language was always the companion of empire." Along with Christianity, it would enable the queen to "put under her yoke many barbarous peoples and nations of alien languages." With physical conquest came linguistic and hence codified rule (2016: 202, 204).

The outcome was religious violence and conversion, a cohort of satraps doing the work of Eurocentrism, and a forceful reaction against foreign cultural domination that has never subsided, exacerbated over the last century by the global entertainment demesne of the United States (Mowlana 2000). This latter element is especially strong in Latin America, in keeping with the Monroe Doctrine, which was enunciated almost two centuries ago to keep Europe out of the Americas by declaring anything that went on in the region's new states to be the business of the United States:

> The Governments who have declared their independence and maintained it, and whose independence we have, on great consideration and on just principles, acknowledged, we could not view any interposition for the purpose of oppressing them, or controlling in any other manner their destiny, by any European power in any other light than as the manifestation of an unfriendly disposition toward the United States. (Richardson 2004: 1038–1039)

The Colombian government embraced this policy in 1826, referring to it as the "gospel of the new continent" (quoted in McPherson 2016: 17). And by midcentury, the now-established independence elites sought their own hegemonic *civilización mestiza* (mixed civilization). It would transcend the country's "black and indigenous past" through education, faith, fashion, and conduct (Rojas 2002: xxvi).

Critiques of cultural imperialism have found significant uptake throughout the Global South—not least for their focus on the machinery of propaganda sold to ordinary people by powerful sovereign-states. Such arguments have resonated in everyday talk, broadcast and telecommunications policy, unions, international organizations, nationalistic media and heritage, cultural diplomacy, anti-Americanism, and postindustrial service-sector planning (see Dorfman and Mattelart 1971; Beltrán and Fox de Cardona 1980; Schiller 1976, 1989). They are exemplified by Armand Mattelart's stinging denunciation of external cultural influence on the Third World:

> In order to camouflage the counter-revolutionary function which it has assigned to communications technology and, in the final analysis, to all the messages of mass culture, imperialism has elevated the mass media to the status of revolutionary agents, and the modern phenomenon of communications to that of revolution itself. (1980: 17)

The concern is that popular culture exported from the Global North transfers its dominant value system to others, through hegemony over news agencies, advertising, market research, public opinion, screen trade, technology transfer, propaganda, telecommunications, and security. There is a corresponding diminution in the vitality and standing of local languages, traditions, and national identities. As Herbert I. Schiller expressed it, "the media-cultural component in a developed, corporate economy supports the economic objectives of the decisive industrial-financial sectors (i.e., the creation and extension of the consumer society)" (1991: 14).

It can be no surprise that Latin Americans generated the theory of dependent development in the 1940s to explain why the industrial takeoff experienced by western Europe and the United States had not occurred elsewhere. It gained adherents across the Global South over the next three decades in reaction to the fact that rich societies at the world core had become so through their colonial and international ventures—*im*porting ideas, fashions, and people from the periphery while *ex*porting manufactured popular culture (Prebisch 1982; Cardoso 2009). When UNESCO formed its International Commission for the Study of Communication Problems in the 1970s, chaired by Séan MacBride, García Márquez was a member. Its landmark 1980 report, *Many Voices, One World*, resonated across the globe. Britain and the United States withdrew from UNESCO, in part because the Commission's radical findings and proposals fell victim to the Cold War (Preston et al. 1989). This critique has enjoyed particular purchase in Latin America and other postcolonial states whose traditions and languages tie them to texts exported from the metropole. That analysis is of value for Colombia, given the oligarchies that run politics and the media and a dependent relationship on U.S. screen drama and music, albeit leavened by black, indigenous, and mestiz@ cultural production. Foreign influences have been enabled by successive generations of local policy makers following the Yanqui dictum of open communications technologies but copyrighted textual markets as a means to development and modernization (Dorfman and Mattelart 1971; Segoviana García 2011; Barranquero Carretero et al. 2017).

And there remains a paradox—possibly a contradiction—in critical engagements with the popular. Whenever spectacle is used effectively by social movements, advertising agencies "borrow" what they see. The fashion and music industries dispatch spies to watch and listen to the popular as part of a restless search for new trends to market. Capitalism appropriates its appropriators, and so do its lackey governments, as per the transmogrification of the term "culture industries" into "creative industries" (Miller 2012) (of which more below).

Popular culture around the globe has become ever more central to economic and social life: world trade in culture increased from US$559.5 billion in 2010 to US$624 billion in 2011 (United Nations Conference on Trade and Development 2013). Popular culture has internationalized, in terms of the export and import of texts, attendant fears of cultural imperialism, and a New International Division of Cultural Labor (NICL) (Miller 2018b). A prosperous economic future supposedly lies in finance capital and ideology rather than agriculture and manufacturing—seeking revenue from innovation and intellectual property, not minerals or masses.

Popular culture offers important resources to markets and nations—reactions to the crisis of belonging and economic necessity occasioned by capitalist globalization. It is crucial to advanced and developing economies alike, and can provide the legitimizing ground on which particular groups (e.g., African Americans, lesbians, the hearing impaired, or evangelical Protestants) claim resources and seek inclusion in national and international narratives (see Yúdice 2002 and Martín-Barbero 2003 on Latin America; Colla 2012 and Pahwa and Winegar 2012 on Egypt; Yang 2009 on China; Boateng 2011 on Ghana).

Latin American cultural policy has gone through several transformations in response to this commodity fetishism. The rather musty, dusty sphere of arts policy has become subject to intense criticism for its failure to encompass the popular-culture industries and their relationship to development (Yúdice 2018). But Latin American critics of the old patrimony approach to cultural policy—arts and crafts—did not all wake up with sore heads from a wine-and-cheese gallery opening and turn into prelates of the putative creative industries. Many maintained and even developed their concerns about neoliberalism as it turned its lustful gaze toward culture. They favored an approach that blended solidarity and difference, through a mixture of regional policy making and taking culture beyond markets to recognize the issues confronting indigenous and Afro-descended peoples (Yúdice 2018).

Methodologically and theoretically, we need to be aware of the double-edged side to cultural commodities, as objects of resistance whose very appropriation can then be recommodified. That makes socioeconomic analysis via critical political economy a good ally of representational analysis via close reading. But a certain tendency on both sides has maintained that the two approaches are mutually exclusive: one is concerned with structures of the economy, the other with structures of meaning. That need not be the case. Historically, the best critical political economy and the best close reading have worked through the imbrication of power and subjectivity at all points on the cultural continuum, bringing together the insights of Gramsci and Frankfurt. Such examples help animate what follows, together with an appreciation of history.

HISTORY

Eduardo Galeano put it well when he wrote that "Colombians suffer violence like a disease, but they do not wear it like a birthmark on their foreheads. The machinery of power . . . is indeed the cause of violence" (2013: 426). For like most sovereign-states, the nation's history has been contoured by the earth-shattering concatenation of political-economic events since the eighteenth century:

- The shift from absolute monarchy to parliamentary democracy
- The social upheavals of imperialism, colonialism, slavery, war, postcolonialism, industrialization, urbanization, human rights, feminism, and climate change
- The expansion of global capitalism

Against that heady history of exploitation, productivity, democracy, and destruction, one scholarly tradition, populated by conservative ethnonationalists, argues that nations are constants across history, albeit changing their morphology with time and circumstance (Smith 2000). The nation is sustained through supposedly indelible ties: origin myths, languages, customs, races, and religions (Herder 2002).

For those more in thrall to modernity, such "ties" are invented traditions (Hobsbawm and Ranger 2002). Far from being the outcome of abiding mythologies, the materiality and idea of the nation derived from the Industrial Revolution and imperialism, which brought places together that had not previously deemed themselves linked in any way. Relatively isolated, subsistence villages were transformed by the interdependence engendered by capitalist organizations, the commodification of everyday relations, and the sense of unity generated from nation-binding technologies and institutions, most notably print and public education (Gellner 1988). Since that time, the state articulates the nation as a spirit-in-dwelling, which gives it legitimacy, but which it nonetheless reserves the right to name and monitor; for nations are coterminous with systems of government. Even as the nation is manufactured, it is said to be an already-extant, authentic essence of statehood and personhood.

Discussions with *campesinos* (peasants) about political violence in Colombia generally return to one point of origin: the clearance of the poor from land by murderous means, at the hands of state, *guerrilla,* and *paramilitar* alike (Molano 2001). That suggests the nonessentialist account of nationalism can best help us understand Colombia's history—that is, in the light of the development and reproduction of national, regional, and global capitalism (Giraldo Durán and Álvarez de Castillo 2018).

Prior to its conquest in the first quarter of the sixteenth century, the area we know today as Colombia comprised distinct peoples. Those distinctions were ramified with the administrative geography imposed by Spain, which created western and eastern spheres of control (Safford and Palacios 2002). It soon imported West African slaves to mine gold, leaving the agricultural east largely intact, where indigenous populations generally survived. The colonists' basic unit of social control and economic production alike was the hacienda, a sphere of living and working for slaves and First Peoples. The latter were required to pay tributes to the Spanish Crown. They lived somewhere between servitude and slavery throughout the colonial period (Celis González 2018: 32–33).

The Colombian nation-state was birthed, like many others, in revolutionary struggle over the long period of 1810 to 1824 when the Republic of New Grenada (now Panamá, Venezuela, Ecuador, and Colombia) won independence. The major beneficiaries were hacienda landholders, whose power over people and territory was consolidated at the expense of those with smaller holdings. The requirement to 'pacify' hitherto-neglected terrain as part of this process made violence a core part of extending the authority of state and capital alike and paying the costs of the war by selling off cultivable land. The formalization of land ownership and use militated against the peasantry, who lacked the finance to purchase what was physiocratically theirs. The nation's wealth was being integrated into the world economic system after a period of economic contraction following independence, and class exclusion via race was a core component of ensuring restrictions on how that wealth was distributed internally. The process was in turn colored by divergent interests—conservative Catholic landowners and liberal urban businessmen. Manumission was achieved in 1851 and helped motivate intense struggle. Liberal and Conservative blocs and parties formed to represent different fractions of capital and relationships to religion (Bergquist 1991; Green 2000; Rojas 2002: xxiv; Bértola and Ocampo 2012: 66; Comisión Histórica 2015; Celis González 2018: 33, 35; Pino Uribe 2017).

That binary party system has plagued the country ever since. The power of the two blocs has essentially precluded electoral uprisings and economic redistribution alike; conservative, Spanish-oriented Catholics opposed British-leaning liberals and radicals via their infamous tendency to divide people and formations as *amigo-enemigo* (friend-enemy) (Rojas 2002: xxvii; Giraldo Durán and Álvarez de Castillo 2018). Although this division applied in much of the region, it was nowhere so deep or violent as in Colombia. The blocs fought ten civil wars in the nineteenth century over slavery, land reform, and new institutions, driven in part by U.S. intervention in Panamá's isthmus (then part of Colombia) (Deas 2015).

At the close of the colonial period, the nation's export base was dominated by gold and silver mined in the eastern highlands. It soon diversified, thanks to coffee, tobacco, and quinine, while hitherto-limited imports grew through consumer goods, particularly luxury items. What had been a country in name only—it was more a set of autonomous regions, and frequently lamented as such by urban intellectuals—was now subject to struggle by competing capitalists, governments, and social groups, alongside the denunciation of indigenous and Afro-Colombians as degrading development and national identity alike. In addition, there came to be not only industrialization and repositioning within the world economy, but also an emergent capitalist imaginary. It drew on reactionary Christianity as a moral technology but allowed for cultural heterogeneity as a means of justifying class hierarchies (Pécaut 1987, 2001; Bulmer-Thomas 2003: 25, 43, 143; Castro-Gómez and Restrepo 2008; Alvarado 2012).

Colombia became one of the least secular countries in the region, in keeping with the large number of Church officials and priests from the colonial era. Its first Constitutions disavowed religious tolerance, until liberal hegemony from the 1850s undermined Catholic exclusivity, legalized divorce, and cut previous tithes. The 1860–1863 war saw liberalism triumphant. Armed with a new Constitution, Liberals exercised political dominance through the mid-1880s, when they were displaced by another civil war and a revised Constitution that favored the Catholic Church, granting it suzerainty over education and religious control of a third of the country. Uniquely across the region, a concordat was signed with the Vatican in 1888 that institutionalized Church hegemony until the 1970s, by which time 95 percent of Colombians affiliated with Catholicism, up from 80 percent in 1910 (Freston 2004: 228; Schwaller 2011: 154–56, 181; Pew Research Center 2014: 27; de la Torre and Martín 2016: 476).

Conservatives ruled until 1930 in concert with the Church, punctuated by the horrendous 1899–1902 War of the Thousand Days, which claimed the lives of a hundred thousand people from a population of four million and saw the Panama Canal ceded to Washington. Theodore Roosevelt regarded the Colombian government as "homicidal corruptionists." He insisted that the "Bogotá lot of jack rabbits" must not be permitted to "bar one of the future highways of civilisation" (quoted in McPherson 2016: 57). The period also saw chaotic currency movements. Conservatives and Liberals both issued paper money, and the peso's value against the gold standard fell from 30 to 0.4 cents over the three years (Bulmer-Thomas 2003: 111 n. 96).

Conservative control fell into disrepute during the Depression, even though the latter's economic effects were relatively mild. When the government slaughtered up to three thousand banana workers who were striking against U.S. capital on the Caribbean coast, this helped stimulate the Communist Party's organization of the rural and urban poor. Violence between Conservatives and Liberals emerged again under Liberal hegemony from 1930, and a new bloc erupted, the Unión Nacional Izquierdista Revolucionaria (National Union for Leftist Revolution). Vicarious tensions arose during the Spanish Civil War, when Conservatives favored Francoist and Hitlerian demagoguery. Liberals removed the Church from its privileged position in favor of a nonsectarian and secular approach to daily life and public education. Meanwhile, an urban proletariat was forming, with the rise of textile manufacturing and government public-works programs designed to offset the loss of export revenue to the Global North. Through it all, extravagant claims were made for coffee as a panacea that could bring Colombians together pacifically in an idyll of decent work and just rewards (Bergquist 1991; Galeano 1997: 102; Bulmer-Thomas 2003: 230, 247; Schwaller 2011: 195; Comisión Histórica 2015; Aranguren Romero 2017: 7–8; Guerrero and Fandiño-Losada 2017).

In 1946, the twenty-year *Violencia* began, as the different interests of peasants, workers, politicians, soldiers, and fractions of capital were drawn into conflict. Conservatives used their electoral success to displace and persecute Liberals, who revolted. The radical presidential candidate Jorge Eliécer Gaitán, a brilliant radio orator and arguably the Colombian politician who has resonated most with the popular classes, was assassinated. Bogotá burned, though the main areas affected were in the countryside. General Gustavo Rojas Pinilla's military coup in 1953, and associated anti-leftist rhetoric, bundled opposition groups together under a putatively socialist barrier. The Conservatives rolled back minimal agrarian reform in a welter of Cold War panic mixed with opportunism, slaughtering *campesinos* in the process and initially identifying Protestantism with the Soviet bloc. Colombia led the way when the Organization of American States expelled Cuba in 1962. By that time, Christian groups had combined in their opposition to the Left, though liberation theology was also emerging within Catholicism (Bergquist 1991; Roldán 2002; Freston 2004: 229; Brands 2010: 51; Schwaller 2011: 197, 244; Deas 2015: 97; Guerrero and Fandiño-Losada 2017; Celis González 2018: 36; Giraldo Durán and Álvarez de Castillo 2018). Meanwhile, Frantz Fanon fondly imagined Colombia's *campesinos* interpreting national radio against the grain and taking revolutionary direction from Cuban and Chinese broadcasts instead (1965: 6–7).

The period from 1946 to 1966 cost three hundred thousand Colombians their lives, displaced two million others, and stole four hundred thousand plots of land from indigenous people. The *Violencia* ended when the junta installed a collaborative front, the two major parties agreed to take the presidency in turn, and Liberals purged progressives and minorities from their ranks. The accord suited an emergent international division of labor that set citizens of the periphery to work as extractors of primary goods and consumers of secondary ones, dragging peasants toward either regional production of cement, energy, and textiles, or industrialized food for export, notably bananas and coffee. As coal and petroleum grew in importance for the nation's balance of trade, agriculture's share diminished, and *campesinos*' economic prospects worsened. The demographic corollaries were intense: Colombia's rural dwellers formed 70 percent of the population in 1960, less than 25 percent at the end of the century, and 20 percent in 2018. Food aid across the 1950s and '60s had impoverished the rural sector by driving down the price of local commodities versus imported wheat, dispatching *campesinos* to the cities. Primary products accounted for 80 percent of exports in 1980 and 66 percent in 2000, drawing level with manufacturing in their contribution to gross domestic product (GDP) (Orlando Melo 1998: 65; Ocampo and Tovar 2000: 240; Pécaut 2001; Dennis 2006; Comisión Histórica 2015; McMichael 2017: 68; Economic Commission for Latin America and the Caribbean 2019a: 13).

These changes birthed and developed today's principal *guerrilla* and propelled the nation into collective traumas that have never truly ended. Political violence took a new turn from the 1960s due to insurgencies. In keeping with Cold War norms, Washington successfully urged violent repression on Bogotá. They jointly bombed resistant peasant groups and set up militias to persecute leftists. That set the precedent for *paramilitares*: Las Autodefensas Unidas de Colombia (AUC) (United Self-Defense Force of Colombia) (Dugas 2005; Hunt 2009; Brands 2010: 60) and Las Autodefensas Gaitanistas de Colombia (AGC) (United Self-Defense Gaitanistas of Colombia), their successors following a putative demilitarization in 2007. These forces have also done the dread work of corporations and ranchers (Hellinger 2015: 311). The AGC exploits the revered memory of Gaitán to reverse his politics, invoking populism while serving established interests.[8]

As in many cases across modern history, the relationship of such militias to the state is ambiguous (Carey et al. 2015), and there has been a tendency for the media to emphasize the horror of guerrilla atrocities by contrast with those committed by paramilitary forces (García Marrugo 2017) despite the latter's intense brutality, from rituals of initiation to forms of torture and combat (Whitehouse and McQuinn 2013). And when a leftist political party ran for office in the 1980s, it was decimated by what the Centro Nacional de Memoria Histórica (National Center for Historical Memory) now refers to as a genocide (2018a).

The Colombian government has sponsored three major studies into the causes and effects of this violence, in 1958, 1987, and 2007. They betray the lineaments of their time. The 1958 Comisión Nacional Investigadora de las Causas y Situaciones Presentes de la Violencia en el Territorio Nacional (National Research Commission into the Causes and Current State of Violence in the Nation) comprised men from politics, the military, literature, and Catholicism. It attempted to put a bipartisan end to bipartisan violence, referred to as "a widespread cancer" that could be overcome by cathartic confrontation and ameliorative social policies (Jaramillo Marín 2015).

The 1987 Comisión de Estudios Sobre la Violencia (Study Commission into Violence) saw membership shift to public-university faculty from law, anthropology, sociology, and engineering, plus one retired officer; all were men. Because the agents of violence had become so varied and intense, it had to manage events that went beyond disagreements between elites that might be resolved technocratically. A discourse of bipartisanship neither described nor explained the numerous guerrilla and paramilitary groups plus narco gangsters generating what was now referred to as a "dirty war." Whereas the 1958 group looked at policies, the 1987 team focused on classification, generating taxonomies rather than programs, predicated on the belief that a renewed democracy would bring peace. A penny for your Habermas, since the evidence suggests that opening dialogue and interaction escalated the violence from 1985, when mayors were directly elected and a leftist political party made legitimate, and 1991, when a new Constitution increased decentralization (Steele and Schubiger 2018). Narcoterrorism emerged and the *paramilitares* and *guerrilla* alike killed and terrorized more and more people in struggles for these new political-economic resources, defying the assumptions underlying democratization. That said, the Commission marked a key moment in the advance of human-rights discourse in Colombia, which remains an intermittently potent tool of denunciation to this day (Jaramillo Marín 2015).

Its successor, the Subcomisión de Memoria Histórica (Subcommission into Historical Memory) (2007–2012), comprised scholars and activists. It sought to monitor the supposed integration of armed groups into civil society and justice for their victims. Memory became a key concept, not merely as an aspect of knowledge but as a performative right in itself. It was to be used as proof of suffering and to shed light on sociocultural experiences of loss and grief. But the Subcommission's work was overdetermined by an administration dedicated to violent destruction of the *guerrilla* and the assertion of nationwide state power (Shapiro et al. 2014; Jaramillo Marín 2015).

In summary, the various official inquiries, like academic work, tend to converge on certain topics as explanations of violence in Colombia, albeit with differences attributable to their governing conjunctures. But most agree that it results from elite desires and disputes, profound social inequality, disparities in living conditions between urban and rural life, the structure of political parties, failures of democratic will and participation, and narcotrafficking (Celis González 2018: 28).

DRUGS

Narco has become the prefix to much of contemporary Colombian life—narcotrafficking, narco-war, the narco-state, narco-culture (Lezcano 2018). Cocaine runs across the recent history of national violence, largely determined by the drug's labor process, which has diversified over time with industrialization and as the gangs hired by cartels become actors in their own right. For some critics, the nexus of cocaine and violence is a gruesome neoliberal project "in conjunction with both civil society (social capital) and the state, to forge both a model and a mythology of development whilst waging a phony war on drugs and drug dealers who have been incorporated into, and/or deployed by, elites in their genuine wars to dispossess rural citizens" (Fine and Durán Ortiz 2016: 14). The notion is that oligarchs, drug dealers, *paramilitares*, the United States, and Colombian national and departmental governments conspired to seize land, develop the corporate sector, and discredit the Left. That may be true, but the history is longer than it might suggest.

Andean coca leaves, which naturally abound in Bolivia and Perú, were immediately seized on by the conquistadores as a means of controlling and stimulating their indigenous silver-mine workers. Coca was inserted into world capitalism in the mid-nineteenth century, though its industrial alkaloid derivative cocaine was fairly insignificant globally until the 1970s, other than for anesthetic purposes and as a creative and sporting stimulant. Legal commodity chains operated from 1860 to 1910, connecting Europe and the United States to Andean suppliers. Then criminalization took hold, and the trade internationalized as contraband through the Dutch, Japanese, and U.S. empires until World War II (Gootenberg 2006).

From the mid-1970s, Colombian gangsters imported coca paste from the Andes and chemical-processing elements from the Global North, using a complex supply chain of many small, informal businesses. The cartels set up cocaine factories in urban and then jungle laboratories, sending the product to Europe and the United States on passenger flights or light planes (Orlando Melo 1998: 68). Coca leaf was successfully transplanted en masse to Colombia in the 1990s from Bolivia and Perú, which were gradually overrun by Yanqui interdiction. In 1994, 20,000 hectares in Colombia were dedicated to coca. By 1996, the figure was 200,000. During initial production, indigenous and *campesino* rural dwellers were attacked to subdue or clear them out. Once cocaine was in play, intense violence proliferated across numerous sites (Bergman 2018: 5, 30, 51, 102):

- Distribution markets and routes
- Among traffickers
- With the state
- During retail on the street
- In related fields (football, oil, and minerals)
- Caused by addicts

By the twenty-first century, cocaine accounted for a quarter of the country's exports and three percent of its GDP (Bulmer-Thomas 2003: 9). Coca cultivated in Colombia virtually halved between 2000 and 2013; but that was followed by massive increases as a consequence of failed compensation schemes for farmers, new cartel tactics, and diminished interdiction. The amount grew by a third from

2015 to 2016, to almost nine hundred tonnes. Two-thirds of the globe's hectares dedicated to coca (170,000) are in Colombia, the majority in the Pacific and central zones. Thousands of laboratories convert the raw material (United Nations Office on Drugs and Crime 2018a: 8, 29; 2018b: 11). There are gun battles in Bogotá and Medellín between rival gangs and the police, threatening the relative calm in big cities as assault weaponry proliferates via FARC cast-offs and Venezuelan military sales. Meanwhile, cartels compete for domestic as well as international demand (Ávila 2019).

As a consequence of cocaine, what had been largely political struggles branched out and deepened in both their violence and their overall impact. The blend of organized, non-ideological, criminal violence and organized, ideological, militia/guerrilla/state violence is unprecedented in Latin America since independence. New fractions of capital have become involved via the financial sector's invention of monetary instruments to launder plunder (Alvarado 2012; Kacowicz and Mares 2016: 16; Aranguren Romero 2017: 9–11; Guerrero and Fandiño-Losada 2017; Giraldo Durán and Álvarez de Castillo 2018).

As a consequence, whereas violent crime and systematic conflict are generally quite separate, that is not the case in Colombia. During the 1980s, the cocaine trade stimulated the rise of powerful, ruthless cartels, notably in Cali and Medellín. They ruled as alternative governments, vying with each other and the state for control and authority: the informal economy rearing up to challenge all comers and seize the mythology of populism. The power of the narcos derived from many factors (Atehortúa Cruz and Rojas Rivera 2008; Castells 2010: 205):

- Support for the trade in drugs by the U.S. government during the Vietnam War as a means of funding proxy local actors, who quickly perceived potentially powerful market forces at play among the U.S. military and fueled a demand that was soon repatriated
- The counterculture's fantasy of alternative consciousness
- Favorable climatic and agricultural conditions
- Peace Corps veterans' taste for "Santa Marta Gold" *mariguana*
- Capacity, based on generations of coca production
- Proximity to U.S. ports
- Smuggling skills garnered from transporting contraband over generations of piracy and catering to legal addicts (of tobacco)
- The ease of transporting large amounts of powder by contrast with weeds
- Interest from U.S. mafiosi
- Lack of interdiction, facilitated by police who were for sale

Since the Cold War, the conflict has transformed from a desire for land redistribution to human exploitation via narcotics and sequestration, as inspiration for the *guerrilla* switched from Marxism-Leninism to wealthy nasal passages

(Moser and McIlwaine 2000: viii, 7). Today, drug traffickers and rebel groups of all kinds are often one and the same—by turns rivals and collaborators in a trail of cocaine that is harvested and manufactured in Colombia then moves through Ecuador, bordering the Pacific en route to the United States. This fragmentation of gangsters leads to massive violence between rival groups, as yesterday's cartel enforcers become tomorrow's new cartel (Bergman 2018). Gangs and guerrillas, inhumanness and ideology, kidnapping and cocaine overlap in an "age of violence entrepreneurs" (Organisation for Economic Co-operation and Development 2016: 27, 2009: 39).

New and transformed occupations and formations proliferate and transmogrify: assassins, militia, gangs, mafia, and corrupt administrations, churches, football clubs, universities, press, politics, police, the FARC, the Ejército Popular de Liberación (EPL—Popular Liberation Army—Maoist then Marxist-Leninist), the Ejército de Liberación Nacional (ELN—Army of National Liberation—a Guevarist group originating among urban students), and its dissidents, who formed the Ejército Revolucionario del Pueblo (ERP—People's Revolutionary Army) (Pécaut 2001; Celis González 2018; Oquendo 2019).

"There are no 'good guys'" (Meltzer and Rojas 2005: 1). As a consequence, the association of Colombia with the drug has become magnetic for outsiders. To give just one instance, John Oliver's liberal HBO satire *Last Week Tonight* (2014–) dedicated a 2018 episode to Venezuela's political economy, in a way that was remarkably balanced for bourgeois Yanqui (U.S.) television. But almost inevitably, in order to provide some context to that nation's level of corruption, Oliver compared it to Colombia, "a country where the only campaign finance law is 'please report all bribes consisting of more than 10 kilos of cocaine.'"[9]

Beyond ideology and social structure, cocaine has transmogrified the country. It represents the collision of rural resources and poverty, urban mafia and commerce, corrupt and fragmented *guerrilla*, and international demand for distraction and addiction (Hobsbawm 1995: 366). The governmental context for all this is a state that is by turns overly present (as a threat) and overly absent (as a source of protection).

THE STATE

The state can be forcefully present in Colombia through the police, the military, and proxy AUC/AGC *paramilitares*. As already noted, the militarization of Colombian society was undertaken at the partial expense and behest of the United States, which preferred state-sponsored violence to development aid as a route to control cocaine traffic and political insurgency (Tokatlian 1997; Rosen and Kassab 2019: 61). The bilateral "Plan Colombia" shifted the battleground states for cocaine export elsewhere and led to a vast array of extrajudicial killings and other crimes: former members of the AUC/affiliates of the AGC now harass and kill indigenous, peasant, and Afro-Colombian activists, while others have been extradited to the United States for drug trials to avoid implicating establishment co-conspirators. The record shows that the *paramilitares* are emboldened to commit more and more killings with increased "military assistance," as it is coyly known. They have a particular taste for assassination during elections (Dube and Naidu 2014).

At a geopolitical level, Colombia is celebrated by DC as a successful junior partner in defeating the *guerrilla*. The U.S. and Colombian militaries position themselves as joint masters of drug interdiction, protecting their budgets and numbers by offering such services around the globe (Lindsay-Poland and Tickner 2016; Sontag 2016). This is known as "risk-transfer militarism" (Smith et al. 2014). It serves as a model for U.S. intervention in conflict from a distance: select, train, and arm foreign militias, police, and armies, tell them whom to kill—then sell them materiel that had once been distributed as aid (Lindsay-Poland 2018: 7–8, 11).

U.S. nationalists regard Colombia "as perhaps the U.S. military's greatest human rights success story in Latin America" (Laurienti 2007: 62). Amateur-hour foreign-policy experts, informed by helicopter visits rather than scholarly or practical knowledge, declared a "Colombian miracle" a decade ago (Boot and Bennet 2009). John Kerry's 2013 confirmation hearing as secretary of state featured astonishing claims to this effect, capable of coming only from someone ignorant of the language, life, geography, history, and contemporaneity of the nation. He called Colombia "[o]ne of the great stories of Latin America," praising ultra-rightist ex-president, rentier-class propagandist, and paramilitary patron and pardoner Álvaro Uribe Vélez for "rescuing that nation." Kerry euphemized these changes as a tribute to DC's "citizen security partnership" ("Nomination" 2013: 19, 80). For their part, coin-operated liberal think tanks such as the Brookings Institution speak of the Plan as offering "much to celebrate"; it may be "too soon for America to declare victory and forget about Colombia," but Uribe's "personality and energy" are prized along with his ability to develop tighter links between the military and citizenry (O'Hanlon and Petraeus 2013). This is pomposity as per the discourse of these bodies during the Cold War, an arrogance that Hannah Arendt sought to puncture (1970: 14–16) but which has never been deflated. In the similarly bizarre world of orthodox international-relations scholarship, Plan Colombia is understood as the successful disciplining of an errant child: "a combination of rewards, punishments, and capacity improvements" (Vaughn 2019: 80).

A breathtaking blend of solipsism and ignorance forms the substructure of such great-game international strategizing. In that world, the putative task of foreign policy is to stabilize conflict to the satisfaction of the leading powers, acting in the name of principle and commitment but favoring the satisfaction of one's own interests in restricting the spread of unrest. That is how Colombia appears in the literature of U.S. policy (Morgenthau 1969: 26–27). It has nothing to do with proletarian and peasant views, nothing to do with languages beyond English, nothing to do with material life, nothing to do with the cultures being tossed about like so many suddenly worthless cards in a hand. The continuity is obvious: the desire of Western powers to create a form of stability by selecting, encouraging, and securing comprador elites. This doctrine is a regrettable and seemingly unstoppable legacy from imperial order and international-relations discourse.

The Colombian corollary is that successive administrations in Bogotá picked up on Washington's post 9/11 fetishes and redefined the FARC and others as terrorists, thereby expanding U.S. aid by enveloping the conflict in the putative "war on terror" (Rosen and Bagley 2015). Uribe colluded with the worst of the worst. Hundreds of politicians had "relationships" with the paramilitary and cartel worlds (Romero 2007; Acemoglu et al. 2013; Fine and Durán Ortiz 2016).

More generally, Colombia is a "paradoxical marriage of a state of continuous violence with the hallmarks of democratic civilization" (Rojas 2002: xxii), "an extreme example of the contemporary unpicking of the so-called Westphalian model of territorial states that monopolize violent resources" (Keane 2004: 179). This is true in terms of both the impunity of violent actors and the failure to deliver basic social services to citizens. But there *is* a national government, which has been almost exclusively democratic in form, unlike many of its neighbors (Karl 2017: 1) (albeit routinely put into a state of exception to permit repression [Aranguren Romero 2017: 12]). It is putatively held to account by an independent press. International obligations are entered into, whether bilaterally with the U.S. military, or multilaterally, in the form of commitments to neoliberal economic restructuring. In terms of the chapters to come, there is intense nationalism, on display in football fandom. Hugely popular televisual dramatizations invoke glamorous and easy (albeit illicit) lives. And Bogotá's policies stimulate and govern tourism and claim to protect the environment.

With a large, educated middle class and significant resources suitable for secondary accumulation, Colombia is supposedly poised to open its newly secure, bountiful territory to increased foreign investment, extraction, construction, and natural and human exploitation. Hence the tourism slogan adopted by the government in 2012, "La Respuesta es Colombia" (The Answer Is Colombia), displacing the idea of the nation as a problem with the conceit that it is instead a solution—rebranding the country as enduringly appealing and now safe. Once the drug cartels and terrorist *guerrilla* were dispensed with, it was said, Colombia would enter a new golden age. This would counter such stereotypes as being the "Tibet Suramericano" (the Tibet of South America) in the 1980s and a *narcodemocracia* (narcodemocracy) in the 1990s. Instead, the nation seeks to define itself as "una estrella que brilla" (a shining star) and the new "tigre de Latinoamérica" (Latin American tiger), troping the booming Southeast Asian economies of the

1980s. Colombia stands ready and able to help meet the world's economic needs—and focuses, in dutifully neoliberal fashion, on labor-market training rather than guaranteed income, agrarian reform, or job creation (Economic Commission for Latin America and the Caribbean 2019b: 392), obediently liberalizing, deregulating, and privatizing to satisfy its northern masters (Rodrik 2007: 20).

Here is the current economic reality. By the end of 2018, Colombia's (formal sector) GDP measured by purchasing-power parity stood at well over US$730 billion. Petroleum, petrochemicals, coal, and coffee were its major exports, principally to the United States, China, and Panamá (Economist Intelligence Unit 2019). Yet despite these numbers, a lengthy period of significant economic growth, and virtually zero inflation, the country is as unequal as when the conflict began. Two decades of neoliberal policies have slowed growth, increased unemployment in the formal sector—and brought double-digit percentage job growth 'thanks' to cocaine (Hellinger 2015: 326).

The supposed national interest serves a small ruling elite of ranchers, politicians, moguls, and *narcotraficantes*, buttressed by state violence (Hunt 2009; Aranguren Romero 2017: 14). Oxfam estimates that "over 67 percent of productive land is concentrated in 0.4 percent of agricultural landholdings" (2016: 5–6) and Thomas Piketty and the World Top Incomes Database list Colombia's elite receiving a fifth of all national income between 1990 and 2010—more than is the case in the United States (2014: 327).

Waves of fixed capital formation investment and contraction cycling with international demand for oil and related commodities have done little for the popular classes, while public works have generally been undertaken to enable capital or recover from environmental disasters (Bulmer-Thomas 2003: 8, 10, 387; Economic Commission for Latin America and the Caribbean 2018: 498–499, 505). The tax system minimizes corporate contributions to government revenue and maximizes indirect taxes. Corporate taxes and surcharges plunged from 40 percent in 2017 to 33 percent in 2019. Indirect taxation soared to 19 percent, the highest rate ever (Economist Intelligence Unit 2019; International Monetary Fund 2019), thereby aiding the wealthy at the expense of the poor. The economy had already slowed down due to levies on consumption, while unemployment was just below ten percent (United Nations Economic Commission for Latin America and the Caribbean 2018).

Almost half the population is stuck in the informal sector. A third lived below the poverty line in 1980; half did so twenty years later. Lower-income people improved their income relative to the wealthier in 2017, but the tenth of Colombians living in extreme poverty was double the proportion of Brazilians and many times the percentages of Chileans and Argentines (Hellinger 2015: 320; Organización para la Cooperación y el Desarrollo Económico 2015: 8; Economic Commission for Latin America and the Caribbean 2019b: 110, 234).

Nor is there a national popular identifiable with the needs and hopes of the majority. Rather, it is animated by entitled classes, many of whose forebears gained authority and wealth from colonial dispossession and enslavement. This has accentuated regional and other differences. No wonder so many people shrugged their shoulders when they were promised that the peace would see a true exchange of armaments in favor of votes: two-thirds of the electorate did not participate in the 2016 plebiscite to endorse the accord with the FARC (Magallón 2016).

The lack of trust in major institutions has spread to religion: Catholic hegemony has come under challenge. About 60 percent of the population are practicing Christians, while over a third say they embrace God but do not attend church. Seventy percent are Catholic. Atheism and agnosticism are marginal, and just a quarter of people adhere to the theory of evolution. But the period since the 1990s has seen a wave of Pentecostalism in both urban and rural Colombia, especially among women and young people, to the point where around a sixth of the population identify as evangelical, three-quarters of whom were raised Catholic (Beltrán 2012; Pew Research Center 2014: 5).

There are profound contradictions at play here: a country with one of the longest-running conflicts in history is technically a stable democracy. Cocaine and mining are a toxic mixture for defenders of indigenous and peasant lands, who face execution by means up to and including decapitation, deeds undertaken with impunity as the paramilitary assert authority over terrain in ways reminiscent of the 1990s. The number of indigenous, human-rights, and environmental activists murdered has multiplied massively since the peace accord was endorsed, while corporate geologists and others involved in gold exploration have been killed or kidnapped by groups seeking hegemony over illegal mining and corruption and killing—directed by rivalrous multinationals (Dennis 2006; Sheinin 2015; Pino Uribe 2017; Chaparro and Yagoub 2018; Goldberg 2018; McEvoy 2018; Rueda De la Hoz 2018; Saavedra 2018; Sánchez-Garzoli 2018; Peláez Sierra 2019).

The cosmic failure of the Colombian state and oligarchy to produce a substantive and inclusive national popular has seen violence fill that gap, as the seeming essence of the nation and its people. Elsewhere, such traumas have produced a solemn public and elite determination to turn tragedy into myth in the name of unity. Not in Colombia. Instead, the violence has taken numerous grotesquely targeted forms.

GENDER AND RACE

Violence against women is more common in Latin America than in the rest of the world, as are female deaths from firearms (Small Arms Survey 2016). Colombia's many extreme forms of gendered violence feature rape, disfigurement, and femicide (Moloney 2015; Huertas and Jiménez 2016). The Instituto Colombiano de Medicina Legal reported 21,115 cases of sexual violence in 2014, with 85.05 percent of victims being women (2015). As in many countries, over 90 percent of homicide victims are men, but unlike women, generally not as a consequence of violence undertaken at home, or with a sexual element. Women are frequently killed by people they know—attacked by family members rather than strangers (De la Hoz Bohórquez and Romero Quevedo 2016). A full 39 percent of Colombian women report violent treatment from male partners, and a spate of acid attacks by men on women over the last five years has affected thousands (Guerrero 2013; "Alarma y repudio" 2014; Gaviria Castellanos et al. 2015; "Wonder Women" 2015). Public-health experts argue that a failure to consider historical patterns of oppression downplays the statistical significance of such violence (Bello-Urrego 2013).

All sides in the conflict have engaged in sexual torture, with women and sexual minorities targeted for humiliation as part of a violent clearance aimed at sex workers, street retailers, and other people on the margins of power, who are assaulted by armed groups when in public space (Oxfam 2009; Suárez-Pinzón 2015; Serrano-Amaya 2018). Colombia Diversa, a human-rights organization dedicated to lesbian, gay, bisexual, transgender, and intersex issues, estimates that over a thousand queer people were killed between 1993 and 2017. Many victims are unidentified, and perpetrators remain free.[10] Statutory rape is routine practice for the *guerrilla* and *paramilitares* alike (Human Rights Watch 2019).

Colombian women played key roles in the struggle for independence and have formed social movements to define and defend their rights and publicize their experiences over the past two centuries (Villarreal Méndez 1994; Solano 2003; Lamus 2008; Puello Sarabia 2017: 84–85; León Soler 2019). But state policies designed to alleviate systematic gender discrimination and inequality have been inconsistently applied and largely ineffective (Gómez Cano et al. 2015). And there has been a wave of U.S.-inspired evangelical opposition to women's and queer rights, culminating in the defeat of the peace plebiscite: Pentecostals are distinguished by their heterosexist and patriarchal politicization, and the process had dared to guarantee marriage equality and other citizenship norms. These evangelicals closely follow leaders' instructions, which promise health and prosperity as quae pro quibus.[11] Those hegemonic intellectuals also engineer events understood as "divine healing," which three quarters of their flock say they have witnessed. Half deem themselves to have been present at exorcisms and a quarter to have spoken in tongues (Beltrán 2012; Pew Research Center 2014: 15, 65–66; Marcos 2016). The Pentecostals seem less concerned that a third of women in their twenties are subject to child marriage than with their exercise of sexual and reproductive rights (UN Women n.d.).

Women's health and participation in the workforce, education, and politics saw Colombia ranked 42nd of 145 countries in 2015, descending from the 22nd spot it attained in 2006 (World Economic Forum 2015). The Human Development Report's index of gender inequality reveals that Colombian women encounter serious difficulties in securing positions of public leadership (Programa de las Naciones Unidas para el Desarrollo 2015). More than four out of five seats in the congress are held by men (Economic Commission for Latin America and the Caribbean 2019a: 27). A decade ago, the United Nations noted a stark gendered difference in the unemployment rate: 11.5 percent for women as opposed to 6.9 percent for men (2010). That disparity continues today (Economic Commission for Latin America and the Caribbean 2019a: 17). Women are likely to be stuck in the informal sector and secondary labor markets, especially if they are indigenous or black; and those groups have disproportionately high levels of maternal mortality (Organización para la Cooperación y el Desarrollo Económico 2015: 34; Cabezas Cortés 2016; Perazzi and Merli 2017; Economic Commission for Latin America and the Caribbean 2019b: 472).

Ethnicity/race are defined differently from the norms of the Global North. The state counts much of the population as mixed race—a single group that would be disaggregated as indigenous, black, Asian, and so on in western Europe and its settler colonies. The latest census (2005) considers 37 percent of Colombians to be white and 49 percent mestiz@ (mixed)—a distinction that is itself not always clear (Hudson 2010: 10). It identifies three non-mestiz@ minorities: 87 national indigenous groups, comprising 1.4 million people who live communally and use their original languages (3.4 percent of the overall population); 4.3 million Afro-Colombian descendants of slaves (10.6 percent); and 5,000 Gitano (Roma) (0.01 percent) (Departamento Administrativo Nacional de Estadística 2007: 33).

The majority is therefore defined as largely unified in racial terms, despite being a blend of indigenous, Afro-Colombian, Asian, European, Sephardic, and Arabic heritage. The prevailing ideology of *mestizaje* assumes a norm in which Colombians form a mosaic of racial intermarriage and respect. As the popular saying goes, "Aquí en Colombia somos muy mezclados" (Here in Colombia we are very mixed) (quoted in Restrepo et al. 2014). Recent scientific, political, and commercial investments in genomics seek to confirm Colombia's hegemonic cultural landscape. Results are pored over to reveal that most people have indigenous heritage—downplaying Africanism—and that the dominant *fons et origo* was sexual liaisons between *conquistadores* (conquerors) and *indigenas* (Wade 2013).

Here's the real deal: descendants of the original inhabitants who survived colonization and capitalism mostly occupy peripheral areas, through isolation or exile (Stavenhagen 2002). Indigenous and black minorities suffer massive inequality, and whites and mestiz@s dominate political, economic, cultural, and social life (Cabezas-Cortés 2016; Perazzi and Merli 2017. Black lives are cheapened by state actors and others—not just in colonial history or contemporary tourism, but through violence that targets them from all sides (Vergara-Figueroa 2018).

This social structure follows a familiar history throughout the region—an elite defining itself against indigenous and black peoples while relying on slave labor, forcibly dispossessing native peoples, and raping and marrying indigenous women. South American movements for independence from Spain and Portugal were not about distancing oneself from Europe and integrating with original owners. The revolutionaries favored Westphalian nation-building, U.S. political republicanism, British economic liberalism, Prussian militarism, and social Darwinism.

In sum, Colombia's problems arose before it did, with the horror of empire and slavery. They concatenated with the formation of a powerful oligarchy, which continues to this day: obsessed with the rule of law, dependent for its *origins* on stolen lands worked by slaves, and for its *continuation* on clientelism and control of the formal economy and politics. That has left little opportunity for a vast number of poor people other than in the informal sector, where they frequently operate through criminal, violent means, sometimes with and sometimes without ideological alibis.

That macrohistorical account gains human contour in the remarkable work of Miguel Ángel Beltrán Villegas (2018). Incarcerated for many years as an alleged FARC ideologist, Beltrán Villegas spent his time interviewing fellow-prisoners from across the spectrum—*guerrilleros, paramilitares,* soldiers, and their visitors. The result is a profound work of participant observation that finds much in common among fellow cellmates: they combined a lamentation for the pain they had caused with a disgust for the corrupt oligarchies running corporate and state life.

COLUMBIA AND THE POPULAR

Iván Duque Márquez, an invention/political creature of Uribe, was elected Colombian president in 2018, having spent many years in the Inter-American Development Bank's Division of Culture, Creativity and Solidarity. During his time in DC, he became a fervent disciple of an English conceptual export to the world, the fantasy of a creative economy—a postindustrial, post-polluting world. Duque is coauthor of the Bank's book, *Orange Economy: An Infinite Opportunity* (Buitrago Restrepo and Duque Márquez 2013). The choice of the word "orange" derives from pharaonic tombs, but for me, it invokes Benjamin's distaste for the nation's 1930s stamps: "the postal parvenus . . . large, badly perforated, garish formats" (2016: 82).

I remember, with a stiff stomach, a congress in Lima when Felipe Buitrago Restrepo, Duque's coauthor, presented their extravagant promises, obediently copied from the British Council: a secular religion that offered transcendence in the here and now through a world blessed for workers, consumers, and residents, where waste would be code rather than carbon. Other participants tried to foment discussion on the subject, but it was almost impossible. We were in the presence of a true believer and an audience keen to see itself transferred from welfare recipients to economic agents. Six years on and his reward was to be Duque's Viceministro de Creatividad y Economía Naranja (Deputy Minister of Creativity and the Orange Economy), responding to what Buitrago describes as the challenge to "hacer digerible, sexy y provocativa a la economía naranja" (make the orange economy digestible, sexy, and provocative) (quoted in S. Rincón 2019).

The latest fetish among the sacerdotes of creativity is the putative "collaborative economy." A cybertarian fantasy of pre-capitalist bartering is brought to bear on supposed new liberties occasioned by digital communications and economic deregulation, but with monetary incentives for brokers (think of lonely-hearts club Internet dating, bed and breakfast services that don't pay taxes, or underregulated door-to-door driving services).

Unsurprisingly, Duque's administration emphasizes the financial value of the sector:

> La economía naranja está en camino de convertirse en uno de los principales motores económicos de Colombia: el mundo de la iniciativa empresarial, la tecnología y las industrias creativas ya representa casi el 3% del PIB del país latinoamericano, lo que representa tres veces la contribución del café y casi 1,5 veces el aporte de la minería. Colombia quiere posicionarse como símbolo naranja, color de la cultura y creatividad.
>
> "Impulsar la economía naranja es una de las prioridades del gobierno. En ProColombia, hemos identificado grandes oportunidades de ventas en el desarrollo de software, películas, televisión, animación y videojuegos. Estos son sectores que han crecido más de un 30% en exportaciones," explica Flavia Santoro, presidenta de ProColombia, la entidad del Gobierno de Colombia que promueve las inversiones, las exportaciones, el turismo y la marca país en el exterior. "Colombia se está convirtiendo en un lugar ideal para filmar industrias como Hollywood. Antonio Banderas, Tom Cruise, Will Smith o Mark Wahlberg son algunos de los actores de talla internacional que en los últimos años han filmado películas en territorio colombiano."
>
> (The orange economy is on the way to becoming one of Colombia's principal economic engines: the world of entrepreneurship, technology and the creative industries already represents almost 3% of the GDP of the Latin American country, which represents three times the contribution of coffee and almost 1.5 times

the contribution of mining. Colombia wants to position itself as an orange symbol, the color of culture and creativity.)

("Promoting the orange economy is one of the government's priorities. At ProColombia, we have identified great sales opportunities in the development of software, movies, television, animation and videogames. These sectors have grown more than 30% in exports," explains Flavia Santoro, president of ProColombia, the Colombian Government body that promotes investment, exports, tourism and the country brand abroad. "Colombia is becoming an ideal place for film industries like Hollywood. Antonio Banderas, Tom Cruise, Will Smith and Mark Wahlberg are some of the actors of international stature who in recent years have made movies in Colombian territory.") ("Orange Economy" 2018)

Again, there is a space between governmental rhetoric and reality. The United Nations Conference on Trade and Development's comparison of Colombia's cultural import-export performance in 2003 and 2012 discloses a serious and growing trade imbalance in the culture industries, with the U. S. an increasingly powerful influence (2015: 36–37). The nation's own accounts indicate that the area's contribution to GDP in a period of strong overall economic growth (between 2001 and 2007) went from 1.6 percent to 1.8 percent, though that represented a doubling in value, from under three and a half billion pesos to over eight and a half billion (Oxford Economics 2014).

Colombia has issued the world's first bonds to develop cultural infrastructure, to the value of four billion pesos ("Colocados" 2018). Duque spoke at the auction, indicating that he wanted his invented "Orange Economy" to contribute a tenth of the nation's GDP, akin to the contribution from manufacturing. Ironically, the model was Holland—very orange. Given that proletarian labor costs are higher than in many Asian economies, Duque sees Colombia's urbanism and digital connectivity as key competitive advantages—and supposed safety from the violence that disrupts the extractive sector in remote areas (Sonneland 2018). The generous state underwrites/materializes Duque and Buitrago's *desiderata* via fiscal, monetary, and taxation incentives designed to encourage the NICL by promising foreign investors that they will pay no income tax for seven years and receive a 19% break on indirect taxes for exported texts. The government allocated half a billion dollars towards this extravaganza for 2019, thanks to the formation of Duque's very own Consejo Nacional de Economía Naranja (National Orange Economy Council) (S. Rincón 2019; "Consejo Nacional" 2019).

So Colombian popular culture is reborn as a set of creative industries; subordinating inalienable heritage, craft production, and the refusal of racism, sexism, and nationalism to avaricious capital. It seeks to make things in similar ways to the manufacture of an automobile or artificial knee, producing objects for consumption in the so-called magical operation of supply and demand. Consider the New Cinema and Location Colombia laws. Taking advantage of the growing number of technical and university degrees that school the willing and worthy in film and television, Location Colombia was enacted to lure international productions. It copied similar actions elsewhere: cash rebates and tax returns to foreign companies (AKA Hollywood) willing to relocate production. The lure included a new El Dorado of cheap labor, beautiful scenery, and industrious servitude—the classic NICL. It is creating primary (international) versus secondary (local) audiovisual labor markets: international productions increase the quality of life for audiovisual workers in an environment that is out of reach for those employed in Colombian screen drama. For example, Dynamo, a Colombian production company that has profited from the new legislation, has done little to support local talent or national films (Rocha 2018: 363). Despite the increasing numbers of Colombian films and audiences for them, the local industry remains a site of precarious work and difficult working conditions (Arias et al. 2018). And runaway productions promote the exploitation of local workers by local producers, since foreign producers are required to hire Colombian firms, which profit most when expanding their overheads and reducing local costs, generating those primary versus secondary labor markets that separate foreign from domestic crews (Uribe-Jongbloed and Corredor-Aristizábal 2020).

Like the orange economy in general, the benefits are unevenly distributed, because they require technology and English. Twenty million Colombians do not have access to the Internet and well under a fifth of the workforce is bilingual (S. Rincón 2019). At the high end financially, this means that Colombian settings and actors are used to represent Venezuela in the second season of Amazon's *Jack Ryan* (2019), its highest-rating series ever, with virtually no one aware of the part played by the NICL. In case anyone imagined that Bogotá standing in for Caracas was dubious, lead actor John Krasinski was on hand to reassure viewers that filming in Colombia was "genuinely dangerous" (quoted in Griffiths 2019). Conversely, Colombia becomes the diegetic source of a rampaging imperialism in season five of *The Last Ship* (TNT, 2018)—shot in California (Richford 2018; Thorne 2019; Debnath 2018)—to match its lawless, leftist reputation.

Despite this oleaginous political economy, other cultural practices—heritage, craft, the avant garde, contemporary dance, and activism—are not mere crumbs scraped from the chopping board of a 'creative' corporate bakery.

Consider the century-long career of José Eustasio Rivera's 1924 modernist classic of the jungle novel, *La Vorágine* (*The Vortex*) (1985). It details the elopement of a young couple from Bogotá during the 1879–1912 rubber boom. They make their way through violent gangs and rough terrain, all the while observing the hell of daily life for enslaved indigenous plantation workers. The vortex of the Amazon ultimately claims the protagonists: they can neither find a way out, nor be found by others.

The story borrows from an array of influences:

- A Greco-Roman tragedy of an inferno claiming star-crossed lovers
- The avant garde
- The fearful encounter of *mestizaje* with the environment
- The horror of forced labor
- The destructiveness of industrial lust for natural resources

La Vorágine is regularly reimagined in commercial screen forms via Colombian film and TV adaptations—part of a constantly developing national tradition of rap music, plays, poetry, and drama that places the horror of violence and the hope for peace at its core. Again and again, the theme is the seeming inevitability of conflict, the desire to end it, and links between corporatized crime, ideological violence, the state, and mainstream civil society (Oslender 2008). The nation's novelists and short-story writers in particular frequently use first-person narration, offering horrified wonderment at their survival, or feature protagonists making their way across the country who are bewildered by its "ubiquitous tragedy" (Chaparro Valderrama 2007: xviii).

This literary fascination is not always critical or progressive; the popular is also crucial to gendered violence. So memoirs by Colombian assassins articulate masculinity to violence through pleasure—a hedonistic cathexis onto motorbikes, guns, and clothes as signs of virility obtained through death (Franco 2001). Consider the textualization of Jhon Jairo Velásquez, a key assassin for the Medellín cocaine cartel in the 1980s. He was personally responsible for killing hundreds of people, and managed the assassination of thousands more. Jairo Velásquez became known as Popeye due to a supposed resemblance to the cartoon character—a typical *sicario* (assassin) appropriation of popular culture to leaven and lighten their image (Uribe 2018). Following his release from prison in 2014, Popeye's YouTube channel exploded in popularity, gaining well over a million subscribers.[12] He remade himself under the soubriquet "Popeye Rependido" (Repentant Popeye) and claimed redemption through apology, even as he started his videos with bullet holes and gunfire, proudly admitted to mass murders, and interpellated his ultra-right followers as political *confrères* (compatriots) (Mele and Garcia 2016; Anderson 2018). Netflix merrily parlayed a Colombian adaptation of his memoir, *Sobreviviendo a Escobar* (*Surviving Escobar*) (2017) and a reactionary Spanish province hired him to promote its setting and cuisine.[13] *Rolling Stone* and the *New Yorker* profiled him (Glade 2017; "Popeye" 2018) and Russia Today released a bizarre documentary, *Escobar's Hitman* (2017), which trailed Popeye around Medellín as he encountered victims and their families and was hailed on the streets by the popular classes.[14] Throughout, the carefully curated image is of a paradoxically dependent man's man, indebted to hegemonic masculinity, craving the approval of his chosen chief, and eschewing introspective males and 'scheming' women (Bialowas Pobutsky 2013). In 2018, he was back in the joint, accused of extortion, intimidation, and leading a group of bagmen for the mob. The following year, he was charged with human-rights violations for his part in the 1986 murder of the prominent newspaper editor, Guillermo Cano Isaza (Higuera 2019).

To understand how vanguardist prose and a mass murderer can be so influential, we must travel beyond material macrohistory and enter the seemingly ephemeral world of popular culture. Gabo's thoughts about the binary contradictions of Colombian subjectivity apply tellingly to both a modernist classic's intertexts and remakes, where an intolerable, inevitable fate is part of the ecstasy of love, development ruins the environment, and labor is forced and painful—and to a crude, cruel, coarse assassin who draws on so-called social media for self-aggrandizement, incitement—and renewed criminal organization.

La Vorágine instantiates and criticizes hegemonic forms of racial, ecological, and gender power in a way that presages both the magical realism of Gabo and his list of binaries: paradoxes of gentle and harsh people and places, where comfort and ease are cheek by jowl with pain and suffering for humans and the natural world. Those paradoxes are homologous with the novel's industrial history, which crosses ancient European myth-making, modernist literature, and popular cinema and television. For his part, Popeye's brazenly murderous narcissism appeals to young men, publishers, and Hollywood alike in its quasi-humorous deadly outrage at the world—and right-wing bling.

Comprehending the life of these commodified cultural signs is part of understanding Colombia's persistence of violence, especially now that there is such adoration of culture's commercial potential via the putative orange economy.

THE BOOK YOU HOLD IN YOUR HANDS

I write as someone who has been heavily influenced by Latin American social science and humanities and their equivalents in the United States and Europe. Colombian communication studies, which is of particular pertinence to me, is divided into "four fields" (not unlike U.S. anthropology). They include journalism, quantitative method, organizational communication, and semiotics, derived from the intersection of administrative (U.S.) and critical (Latin American) paradigms (Martín-Barbero 2006; Barranquero Carretero et al. 2017). But unlike in the Global North, Colombian faculty and students frequently function across these domains, doing policy-oriented and quantoid work as well as textual analysis and political economy. *The Persistence of Violence* follows that lead in its methodological mix.

The book draws on the accounts and contradictions adumbrated in this introduction to contextualize detailed investigations of key sites in Colombian popular culture that express violence and its counters. I blend political economy, ethnography, and content and textual analysis, mixing philosophical, scientific, and social-scientific approaches through the filter of Latin American studies. Each chapter commences with an account in theoretical and research terms of the general phenomenon of popular culture that follows, in its Colombian context.

Chapter 1, on sports, focuses on the national pastime, association football. It looks at the hypermasculinity embodied by many fans and its imbrication with narcotrafficking, the media, and symbolic ties to militarism. The chapter draws on football's history, its corruption and violence, and a close reading of the game's recent use by television networks and the state to invoke and develop a regressive national popular, as the government seeks to emphasize its monopoly on legitimate symbolic and actual violence.

Chapter 2, on tourism, examines the marketing of Colombia as a brand in the formal and informal economy, with a dual attention to sexuality and history. The sexual component argues that successive tourism policies have emphasized gender and nature via homologies between young women and the environment. This tendency is connected to child sex trafficking in Cartagena de Indias, the incipient violence underpinning the port's gender and racial politics—and resistance to these formations. The historical component focuses on the recent controversy in Cartagena over a plaque erected to attract U.K. tourists that commemorated Britain's blockade of the city during a struggle to control the Caribbean slave trade.

Chapter 3, on the media, is again double-sided. The first side investigates past and present violence against Colombian journalists, using interviews with victims to see how self-censorship arises from newsroom corruption and public threats and what can be done about it. The chapter's second side draws on a content analysis of high-rating broadcast *narconovelas* and their narco aesthetic of light-skinned, blonde, surgically modified femininity, in a country where very few people either resemble that stereotype or can afford to develop it. This popularity derives from production practices within the media, historic tendencies toward machismo and *Marianismo*, domestic violence, and wider debates over gender and *narcocultura*.

Chapter 4, on the environment, looks at the nation's crucial riparian thoroughfare, the Río Magdalena, and its systematic and accidental pollution through industrialization, warfare, and neglect. A content analysis centers on emotions expressed by Colombians in the words they use to describe the river, its meaning, and their feelings about the devastation it has undergone. The context is debates within science, activism, and government over the environment and the violence suffered by the Magdalena from development and conflict.

The book concludes with the notion that García Márquez's oppositions are useful ways to understand the profound duality over violence in Colombian life that is both evident in, and sustained by, popular culture. At the same time, although binaries are good to think with, they are frequently logocentrically interdependent, rather than truly opposed. One can see them more as paradoxes than contradictions.

The liberal/UN mantra of demobilization, disarmament, and reintegration as routes to post-conflict Colombian peace and prosperity derive from postwar western Europe and Japan—taking industrialized fascist countries and reestablishing them after monumental military defeat by state-socialist and state-capitalist ones. The model is barely credible when "reintegration" means returning to a corrupt, hugely unequal, and barely/badly governed nation. The focus on former combatants as problems is understandable, but it misses the reasons for their and others' alienation, and the structural and organizational forces that either incubate or enact violence (Carranza-Franco 2019).

That said, many Colombians are dedicated to peaceful progress. In that spirit, I analyze the book's themes in the context of theories and initiatives for building peace. For there are progressive elements in sports that draw on history and critique to problematize corporate nationalism. In tourism, social movements organize contra child sexual abuse, and there was opposition to the British plaque. Colombian journalists have shown a bravura, inventive response to occupational and physical intimidation, and critical responses problematize the racial and sexual politics of *narcocultura*. Social movements and environmental scientists seek to protect the environment from development.

The evidence of these diverse yet interconnected sites of the popular is that violence is never far from the surface; but nor are alternatives to it. *The Persistence of Violence* sheds light on the nation's scarred bringing-into-being, the strange dialectic of a state that is either too present or too absent—able to coerce/unable to serve—and prevailing economic, racial, and sexual dogmas. It also addresses equally Colombian, pacific, social movements. They are just as persistent as the violence they oppose.

1 • THE ABSENCE AND PRESENCE OF STATE MILITARISM

Violence, Football, Narcos

WITH ALFREDO SABBAGH FAJARDO

Gabo drew on football[1] to lend color and comprehensiveness to his explorations of Colombian life. In *Noticia de un secuestro (News of a Kidnapping),* a fictionalized essayistic ethnography of cartel kidnapping, prisoners and their guards connect with one another through their love of the sport, transcending the haze of violence that otherwise characterizes their lives together (García Márquez 1996).

The talent of football has been to capture quite precisely the popular energies of everyday people, notably men, in most of the world. The obvious task for a nation like Colombia, falling apart again and again and in danger of achieving the status of a "failed state" (Helman and Ratner 1992–1993; but see Ross 2013) has been to harness such allegiances and energies toward a national popular. Colombian football has moved from the periphery of that quest to its core and back again, as different forces have tried to harness, pervert, neglect, and resurrect the sport's role for hegemonic reasons. *Narcotraficantes, guerrilla,* and the political class have all sought to "own" football for one purpose or another, whether to highlight their power, permit the sport's relative autonomy from their struggles, or consolidate public support for national institutions. Throughout, the media and spectators have been coeval partners in this trajectory and the players exploited missionaries, sometimes colluding in their own oppression, sometimes resisting it (Soto 2017).

Our contention is that football in Colombia has zigzagged between being a force for normalcy, routine, and pleasure versus violence, inconstancy, and horror. We focus on a time when the globally well-established nexus of militarism and sports was trumped in Colombia by a narco-trafficking formation that used football as an exhibit in its challenge to the very basis of the state. The sport emerged as an attention-getting means of querying the rule of law, problematizing Weber's definition of sovereignty discussed in the introduction, and stressing the contradictory world of *hecha la ley, hecha la trampa.*

We ask how football became a symbol of one of the three different para-states seemingly running parts of the country, and what changed when those material circumstances shifted, such that Weber's maxim came true once more—on prime-time television, through one of the nation's putative creative industries: sports (Ministerio de Cultura 2014: 28). Prior to that change, we look at the nexus of violence and sport in the *ethos* of football more generally. The origins of the conflict we describe reside not only in Colombia, but in the very sinews of the game's history.

When English and French fans alike sang "La Marseillaise" before their countries met in a football match just days after Paris had been assaulted in 2015,[2] they did so in the presence of the British monarchy, the French presidency, the police, and the military. The event was broadcast on public television and radio (McKenzie 2015). Like the U.S. and Colombian versions mentioned in the introduction, the anthem they shared that night was a notoriously bloodthirsty paean to racism and war: "Qu'un sang impur / Abreuve nos sillons" (Let impure blood / Water our furrows). It is "a pretty nasty song" (Dubois 2013).

That night at Wembley was a manifestation of militarism in its language, hierarchy, conduct, clothing, celebration, and propaganda. The event embodied the persistence of violence in the cultures of these notorious imperial nations and weapons exporters. But the performance was hailed quite differently, as an expression of solidarity, humanness, and caring. It was instantly likened to the tear-jerking sequence in *Casablanca* (directed by Michael Curtiz in 1942) when Paul Georg Julius Hernreid von Wasel Waldingau, Corinna Mura, and Marie Madeleine Berthe Lebeau lead the crowd singing the French national anthem in opposition to Nazism and collaboration in occupied French imperial territory.[3]

But Wembley 2015 would satisfy many definitions of militarism meeting football, given the state presence, the lyrical content, the uniformed imagery, the armed environment, the declaration of war, and the stadium setting.[4] It is telling that in 2001, when Algeria played France in Paris for the first time, "La Marseillaise" was booed by a crowd consisting mainly of postcolonial survivors, and the game was called off following a pitch invasion (Andress 2018). This followed the Front National's leader calling footballers who refused to sing along with the anthem "fake Frenchmen" (quoted in Dubois 2013).

Nationalism, racism, violence, and militarism are incarnate in football, as we indicate through an engagement with its history and theory. In Colombia, as in many countries, no other cultural practice generates as much media coverage, employment, fandom, or sponsorship. Attention orange economy and hegemonic forces in search of money and a national popular respectively!

Polling data say football is of great interest to 94 percent of the Colombian population, and is played by a third of adolescent girls and 85 percent of the Afrocolombian and indigenous populations (Comisión Nacional de Seguridad, Comodidad y Convivencia en el Fútbol 2014: 13). When researchers asked a group of children to define the country, they replied "un partido de fútbol" (a football game) (quoted in Dávila and Londoño 2005: 135). There is a Colombian expression: "en la mesa no se habla de religión, ni de política, ni de fútbol" (one doesn't speak of religion, politics, or football over dinner) (quoted in Santos Gómez 2018).

Our focus here is the 1980s and '90s, an era dominated by putatively progressive *guerrilla*, putatively unofficial right-wing *paramilitares,* and putatively populist *narcotraficantes*/mafiosi. As noted in the introduction, they held sway over rural and urban terrain; ran institutions of civil society; harvested, refined, distributed, and sold recreational drugs; were ruthless and violent kidnappers and executioners; corrupted state officials; and trumpeted inconspicuous battle fatigues and conspicuous consumption, respectively, as signs of legitimacy and triumph. One aspect of everyday life was not entirely shared in their tripartite struggle against each other and the state over who could terrorize the population most—the narcos' involvement in football. Here we see the emergence of a non-ideological alternative government, unlike classic movements of left and right, and a sign of how popular culture can connect to glamorous criminality.

Football in Colombia has long attracted those interested in hegemonic display—spectacle with a message rather than for its own sake—as well as shady operators seeking dark shadows. It is a flashy means of displaying wealth, power, and sovereignty, but equally a way of obscuring the flow of illicit money behind the sport's simultaneously folkloric and glamorous status, as the coevally physiocratic property of fans and capitalist property of owners. And there is a great deal to hide—whereas Colombian coffee sells in the United States for four times the cost of production, the profits from cocaine are a hundredfold (Bergman 2018: 27).

The narcos' non-military violence came to dominate the national game for perhaps two decades. It crowded out the usual propagandistic ties between football and militarism essayed by governments or other actors we have mentioned. When the conjuncture changed twenty years later, because the narcos had ended their showy control of football, the AUC had ceased formal operation, and a peace accord had been signed with the FARC, the military and television governmentalized and commodified football to symbolize a new national unity benignly intertwined with populist capital. The sport's ties to violence were normalized within the conventional policy and rhetoric of a national popular, founded in alliances between governments and media. Did this mark a break in the persistence of violence?

FOOTBALL/CROWDS/VIOLENCE

George Orwell famously described sports as "war minus the shooting" (1945) even though they shared ties to violence and imperialism. His pithy description came from observing a "goodwill" British tour by the Soviet football club, commando Дина́мо Москва́ (Dynamo Moscow) (Dmowski 2015).[5] Orwell feared that such "sporting contests lead to orgies of hatred" because the competitiveness inherent in football symbolizes and stimulates the desire to defeat the other. His colonial and militia experience of football in Burma, India, and Spain was of uncontrolled and passionate derision expressed by one section of a crowd toward another.

Football had evolved from the British middle class pacifying, adopting, and codifying unruly working-class male pastimes. During Britain's revolution, Quaker radicals looked down on it while workers reveled (Hill 1991: 233, 254). E. P. Thompson took the next phase, of rentier control, to typify the sequestration of public space (1979). Lenin feared that England's cultivable land was being wasted, "used for sport, for the diversion of the rich" (1964: 281–282). The nineteenth-century British inspector of schools, poet, and critic Matthew Arnold looked on, bemused but resigned, as the Industrial Revolution created "games and sports which occupy the passing generation of boys and young men" in search of "a better and sounder physical type for the future to work with" (2003). The process saw many contradictions, with social elites gradually losing control of football's "modest subterranean life as a proletarian spectator sport" (Hobsbawm 1998: 63, 65). It spread across the world during that century in close concert with the United Kingdom's colonial, maritime, military, and commercial interests (Elias 1978; Elias and Dunning 1986; Krauze 1994).

Ambivalence and even contempt for the sport has a long and profound heritage. In *Utopia*, Thomas More called for football to be banned because it encouraged the poor to invest their money unwisely (2012: 47). Many distinguished authors and critics have concurred, from Borges loathing sports in general for embodying crass popular tastes to Sánchez Ferlosio deriding them as fascist spectacles (Meneses and González 2013) and Ortega y Gasset (1994) complaining that football fans were incapable of encountering a world of wonder with the truly open gaze of the intellectual. Fred Halliday longed for "a time before public discourse was dominated by footballers" (2009), Sherlock Holmes advised that "football does not come within my horizon" (Conan Doyle 1960: 633),[6] and Queenie Leavis characterized watching it as one of the world's "substitute or kill-time interests" in comparison with crafts or singing (1939: 209). In Latour's eyes, fans are mere atoms, with predictably banal collective responses (Latour et al. 2012), while the passage of European football from a public to a private good via profound governmentalization and commodification is clearly a matter of great regret for Galeano (2016) and Yanis Varoufakis (1998: 230) alike.

For many on the cultural left, football is at best a "popular tonic" (Horkheimer 2002: 289–290); at worst, it warrants Adorno and Horkheimer's famous articulation of "a left-half at football, a black-shirt, a member of the Hitler Youth, and so on" (1979: 164). H. G. Wells drew a homology between football teams and armed divisions (1902: 184). In Marcuse's words, the game represents a "conspicuous social mobilization of aggressiveness, the militarization of the affluent society. This mobilization goes far beyond the actual draft of manpower . . . no longer the 'classical' heroizing of killing in the national interest, but rather its reduction to the level of natural events and contingencies of daily life" (2009: 195). Luxemburg metaphorized it to describe weakness in the face of state and military domination (2004: 218). For example, the valence of matches between Real Madrid and Barcelona has long been supercharged by the Spanish Civil War, the dictatorship's support of Madrid and suppression of *Català* (Catalan), and the rivalries generated by core-periphery relations. Manuel Vázquez Montalbán referred to Barça as "el ejército de un país desarmado" (the army of a disarmed nation) (1987).

Football is said to appeal to base instincts, blinding ordinary people to their real conditions of existence in a mystificatory "collective narcissism" (Burke 2004: 69). Trotsky claimed that working-class revolutionary possibilities were derailed because these "deepest passions . . . [were] skilfully restrained and suppressed" by cathexis onto football and other pastimes (1925). Badiou mocks newspapers comparing popular responses to France's 1998 World Cup triumph to liberation from the Nazis. He regarded the celebration as a "counter-demonstration" (2007: 107).

In at least semi-jest, Terry Eagleton (2010) has called for the sport's abolition in order to liberate the minds of the people. Agnes Heller worried about the spectator who compensated for "disappointments and failures by identifying with a top football team" and thereby became "a slave to play" (1984: 231). No surprise, then, that in *Nineteen Eighty-Four,* "the proles" were fascinated by football; it "filled up the horizons of their minds" (Orwell 1949: 41). Bourdieu argued that sports' blend of violence and discipline generated a classic working-class pastime—fatally so in terms of political efficacy (1978).

For Irigaray, football is a route to masculine dominance. It "encourages the stereotypes of the male world: a competitive relationship between the same—one organized around the appropriation of an object belonging to one and all, yet none" (2004: 93). Elena Poniatowska's account of the horrendous Mexico City earthquake of 1985 includes a telling remark on national and international footballing authorities reassuring themselves that the 1986 men's World Cup could go ahead despite the chaos, and bring much-needed foreign investment and local joy and pride. She wrote "Yeah, sure" (1995: 101). Iris Marion Young derides the idea that a sports club can "enhance democracy or contribute to a solidarity of strangers" as absurd (2000: 162), while Michael J. Sandel criticizes the aggressive vicariousness on display when touchline parents routinely abuse players, referees, and others (2007: 53).

Adorno thought simply watching football promoted "a retrogressive and sometimes even infantile type of person" (1945: 213) as the game's aggression breached the very "rules of hospitality," with visiting fans ignored or jeered by their hosts (2005: 118). Guattari said that the fleeting moments of jouissance in spectatorship, when the self is lost in orgasmic joy through identification with collective triumph, are forever scarred by violent capitalism because of their necessary link to an inferior other (1996: 156). Hobson referred to a "hygienic necessity" that imperial Britain channel its people's "savage instinct," which was expressed abroad through the oppression of others and domestically in football matches (1902: 213).

Such critiques are typical of progressive activists in the late nineteenth and twentieth centuries, as part of their frequent contempt for working culture and concerns about false consciousness (Hobsbawm 1998: 71). They also fit Eco's concept of sports cubed: multiplied first by media coverage per se and then by coverage *of* that coverage, putting us progressively at further removes from social issues (1987: 162–164).

Other observers allow football a relative autonomy from this flattening of perception and sharpening of chauvinism. Functionalist theorists argue that sports in general provide a physiological, psychological, and sociological outlet for tensions, especially for young men, while team games help form a healthy civil society (Parsons et al. 1955: 129). For Simmel, sports both reflected and incarnated the social order and its disorder (1949), while Durkheim thought they could "balance and relieve . . . serious life" (1961: 361). Richard Florida, the Anglo world's leading prelate of the creative-industries discourse that we encountered in the introduction, drools over "soccer moms" showing civic commitment (2009: 268), arguing that the beneficiaries of the orange economy will include cosmopolitan, internationally minded football aficionados (2012: 141).

Norbert Elias discerned a largely agreeable sublimation and civilization of dangerous drives—both a sanctioned release from the travails of life and a means of generating profit:

> Battle lust and aggressiveness . . . find socially permitted expression . . . in competitive sports. And they are manifest above all in "spectating" . . . the daydream-like identification with some few people who, in a moderate and precisely regulated way, are allowed to act out such affects . . . active, pleasurable aggression is transformed into a more passive and restrained pleasure. (1978: 240)

In Weber's words:

> where violent conflict changes to "competition," whether for Olympic wreaths or electoral votes or other means of power or for social honor or gain, it is accomplished entirely on the basis of a rational association, whose regulations serve as "rules of the game" determining the forms of conflict, thereby certainly shifting the conflict probabilities. The gradually increasing "pacification," in the sense of the reduction in the use of physical force, only reduces but does not ever wholly eliminate the appeal to the use of force. But in the course of historical development, its use has been increasingly monopolized by the coercive apparatus of a certain kind of association or consensus community—the political—and has been changed into the form of the regulated coercive threat by those in power and finally into a formally neutral force. (1981: 173)

Further to the left, Williams warned that "we mustn't be snobs . . . football is indeed a wonderful game" (1963: 364), while Brecht joyously said, "We pin our hopes to the sporting public. We have our eye on those huge concrete pans, filled with 15,000 men and women of every variety of class and physiognomy, the fairest and shrewdest audience in the world" (1964: 6). He saw great potential for political vibrancy and even revolution, akin to the political pleasure that John Lennon experienced when football crowds chanted the Beatles song "All Together Now" to express solidarity (1971). Lukács held that only proletarian crowds truly understood the importance of football, because it was an extension in spectacular form of their industrial experience (1972).

The Situationists celebrated the *soixante-huitards* (French activists of May 1968) taking over the offices of the Fédération Française de Football (French Football Federation) (Solidarity 2001: 92). Boaventura de Sousa Santos argues that popular resistance to the 1964–1985 Brazilian dictatorship, which led to progressive local government, was fomented by the formation of clubs, inter alia (2007: 311–312), while Amilcar Cabral took football teams as models for the unity of purpose and diversity of identity needed for revolutionary change (1979: 4).

Kristeva delights in a "footballer's body" as a sign of male modernity (Kristeva and Sollers 2016: 22). América Larraín overcame her intense antipathy to football through its association with dance, in terms of the body encapsulating identity—and how Colombia's national team celebrates on the pitch (2015). Jean Rouch's cinema illustrates the ties between dance and football (2003), and the white proletarian bigot Alf Garnett of British television's *Till Death Us Do Part* (1965–1975—remade in the United States as *All in the Family* [1971–1979])—described football as "working-class ballet" (quoted in Rentoul 2011).[7]

Interesting contradictions arise: militant nationalistic men cavorting in stadia against "the other" are drawn to symbols that engulf them and are often international; the sport embodies global culture as much as do the English, Arabic, or

Spanish languages (Hobsbawm 1998: 6). Ulrich Beck (2002) avowed that football counters nationalism thanks to its postcolonial/global capitalist ecumenism, and can work for multicultural peacefulness—the positive side of multinational capital striding the stadia of the world. The nationalism expressed by fans in regional and global contests can transcend the pressures of globalization, reasserting local identities (Velasquez Forero 2010). Néstor Garcia Canclini notes that teams are "key sites of imaginary identity," capable of producing "a durable, affective investment of loyalty and solidarity" (2008: 393).

Jacques Attali argues that football is one of the few topics that can generate discussion in almost any venue, potentially leading to a common understanding where none had seemed possible (2001: 262). And even Orwell referred admiringly to a miner who emerged from the pit covered from head to toe by coal dust, then proudly washed and changed into his best clothes to attend a match, imagining a socialist future that would sparkle with the pleasure of watching football (1937: 3, 11).

Eisenstein offered a dialectical explanation of the sport's popularity: "the symbol of joint battle and cooperation is embodied in it very strongly and magnificently, which forces one to pass on personal initiative" (1987: 284). Despite her reservations about spectatorship, Heller took the playing of football as a site where "the individual grows into the group"; an exemplar of collective, interdependent action that assumed reciprocity as much as competition (1984: 31, 221). She has this in common with Laclau and Mouffe (1987: 82), Donzelot (2006), and Castoriadis (2010: 92).

The idea of a struggle over violence and order, pleasure and passivity underpinning football and its spectators goes back centuries (Weber 1992: 112). T. H. Marshall regarded attendance at matches as a "common right" (1950: 82), Stuart Hall discerned an "overwhelming mirror of football" refracting society (1998: 191), and Althusser viewed stadia as sites of oscillation between exuberant arrogance and gormless conformity (1971: 162).

In their different ways, all these writers were trying to understand bodies at play, beyond the confines of the field, factory, or office and in moments of power and weakness, strength and failure, control and excess (Miller 2001), as per Adrienne Rich's celebration of "what makes the body shoot . . . [i]nto its pure and irresistible curve" (1997). That semiotic system routinely cross-validates sports and nations via myths of representativeness, justice, and upward mobility that idealize existing political, economic, and social life—distorting conflict, then resignifying it. The sporting body is an always-already mediated object, rearticulated with the supposed essence of the person via training and play.

Footballers instantiate the possibilities and limitations of life within formal and informal rules and expectations. We know almost too much about them, most notably what they look like in extremis: dirty, sweaty, teary, demoralized, undressed, furious, joyous, unguarded, unconscious, and otherwise injured (like ourselves when vomiting or coming).

Assumptions of omniscience and failure flow from their visibility, liveness, repetition, difference, and discourse. Football's link to violence is ongoing, from fields of play and stadium spaces to streets, bars, homes, and television programs. When Wittgenstein problematized the seemingly synonymous use of the word *good* in the formulations, "a good football player" and "a good fellow," he was referring to the complexities that arise when words are redisposed to connote ethical value rather than empirical description (1965: 9). This has significance for social distinctions, as when middle-class British children internalize the importance of not playing football in the street; their working-class equivalents, not so much. These inhibitions are tied to 'correct' conduct rather than to safety (Bernstein 2003: 153).

Of course, the pacification outlined above was uneven. Football seemingly returned to its ungoverned origins in 1970s Western Europe. The stagflationary chaos of that period saw jobs lost, social services compromised, unemployment risen, and immigration turned into a tinderbox, as people from former colonies came (in small numbers) to reactionary deindustrializing metropoles. The sport became a place of spectacle to enact these tensions in Britain, the Netherlands, Italy, and the then Federal Republic of Germany. Stadia were transformed into crucibles of nationalistic, racist, misogynistic, and hypermasculine conduct ("hooliganism") and the countervailing desire to control such urges by both state and commerce.

The term *hooligan* was an Irish/Marxist concept describing:

> foul and adventures-seeking dregs of the bourgeoisie, . . . vagabonds, dismissed soldiers, discharged convicts, runaway galley slaves, sharpers, jugglers, lazzaroni, pickpockets, sleight-of-hand performers, gamblers, procurers, keepers of disorderly houses, porters, literati, organ grinders, rag pickers, scissors grinders, tinkers, beggars. (Marx 1987: 63)

Scholarly investigations of football hooligans incarnate both their criminalization via moral panics and their romantic annunciation as working-class scions, while the psy-function strives to correlate heightened testosterone with victory (Armstrong and Young 1997; Armstrong 1998; Bernhardt et al., 1998).

Debates thrive between those who see redeeming features in this violence, or at least some critical symbolism, and those who straightforwardly condemn it. Progressives draw on Thompson's insight that crowds may be animated by economic conditions, sexual urges, or blind rage, but also by ideological commitments and desires to comment, maintaining that anomie produces indexical resistance and criticizes the panoptic design of contemporary stadia (1971). Conversely, conservatives see hooliganism as the outcome of permissiveness leading to loose-willed, tight-limbed lawlessness (Giulianotti 1999: 80–82;

Meneses and González 2007; Schimmel et al. 2007). The reality probably lies in some mixture of these accounts; British football hooligans appropriated cultural style and social space to compensate for their exclusion from dominant norms, but did so to revolt against difference as much as uniformity, because their solidarity was to do with gender and class sameness expressed against gender and racial difference (Hall 2016: 195).

The increasingly centralized nature of football is equally complicated. World football's governing body, the Fédération Internationale de Football Association (FIFA) routinely rides roughshod over international organizations, national sovereignty, and tricky little things like democracy (Bond 2010; Hyde 2010)—consider the way it brokered power-sharing in Bosnia-Herzegovina, transcending the European Union (Cooley and Mujanović 2015). FIFA fiefdoms are painful, pitiful, but powerful hangovers from the amateur good-old-boy networks that ran the sport before its wholesale commercialization. We should not be in thrall to this self-anointed elect's control of football, especially when it is deeply connected to capital: the Association represents the ultimate in corrupt commodification and governmentalization—but it is not alone.

There are coefficients in the transmogrification of national organizations. Most prominently, Western European football clubs were once small, city-based businesses, drawing on athletes who had grown up close to their grounds. They were run rather like not-for-profits, representing and regenerating local cultures, albeit sometimes dominated by corporations (in Germany) or petit-bourgeois *machistas* (male chauvinists) (in Britain). By the 1990s, many had been commodified into creatures of exchange. In the course of this radical transformation, they fell prey to fictive capital, becoming sources of asset inflation used by rentiers to service other debts through the cash flow of television money and merchandising, and governed by growth evangelists who sought an ever-greater expansion of their associations. A similar illicit story unfurls in the pages to come.

COLUMBIA

The remainder of this chapter addresses the following quandary: why close ties between state-based militarism and football have not always applied in Colombia. For while militarism obviously occupies an important role in the mental map of Colombians (Lindsay-Poland and Tickner 2016), it has been largely absent from football. Institutional violence and its symbolism have not. We speculate that this is the consequence of a failed state that has been hugely compromised in its capacity to deliver security to its citizenry, thanks to lawless cocaine dealers and revolutionaries and its own human-rights violations. Only now, with *narcotraficantes* having abandoned the politics of spectacle and the FARC the politics of armed struggle, is the state reasserting its military primacy in association with sports.

Theoretical and policy anxieties and pieties over football's oscillation between passivity and violence attain particular form in Latin America, where state involvement in football is a suitable case for critique. One thinks back to the repatriation of Latin Americans of Italian descent like Enrique/Enrico Guaita to help Mussolini's Italy win World Cups in the 1930s, and 1969's so-called football war between El Salvador and Honduras (Rec.Sport.Soccer Statistics Foundation 2015; Cable 1969; Galeano 2013: 142, 288–289). Fascist dictatorships installed and curated by the United States from the 1960s to the 1980s drew on the sport as legitimating theater, connecting their rule to popular pastimes and support: consider propaganda for the Brazilian and Argentine regimes provided by their teams' international successes (Andrade de Melo and Drumond 2014; Jiménez Botta 2017). Particular attention is often paid to the 1978 men's World Cup Finals in Argentina, which featured a dubious match with Perú; the hosts won 6–0 and hence qualified for the next round. Johan Cruyff, Dutch captain and hero of the left and Cataluña, was (falsely) rumored to have boycotted the Finals because of the dictatorship (Arango Forero 2005; EFE 2007; Cronin 2010).

But Colombia's Comisión Nacional de Seguridad, Comodidad y Convivencia en el Fútbol (National Commission for Safety, Comfort, and Togetherness in Football) forwards the sport's purported character-building qualities of solidarity, health, social cohesion, and pleasure in diverting young people from violence. Its ten-year plan tethers football to the peace process (2014: 17) as a source of integrative transformation (Centro Nacional de Consultoría 2014). Colombian research found no positive correlation between heart attacks, stress, and viewing the 2014 men's World Cup—in fact, to the contrary (Rincón-Escobar et al., 2018). Football relaxes?

But those functionalist claims for sport—that it produces a fitter population, better able to work, and a more pacific one, capable of expressing powerful feelings in law-abiding ways—are brought into question by violence on and off the pitch (Salinas Arango 2018). Cross-cultural research indicates that there are more red- and yellow-card sanctions issued to players for violent conduct in countries with high levels of violence in general than in more pacific locales. This applies to Colombians and Israelis above other nationalities, in both domestic and foreign leagues (Orrego Ramírez et al. 2010; Miguel et al. 2011). And Colombia's *barras bravas* (fan "hooligans") include many violent men characterized by the following:

- Bellicose frames of mind
- Use of alcohol, marijuana, and cocaine before, during, and after matches
- Minimal education
- Maximal alienation
- Domestic violence
- Racist stadium chants and taunts

Numerous *hinchas* (fans) have spent time with the *paramilitares* and narcos; membership of such groups allowed them to establish identities within stadia and feel proudly marked as "same" versus "other." As per hooligans more generally, the scholarly literature is split between critiques of this hypermasculinity and its romanticization as carnivalesque proletarian resistance to middle-class, governmental, and corporate norms (Clavijo Poveda 2004; López-Quintero and Neumark 2012; Villanueva Bustos 2013; Castro Lozano 2013, 2019; Uribe Aramburo and Castaño Pérez 2014; Edgar Galeano et al. 2015; Restrepo Escobar 2015; Castillo et al. 2016; Uribe Aramburo 2018).[8]

The stakes are high: when Asociación Deportivo Cali failed to make the playoffs in 2018, a player was shot at; after the Barranquilla team Club Deportivo Popular Junior FC SA won a match that year, supporters were bombed as they caroused in a Córdoba night club ("Colombian Player" 2018; "13 Wounded" 2018). During the 2014 and 2018 men's World Cup Finals, the rate of domestic violence rose by 38 percent and 25 percent respectively during matches involving Colombia. The figure was 50 percent for the 2015 Copa América, a competition between national teams from the region (Salazar 2018).

This should be no surprise; in Colombia, as elsewhere, women have largely been excluded from football's discourse of vibrancy, nationalism, and disorder, despite its embeddedness in the media as the national pastime and symbol of a virile and skillful unity—and despite women's fascination for the sport (Vélez 2001; Orrego Ramírez et al. 2010). This is in keeping with generations of powerful taboos against women playing games in general, leavened only recently by a development discourse that stresses physical culture as a route to safety, pleasure, and fewer teen pregnancies, but remains dogged by colonial prohibitions (Oxford and Spaaij 2019; Oxford 2019). Meanwhile, the women's national team has struggled in the face of minimal resources. It came to be known as *nuestras guerreras* (our fighters) at the 2015 women's World Cup Finals and the Panamerican games, and the men's team has spoken out against gendered violence (Watson 2018: 608; "Selección" 2014). On the other side of the ledger, one of their number, Pablo Estifer Armero, was arrested in 2016 for sexual assault. When the prominent sports journalist Andrea María Guerrero Quintero criticized his selection for the national team the following year, she received numerous death threats (Salazar 2018).

HISTORY

Colombian football's links to the persistence of violence derive from the twentieth-century diffusion of both the sport and the railway, connecting residents of the sovereign state to one another and the capitalist world economy. These journeys into modernity were equally journeys into violence, via attempts to impose centralized cultural and economic authority on peripheral regions (Quitián Roldán and Urrea Beltrán 2016a).

It is often suggested that football gained its Colombian foothold in Barranquilla, the port city where many British sailors and businessmen alighted, traded, built—and played football (Ruiz Patiño 2017). The mythic formal origin of football in Colombia is an 1892 match between teams from a military college. Organized by a U.S. colonel, it was played in front of President Miguel Antonio José Zolio Cayetano Andrés Avelino de las Mercedes Caro Tobar and covered by the press. The participants continued regular matches until the Thousand Days War (Santos Molano 2016).

The link between violence and football was therefore present from the beginning. Between the 1900s and 1940, the sport emerged from the governmental and commercial elite to become a national pastime. Football democratized in part because the state began a biopolitical regime that institutionalized physical education in schools. Biopower brought "life and its mechanisms into the realm of explicit calculations," making "knowledge-power an agent of transformation of human life." Bodies came to be identified with politics, and managing them equated to running the country, with "the life of the species . . . wagered on its own political strategies." Keeping populations fit for purpose involved assaying them and encouraging recreational activity (Foucault 1984: 143; 1991: 97, 92–95). In this context, Colombian football migrated from gated polo, golf, and gun clubs to public schools and unpaved streets, aided by physical education, radio coverage, and associated gossip (Quitián Roldán 2013; Ruiz Patiño 2017). Its developing strength as a pastime derived from schools and other elements of civil society dedicated to the idea of recreation preparing young men to be disciplined followers rather than dissolute rebels. This in turn drew approbation and support from governments (Torres Velasco 2019).

But football's availability for hegemonic use as part of a national popular was limited. As we shall see, the state's ability to harness the sport symbolically was uneven throughout the century to come, in terms of administration, finance, and lawfulness. To begin with, the relative isolation of the country's distinct topographic regions enabled a racialized discourse of essentialism that tied the power-laden but largely immobile sports of baseball and boxing to the coasts and the intense labor of cycling and running to the interior (Fernández L'Hoeste 2015). This was a striking difference from British football clubs, which mapped almost exactly onto clusters of working-class labor (Hobsbawm 1998: 66).

That said, the early years of *La Violencia* were surprisingly propitious for football. As noted in the introduction, Gaitán's assassination in 1948 marked the infestation of politics by violence—the onset of two decades of open bloodshed. But Colombian football mythologizes the period between 1949 and 1954 as its *El Dorado*. Those years saw the formation of federations, the codification of laws of the game after the British example, the full emergence of professionalism, and the capacity to share scores and highlights via the spread of telex, telephone, radio—and people, with perhaps a thousand footballers arriving to play in the national league from Britain, Italy, Yugoslavia, Hungary, Perú, Paraguay, Argentina, Costa Rica, and Uruguay. One of football's greatest, Alfredo Stéfano Di Stéfano Laulhé, played with Bogotá's Azul y Blanco Millonarios Fútbol Club SA for four years (Quitián Roldán and Urrea Beltrán 2016a; Santos Molano 2016). The period marked the sport's insertion into an emergent NICL through unprecedented salaries (Miller 2018b)—albeit without the payment of transfer fees, and the nation's subsequent exile from international football as punishment. The influx of foreign players ended when European leagues began their recovery from the war and scouted talent that had gone overseas, other South American leagues entered the transfer market, and Colombia sought reintegration into the world game (Fernández L'Hoeste 2015; Santos Molano 2016).

Thanks to this cornucopia of cosmopolitan talent, football was also popularly celebrated for its political neutrality amid the polarization of *La Violencia*. It became a core part of newspaper reportage, which had largely ignored it until then. Radio coverage during *El Dorado* and the bipartisan period of politics between *La Violencia* and the mid-1970s projected football into a nascent national popular. This occurred in dialectical form: the sport was the property and design of elites seeking incorporation of the population into their projects through a sense of carnival and expressivity and football's governing mythology of upward mobility (Jaramillo Racines 2011; Quitián Roldán and Urrea Beltrán 2016a, 2016b; Santos Molano 2016).

That said, the administration of the game was subject to jurisdictional struggles during *El Dorado*. A national competition of commercial clubs commenced in 1948 with the División Mayor del Fútbol Colombiano (DIMAYOR) (First Division of Colombian Football). Its rival for control of the sport was the Asociación Colombiana de Fútbol (ADEFUTBOL) (Colombian Football Association), which had been founded and granted official standing by President Miguel Abadía Méndez in the 1920s and subsequent recognition by FIFA as the legitimate national ruling body (Ruiz Bonilla 2008). DIMAYOR's first divisional title was won by Bogotá's El Club Independiente Santa Fe SA, with Junior the runner-up. In 1949, Brazil hosted the 16th Campeonato Suramericano de Fútbol (South American Football Championship), the equivalent of today's Copa América. ADEFUTBOL was invited to send a representative club team and passed over the national champion in favor of Junior. When the club returned from Brazil, it found itself suspended from competition by DIMAYOR until 1950 (Aguirre Acuña 2003).

By the mid-1950s, these struggles had been resolved and *El Dorado*'s NICL drawn to a close. Meanwhile, the new military junta's modernizing agenda was marked by major infrastructural investments, notably in football stadia. One of these, in Ibagué, was named after Rojas Pinilla; another, in Pasto, for the day he seized power. When a new junta took control in 1957, the former was renamed La Libertad (Freedom) and the latter 10 de mayo (May 10), for the day he left office (Aguilera Peña 1999). So both football itself and its naming rights were objects of hegemony, with various contradictions bringing down efforts to associate military dictatorship with the sport. But other, pressing issues were brewing; Cold-War bipartisanship eventually gave way to the *guerrilla* and the narcos. Football merged with contraband.

NARCOFÚTBOL

In the 1980s and '90s, many clubs in Colombia were dominated by narcos, whose export of drugs and importation of guns made them wealthy and dangerous. Their involvement in football was far from clandestine; it was a bizarre form of civilian militarism, of rule through showy violence (Financial Action Task Force 2009; Martínez Colorado 2013; De Sanctis 2014; Fernández Moores 2014; Fernández L'Hoeste 2015; Marinetto 2015).

As is the case around the world, football was a suitable laundering facility for the vast amounts of *narcotraficante* cash. Governmental audits were limited and the potential for overstatement of attendance figures immense, while the sport itself afforded the narcos cachet with the popular classes. They used clubs to secret and process money, making it appear as though their wealth derived from ticket sales or player transfers—*hecha la ley, hecha la trampa*. This money-laundering emerged into the international spotlight in 1985 when the United States extradited for wire fraud Hernán Botero Moreno, a businessman with a variety of interests and president of Medellín's El Atlético Nacional SA. During a 1981 match between Nacional and El Deportivo Independiente Medellín, he had held up a fistful of dollars to signify that the referee's, shall we say, attentions, had been bought. This was in keeping with long-standing rumors that Moreno was involved in money laundering. His extradition was part of a government crackdown following the 1984 assassination of Justice Minister Rodrigo Lara Bonilla at the hands of hitmen contracted by narcos following his pronouncement that "the mafia has taken over Colombian football" (quoted in Fernández L'Hoeste 2015: 98). When football authorities protested, the government responded by threatening to close down stadia (Fabio Castillo 1987; NULLVALUE 1994; Ruiz Bonilla 2008; Allen 2015).

The state has also sought to use football as a distraction. In 1985, a commando from Colombia's *guerrilla* Movimiento 19 de Abril o M-19 (the 19th of April Movement, or M-19, named after the date of a 1974 electoral fraud) attacked the Palacio de Justicia de Colombia (Palace of Colombian Justice) in the very seat of government. Funded by the narcos as a means of intimidating the judiciary, the *guerrilla* took hundreds of hostages, from Supreme Court judges to clerks, a third of whom died in the ensuing firefight. A match was scheduled nearby between Millonarios and Club Unión Magdalena SA. The government sought to distract public attention by insisting it proceed and be televised (McCausland Sojo 2012; "Noemí Sanín" 2013). Such distractions were even meant to bring antagonists together: at the height of the kidnapping and violence by the FARC and the narcos, TV would preface broadcasts of matches with appeals for the release of victims, often fronted by the players, while captives and jailers watched games in each other's company (García Márquez 1997).

The Medellín cartel's head, Pablo Escobar Gaviria, a fan of Atlético Nacional, was the world's seventh-richest man in 1989. He specialized in populist gestures, such as paying for the importation of exotic animals to a zoo, establishing himself as a benefactor to poor suburbs in Medellín and Envigado, upgrading stadia, inviting football stars to stage matches at his ranch, and providing children with playing gear. He even held elective office, both to shore up these credentials and to ensure immunity from extradition. Other kingpins with footballing interests have included the cartel *capos* (mafia captains) "Don" Miguel Ángel Rodríguez Orejuela from Cali (La Sociedad Anónima Deportiva América SA de Cali) and Medellín's José Gonzalo Rodríguez (Millonarios). When América de Cali returned to the first division for the first time in five years in 2016, fans in Miami created banners thanking "Don" Miguel, long after he had been imprisoned in the United States. On his birthday in 2019, Cali's *hinchas* hoisted a massive banner that read "¡Siempre gracias por todo #DonMiguel, no nos olvidamos de la historia ni la gloria!" (Eternal thanks to #DonMiguel, we'll never forget the history or the glory). His legacy demands adornment (Atehortúa Cruz and Rojas Rivera 2008; Malem Seña 2014; Allen 2015; Cañizares 2018; Lezcano 2018; "El desafortunado" 2019).

Supposed civic mindedness and political ambition almost normalized the narcos as Robin Hood figures: they were regarded by many people as dynamic economic forces at a time when growth was otherwise stilted, and they presented an alternative to the seeming powerlessness of the state in the face of insurgencies (Narvaez Montoya and Romero Peña 2017). Manuel Castells was clearly prey to this mythology when he wrote that their rootedness in local culture and desire for legitimacy "made Colombian football teams (traditionally poor) the pride of the nation" (2010: 57).

Various other key moments illustrate the depth and breadth of sporting corruption and violence. In 1988, referee Armando Pérez was kidnapped by narcos representing as many as seven teams and offered a choice of bribery or death. The League championship was abandoned in 1989. That year, the Copa Libertadores saw various attempts to buy matches, and the Final was subject to threats from Escobar to kill spectators if his preferred team lost. Tanks were called out when he declared "Nacional gana o todos mueren" (Nacional wins or everyone dies). The referee, Álvaro Ortega Madero, was murdered on Escobar's orders, supposedly because he had participated in an *amaño* (a fix) when one narco's team was defeated by another. *El Espectador* called it "El día que mataron el fútbol" (the day they killed football) (González Castaño 2014). Millonarios's president and vice president and the director of Cristal Caldas[9] were assassinated, and the junior league's head resigned after death threats. The Liberal candidate for the presidency, Luis Carlos Galán Sarmiento, was killed two days prior to Colombia's first match in the men's World Cup qualifiers (NULLVALUE 1999; Fernández L'Hoeste 2015). Because of these scandals, the nation was suspended as host of Confederación Sudamericana de Fútbol (CONMEBOL) (South American Football Confederation) fixtures in 1991.

The Colombian national team's great triumph, defeating Argentina 5–0 away in a 1993 qualifying match for the men's World Cup (Silva 2013),[10] continues to be commemorated as an epochal moment of national pride. President César Augusto Gaviria Trujillo unsuccessfully sought to claim it and renew the national popular (Watson 2018). It is less remarked that seventy-six people died and over nine hundred were wounded in the aftermath. While the national team awaited its first game of the 1994 Finals, cartel heads sought and obtained reassurances from the team manager that his selections would not be affected by the *Limpieza del Fútbol Colombiano* (Clean Up Colombian Football) movement (which in any event was rumored to be a front for disaffected gamblers). Juan José Bellini, the head of ADEFUTBOL's successor, the Federación Colombiana de Fútbol (COLFUTBOL) from 1992 to 1995, and president of América de Cali, was convicted of money laundering. It was estimated that 80 percent of shares in the nation's leading teams in 1997 were held by narcos, with many lesser sides involved in trafficking (Fernández L'Hoeste 2015).

COLUMBIA 2001

As part of a regular rotation between members, CONMEBOL selected Colombia to hold the 40th Copa América. A series of conflicts between the government and the FARC cast a pall over the run-up to the event, leading to urgent discussions between the different national federations over whether Colombia could guarantee public safety. CONMEBOL decided to proceed as planned. Then the FARC kidnapped Hernán Mejía Campuzano, vice president of COLFUTBOL. When CONMEBOL announced that it would postpone the Copa, and might hold the competition the following year in Brazil, the *guerrilla* freed him ("Las FARC" 2013). At the urging of President Andrés Pastrana Arango, who hoped to tie this success to his image after unpopular deals with the FARC, and under pressure from television networks and sponsors, the Copa proceeded, with Colombia as host—and the blessing of the *guerrilla*. The Asociación del Fútbol Argentino (Argentine Football Association) decided not to participate, and Honduras only came at the last minute, in a military plane (Fridman Stalnicovitz 2016; Watson 2018). The promotional geniuses who had nominated the event as *La Copa de la Paz* (the Peace Cup) should have been embarrassed (Celis Hernández 2017).

The second match of the competition was between Colombia and Venezuela. When Freddy Indurley Grisales (known as Totono) scored for the host nation, he celebrated by seizing a police officer's helmet and saluting the crowd. This was interpreted as an homage to military and police efforts to keep the population safe against the FARC, his gesture representing a shift in social relations toward a benign view of state power as a force protecting the citizenry, and football as a safe site to honor that monopoly on legitimate violence. Totono initially deflated these assumptions, explaining that he was simply thanking a security guard who had agreed to look after his money while he was on the pitch ("La Copa Rosa" 2001) but later said he wanted to uplift the nation and point out its debt to officialdom in the struggle against the *guerrilla* (Hoyos 2015).

The killing of Pablo Escobar in 1993 and the arrest of many others eventually turned the tide away from ostentatious challenges to the state in the face of sustained Colombian and U.S. interdiction. Over the two decades since, brazen nouveau riche drug traffickers have retreated from football, and public life in general. As we shall see in chapter 3, suppliers to the naughty, needy nostrils of the U.S. and European middle classes changed gear; Colombian narcos became Netflix protagonists rather than stadium *capos*. They continued their involvement in the sport, but as money launderers rather than Flash Harrys[11]—acting clandestinely, quietly, under the radar. *Narcofútbol* has become strictly business, rather than a symbolic show of power aimed at compromising governmental legitimacy.

Clubs have come to rely on youth academies and sponsorship as well as contraband in their search for cross-generational success (MacKenna 2016). The nation's most famous player, Carlos Alberto Valderrama Palacio ("El Pibe") (The Kid) proposed a football match with the FARC as part of the peace process in 2013. And the state reemerged into the narcissistic glow of football's floodlights, despite Uribe's lack of commitment to football as a means of generating a national popular. In 2009, the government established the aforementioned Comisión Nacional para la Seguridad, Comodidad y Convivencia en el Fútbol. Made up of DIMAYOR, COLFUTBOL, and various government ministries, from cultural sectors to the police, it set up national and local laws, guidelines, and agencies to control the *barras bravas* (Aponte et al., 2009; Ladrón de Guevara 2014; Uribe Aramburo and Castaño Pérez 2014).

The playing of "La Marseillaise," with which we began, presaged events in 2016's Copa América. The Juan Manuel Santos Calderón government claimed the team's success at the first major international competition after an outstanding 2014 men's World Cup as a sign of renewed nationhood. It dispatched the side with the good wishes of all (Puentes Sánchez 2015; Watson 2018). The state's advertising campaign interpellated the FARC as patriotic fans who were welcome to root for the national team, alongside the military in helicopters, coffee growers in fields, and supporters at grounds: "Colombia le está guardando el puesto" (Colombia is saving a seat for you).[12] The *guerrilla* issued a communiqué stressing that patriotic fervor for the national team united the country, in the very way needed for a peaceful future ("FARC" 2014). Santos said that Colombians could bask in peace and prosperity if they worked together "como la Seleccion Colombia—¡UNIDOS POR UN PAÍS!" (like the national team—UNITED AS ONE COUNTRY!) ("Alocución" 2014). Football was "el máximo símbolo de la unidad nacional" (our greatest symbol of national unity) ("Palabras" 2014).

During the Finals, the peak organization Comunidades con Paz (Communities for Peace), representing over a hundred groups of Afrodescendant, indigenous, and peasant Colombians, sent an open letter (2014) to the team's emergent star, James David Rodríguez Rubio. It was a poetic paean to football as a potential exemplar of individual beauty and expression harmonized with solidarity, work, discipline, and commitment—a model for what the organization hoped the nation could become via a truly inclusive democratic urge that valued all forms and sources of life, and eschewed violence in ways that were akin to James's own public displays of humility in the face of spectacular success. But the militaristic connotations of football were soon to the fore.

USA 2016

The national TV station RCN (originally Radio Cadena Nacional [National Radio Network]) won the rights to non-broadcast television coverage of the 2016 Copa from traditional holders Caracol (Cadena Radial Colombiana [Colombian Radio Network]); they shared television coverage. RCN joined with the Colombian military to produce stirring commercials of joyous nationalism and militarism that were also implicit promotions for Carlos Arturo Ardila Lülle: a billionaire honoree for services to the armed forces, proprietor of the network (following a notorious privatization) baron of Postobón, a sugary drinks firm, of which more in a later chapter—and owner of Atlético Nacional (López de la Roche 2003; Rodríguez Romero and Duque Oliva 2007; Luna Geller 2016).

Private and public interests aligned in a show of happy state violence, brokered through identification with the national team. The idea was to merge RCN and the military with Radamel Falcao García Zárate, James, and their compatriots in the minds of an adoring public ("El Batallón" 2016). RCN, Postobón, and their kind stepped into the space of spectacle formerly occupied by the mafia, and invited the military arm of the state to join them. In the process, they displaced the regional football identities favored by the narcos with a national one (Fernández L'Hoeste 2015).

The network's five promotional spots for the Copa featured the military under the rubric of the "Himno Copa América Centenario 2016 #YoCreo" (Copa América Centenary Anthem 2016 #IBelieve). When viewed in combination, the various military versions comprise seven minutes of striking propaganda.[13] For a helicopter and parachute commercial, the setting was an airfield. Soldiers dropped to the ground draped in the slogan's flag. Air force planes carried the slogan on their fuselage as they flew by. The navy provided uniformed women and men playing instruments and singing, and a ship with a banner alongside the flag. High school is called up for U.S. viewers in the video where a military college band twirled away, children ready to fight for . . . something; whatever that might be, its iconography was militaristic. Then there was the presidential guard, adorned in remorselessly nineteenth-century attire, part of Colombia's aforementioned mimicry of Prussian uniforms.[14]

These commercials drew on imagery that was familiar to viewers. The long-established local firm Cervecería Bavaria (Bavarian Brewery) was connected to the national football team via a marketing campaign agreed with the corrupt COLFUTBOL official Luis Erberto Bedoya Giraldo ("Bavaria y Colfútbol" 2015), while Postobón sponsors the professional leagues: the company modestly describes itself as "¡El sabor del fútbol!" (The flavor of football) and identifies sports with sugar drinks and treats athletes as warriors.[15]

Nationalism courses through these ventures, and the distinction between straightforward propaganda and news bulletins can be fuzzy, as per RCN's 'journalism' celebrating itself, the team, the fans, and the armed forces as one.[16] For its part, the military's YouTube channel featured three camouflaged soldiers with machine guns taking time to intone to the camera that they wished the team success in the Copa.[17]

Just as the U.S. public assiduously loathes the state while loving the military, and seems blissfully unaware that one is a subset of the other (we'll leave it up to you to decide which is which) so the assumption underpinning these commercials is that the military, football, and RCN between them actually *are* the nation. For the promotional series also includes civil society: happy fans leaping up and down in their team shirts singing the same song, with the same smiles, but in a form of choreographed abandon that showed this was the state both at rest and at play. RCN's show of cheery governmental power, national unity, and corporate advertising raised serious questions about public entities put at the disposal of a private network. It may have breached civil and criminal codes, and was bizarrely exploitative given the network's unabashed opposition to the armed forces' then commander-in-chief, Santos, and his peace agenda with the FARC (Luna Geller 2016). There *was* a nice irony—Caracol won the Copa ratings ("Copa América" 2016).

THE LABOR PROCESS

What do the newly-renovated national popular and ongoing violence and corruption imply for the workers who make football happen? Players and technical staff in Colombian football's labor process have historically suffered major problems with job stability, working conditions, the right to organize, participation in governance, access to the money flowing from proprietary media sales, and the violence outlined above (Bolívar-Ramírez 2018).

Many players have been propelled into a world of corruption and violence, often with dire consequences ("¿Por qué algunas" 2019). When Andrés Escobar Saldarriaga (no relation) was murdered after his own goal consigned Colombia to defeat against the United States in 1994, his death became an index both of how much the sport meant to people—and to the cheapness of life (Chua-Eoan 1994). Today Millonarios fans love to chant: "Andrés Escobar, paisa hijueputa no existes más" (Andrés Escobar, Medellín's son of a bitch, you don't exist any more)[18] (quoted in Vélez-Maya and Arboleda-Ariza 2016). In 1996, national team player Felipe Pérez Urrea was killed for his cartel associations (NULLVALUE 1999; Fernández L'Hoeste 2015). Goalkeeper José René Higuita Zapata de Escobar Gaviria, beloved by fans across the world for his scorpion kick ("Goodness me, have you seen anything like that in your life?")[19] and later imprisoned after acting as a go-between for cartels in a kidnapping, was developing his skills—and commitments—under Escobar (Kuper 2008).

The way to transcend such things is to reward players properly. The Asociación Colombiana de Futbolistas Profesionales (Colombian Association of Professional Footballers) (ACOLFUTPRO) was created in 2005 to seek better working conditions for its members and secure a percentage of television rights in negotiations with DIMAYOR. When nothing happened, ACOLFUTPRO members voted to strike. The strike failed; only América of Cali complied with the decision. ACOLFUTPRO executives denounced pressures and threats from bosses, such as vetoing future jobs for protest leaders ("El último" 2019). DIMAYOR argues that labor issues must be directly addressed with teams as employers, many of whom maintain that football players have no right to industrial action. In 2019, ACOLFUTPRO asked DIMAYOR to discuss these topics again, along with the tournament calendar and the women's league. A general strike was called and the Ministry of Labor commenced mediation ("Reunion de" 2019).

Players have also staged performances to make their point through spectacle. These protests have included "sitting" or making only light touches of the ball during the first minute of matches.[20] Such images have been "banned" from broadcasts on WiN (the official league network) and RCN, which generated some negative public reaction towards such censorship and encouraged alternative-media coverage ("WiN sports" 2019; "Hablan de veto" 2019).

Television contracts and the creation of a premium channel have provoked discussion within DIMAYOR over how to share revenue. In 2016, a group of 'large' or 'traditional' teams requested revisions to the rights system, based on audience and investment criteria. That didn't happen, because 'smaller' clubs—

the majority—were not supportive. It nearly led to a split ("La disputa" 2016) of the kind often threatened in Europe's major leagues. In 2018, new tournament regulations prevented teams from participating in international tournaments, which harmed the 'bigger' clubs ("Liga aguila" 2019).

Players are also asked to do too much. The Colombian professional soccer calendar is one of the most extensive in the world, to the point of clashing with FIFA dates. In 2018, Junior played seventy matches; a figure well above international standards ("El maratón" 2019). Players are largely excluded from planning.

The president of DIMAYOR during strike negotiations, Jorge Enrique Vélez, is a lawyer with a political past. He is close to the Radical Change party, which is led by former presidential candidate Germán Vargas Lleras and opposes the central government. The same party includes the owner of Junior, Fuad Ricado Char Abdala, who has also been an ambassador, minister, governor, and senator, and is the father of Alejandro Char, twice mayor of Barranquilla. Despite this apparent political consanguinity, Junior seeks a new formula for distributing profits from television rights—but one that does not favor players, of course ("Fútbol colombiano" 2019). For even when the good old boys disagree, their interests consistently militate against a fair labor process—one in which the 'talent' would benefit from TV deals and a share in decision-making. They collude to disenfranchise workers, regardless of their own intra-class disputes. And it can be no surprise that Fuad Char has been denied a visa to the United States due to his alleged ties to narcos ("I Have Been Honorable" 2014).

CONCLUSION

The Colombian situation of the 1980s and '90s, a period when many other countries were associating militarism with sports, is an example of what occurs when violence is so institutionalized in the informal economy that the armed forces become just one segment of that quotidian reality. The situation was too overdetermined for government propaganda or even FARC infiltration. Football was a zone of gangster killings, gangster 'welfare,' and gangster popular culture. It signified para-state control of the third sector. Violence was everywhere, from the intimidation of referees to the slaughter of opponents.

Then the era of overt narco dominance of the public sphere ended, transformed into more businesslike, less spectacular norms that were some distance from the cartels' star system and ostentatious penetration of football. But malfeasance continues. In 2007, Luis Eduardo Méndez, former president of the title-winning Club Independiente Sante Fe SA, was sentenced in Florida for trafficking cocaine, and Óscar Ignacio Martán Rodríguez, a member of COLFUTBOL's executive committee, was indicted (Hersh 1990; "Dos primeras" 2001; Quitián Roldán 2007; Redacción Deportes 2012; Martínez Colorado 2013;

Fernández Moores 2014; Iglesias 2014; Malem Seña 2014). In 2010, Colombian authorities found a model World Cup trophy made from cocaine, molded with gasoline or acetate and destined for Spain, and Independiente was investigated for ties to the narcos that saw the murder of several leading figures associated with the team (Brodzinsky 2010; Martínez 2010; "World Cup" 2010).

Since 1995, the U.S. Treasury's Office of Foreign Assets Control has promulgated a *Specially Designated Nationals and Blocked Persons List* (2019). Known colloquially in Latin America as the "*Lista* Clinton," it is a set of names associated with international narco-trafficking. Their assets are blocked, and U.S. citizens, residents, and businesses are usually outlawed from dealing with them (Quitián Roldán 2013). In 2014, the U.S. Treasury named La Oficina de Envigado (the Envigado Office) as a major trafficker, and El Envigado Fútbol Club and its owner, Juan Pablo Upegui Gallego, as launderers. The club's narco links went all the way back to Escobar (Quevedo H. 2012; "Treasury Designates" 2014).

A U.S. indictment of numerous football administrators across the Americas identified Bedoya, a senior officeholder with CONMEBOL and president of COLFUTBOL, as taking bribes to deliver TV and marketing rights. He pled guilty to wire-fraud conspiracy and racketeering and received a life ban from world football (United States of America against various 2015; Homewood 2016). Meanwhile, twenty years after Bellini's disgrace, he was merrily promoting himself as a specialist in sports law and player transfers.[21]

As at early 2019, the Clinton *Lista* was 1,261 pages long (U.S. Treasury 2019). Colombian football clubs and their proprietors still figure prominently. The international image of Colombian football remains scarred by its association with the narcos ("Colombia pide" 2014), and the country continues to struggle with their corrupting power over public life in general (Duncan 2015). As we shall see in chapter 3, screen drama has continued an obsession with Pablo Escobar that has only grown more powerful with the years. Distance from his death in 1993 has allowed the bourgeois media to portray him in fictional terms, even as his family claims the right to police and profit from his image in perhaps the most bizarre material ever published by *TMZ* (Moreno 2014; Strause 2016).[22]

The association of Colombia with cocaine and football in the Anglo mind continues. It was emblematized by the front page of the *Sun* newspaper, owned by Rupert Murdoch, on the day of England's match against Colombia in the 2018 men's World Cup. Troping the name of England's captain, Harry Kane, it depicted him with "GO KANE" the headline, to the outrage of the Colombian embassy and media (Taylor 2018). In response to their complaints, the next day's paper read as follows:

> The front page of yesterday's *Sun* may have given the impression that Colombia is well known for its cocaine trade. This was unfair on the Colombian people, who

are far more embarrassed by the way their cheating, fouling, play acting, mean-spirited national football team played last night.

We are happy to set the record straight (quoted in Neville 2018).[23]

But at home, the sense of a spectacular sporting challenge to government has passed. The FARC promoted themselves as preparing for peace by playing football, supporting the national team, and renewing ties to clubs they had followed prior to self-exile ("Con fútbol" 2016; "Miembros de la FARC" 2016).[24] Football continues its complex movement between pacifying, incarnating, attracting, and repelling violence.

It remains to be seen whether the struggle for legitimacy, once waged by the narcos, can be won by the state, corporations, and social movements, such as women and other players. Weber's maxim may still require some revision: the military allied with commercial partners in using sports to express symbolic violence. This is a far cry from a positive national popular seeking peace and justice.

Football embodies the distinction between a world of domination, scientific management, and an artificially generated dislike of others, versus a world of collaboration, spontaneity, and fellowship. Against such banal competitiveness and disciplinary obsessions stands the untrammeled ecstasy of a lengthy passing movement or dribble—a perfectly material, utopian, snatched alternative to this seemingly most capitalistic of metaphors. Hence the paradox at the heart of sports, its simultaneously transcendent and imprisoning qualities and astonishing capacity to allegorize. As per Brecht, there is so much potential there, if only it could be harnessed toward progressive purposes; beyond hypermasculinity and narco laundries.

2 • INDUSTRY POLICY AND SEX TOURISM MEET THE CASE OF THE DESTROYED PLAQUE

WITH OLGA LUCIA SORZANO
AND ANAMARIA TAMAYO-DUQUE

The Colombian state's proclaimed desire for peace and development through the creative industries has animated a wish to improve the country's standing internationally and generate tourism based on its climate, ecology, and heritage. Tourism holds a special place in this putative era of reconstruction: its emphasis on visitation and civil society incarnates an organic understanding between peoples, sans state interference (Dinnie 2016). Along with sports, the industry is a key component of Colombia's *economía naranja* plans, promoted as pacific, environmental, and growing. Such possibilities encourage bourgeois boosters and carpetbagging consultants alike.

But evidence from Latin America shows that tourism in this brave new world is just as good at expressing and solidifying inequality as it ever was: "old patterns of privileged access for some and denial for others." There is nothing new, inspirational, or particularly entrepreneurial about the services sector in Colombia; it has been around for centuries (Clausen and Velázquez García 2017: 274).

Our contention is that a combination of the informal economy, romanticized/sexualized national imagery, and efforts to dynamize the tourism industry through rebranding are synchronizing in an accidental (but far from incidental) misogynistic, exploitative, neocolonial cocktail of promotional campaigns, child sex-trafficking, and regressive cultural policy that exploits and furthers violence, both physical and symbolic.

The first half of this chapter examines the nation's tourism history and policy, national imagery and gender, the links between these topics and sexual exploitation, and implications for the future. "Explotación sexual commercial de niños, niñas, y adolescentes (ESCNNA)" (The commercial rape of boys, girls, and adolescents)[1] is one of the principal issues confronting the nation's tourism industry, social movements, and government, with numerous agencies and resources dedicated to opposing it.

But in doing so, both industry and state are opposed to some of their own actions, for there is an accidental but semiotically clear connection between these crimes, national branding, and economic policy. That connection derives from decades of imagery romanticizing and sexualizing young women in order to attract visitors. The mixture of these forces and tensions makes the country a key site in the global crisis created by masculine desires to commit statutory rape.

The chapter's second half looks at Twitter and bourgeois-press activism triggered by the unveiling of a controversial plaque designed to attract tourists—this time of the imperialist rather than the sexual kind.[2] It commemorated the failure of British and American troops[3] under the command of Admiral Edward Vernon to seize the Caribbean in 1741, in the face of resistance led by Admiral Don Blas de Lezo y Olvarrieta/Olabarrieta.

The plaque represents the collision of two histories. One is to do with Colombian nationalism prior even to its independence; the other is about late twentieth- and early twenty-first-century tourism planning. One is about repelling the British; the other, attracting them. One celebrates dispatching the British military; the other welcomes their descendants' wealth. One centers around sustaining a blockade, the other opening a city.

In each half of the chapter, our methods include textual and policy analysis, political economy, gender and ethnic studies, and participant observation. Our geographical focus is a Colombian city on the Caribbean.

CARTAGENA

Cartagena de Indias is a World Heritage locale, renowned for its colonial architecture, social inequality, beach culture, and international colloquia. It is the country's principal tourism destination and site of sexual exploitation, a key figure in Colombian history, symbolism, and diplomacy—and a place where over half the population lives below the poverty line (Mosquera and Bozzi 2005; Guerrero-Figueroa Guerrero 2016).

Cartagena is central to García Márquez's *El amor en los tiempos del cólera* (*Love in the Time of Cholera*) (1988). Gabo describes a city that is "the most beautiful in the world" but has been temporarily abandoned due to disease "after three centuries of resistance to the sieges of the English and the atrocities of the buccaneers" (1988: 147). It provides the setting for an implicit male duel that animates the novel in a struggle between tradition and modernity, romance and reason (Martínez 2008).

Founded in 1533 by the Spanish under Pedro de Heredia Adelantado on the site of an indigenous settlement that dated back thousands of years, Cartagena quickly became an entrepôt for silver from Perú to Spain and slaves from Africa to the colonies. Perhaps half a million people were trafficked between 1580 and 1640, seized for their skill in mining gold and as substitutes for a decimated indigenous population (Mayo Restrepo 2009; World Bank 2018: 62). Cartagena declared independence in 1811 and is called *La Heroica* (the Heroic One) because it withstood naval assaults during colonialism and afterward, the two most prominent being brutal blockades by the British and Spanish Empires (McNeill 2010). Bolívar called it "impregnable" (2003: 14). The suffering of Cartagener@s during their resistance is marked in the national anthem ("la abnegación es mucha") (heavy is the hardship).[4]

Cartagena's economy has been a boom-and-bust pattern of growth and contraction. From the late 1890s, the railways enabled transportation of goods between the interior and the port via the Río Magdalena—the subject of chapter 4—and the city's subsequent submergence as a company town of the Andian National Corporation, a Canadian subsidiary of Standard Oil. In 1905, Cartagena had fewer than ten thousand residents, rising to 128,000 in 1951. The country in general urbanized as part of its insertion into global capitalism. This growth was accompanied by public works between the 1890s and 1920s that demolished colonial heritage—as it would now be fetishized by the tourism industry, the state, and the international cultural-policy world—in favor of additional and more modern port facilities. In the late 1950s, development was stimulated by new paved roads linking Cartagena to other cities, a refinery, and broader-based investment—businesses with high levels of automation that did little for local employment (Meisel Roca 1999; Orozco-Triana et al. 2015).

Today's population is well over a million. The city is Colombia's fifth largest, after Bogotá, Medellín, Cali, and Barranquilla (Aguilera Díaz and Meisel Roca 2009; Cartagena Comó Vamos 2017). Approximately 63 percent of residents are defined as mestiz@s and 36 percent as Afro-Colombian. There are small numbers of indigenous people.[5] The conflict has seen many internal exiles flee the center of the country for the Caribbean, where the *guerrilla* and narcos have rarely focused their efforts, but death has still come easily due to the violence of *paramilitares*.

While economic growth has diminished poverty for some, as per the national situation, women suffer disproportionately from unemployment. The informal sector, which includes sex work, accounts for well over half the city's jobs (Rueda de Vivero and Espinosa Espinosa 2008; Cartagena Cómo Vamos 2017).

The formal sector is organized around petrochemicals, plastics, transportation, and tourism. Further upgrades to the city's refinery and port facilities have not assisted social mobility or equality (Meisel Roca 1999; Aguilera Díaz and Meisel Roca 2009; Acosa Ordoñez 2013). Light-skinned mestizo oligarchs dominate finance, business, education, and politics. They deny the structures and causes of racial inequality (Valle 2018). This further complicates the classic Cartagena tendency to speak of people in derisory class terms while avoiding the racial connotations that inevitably involves (Streicker 1995).

Afro-Colombians have lower levels of infrastructural expenditure, education, and wealth than others. They have been racialized ideologically in ways that resonate with colonial times: the state's disrespect for slave-descended peoples has a history that started in chains and continues to be expressed in the absence of opportunity (Maya Restrepo 2009, 2001; España Eljaiek 2017). Meanwhile, parts of the city with a profound and long-lasting black presence are gentrifying to attract tourists. Afro-Colombians lacking wealth and education are being cleared, driven "into poorer, more dangerous neighborhoods" (World Bank 2018: 67). At a cultural level, Cartagena's story is all too often told without using words such as *slave, black*, or *Afro* (Bassols 2019), and the city's streets and neighborhoods commemorate Spanish conquistadores and rulers, with Pedro de Heredia (figure 2) and Blas de Lezo among the most prominent. Black and indigenous leaders are largely invisible.

TOURISM

Tourism has long been a core aspect of development discourse across the Global South, from colonial and postcolonial administrators and politicians to international agencies, corporate interests, academics, and Christians. They have seen it as a route to foreign investment and exchange, employment, and infrastructural modernization. Structural adjustment has been peddled by neoliberal high priests at the World Bank, the International Monetary Fund, the World Trade Organization, and the sovereign states that dominate them. This discourse encourages the Global South to turn away from subsistence agriculture and towards tradable services, beyond manufacturing capacity and in the direction of human exchange. In much of Southeast Asia, for example, tourism policies pushed people across the 1990s into littoral regions in search of work. Fish-farming corporations created a new aquaculture, displacing the natural environment of mangroves and coral reefs that protect people and land. The requirement to reconstitute entire countries as entertaining heritage sites and decadent tourism playgrounds induced Thailand, Indonesia, and Malaysia to undertake massive construction projects, decimating natural protection. They built resorts at the point where high tides lap, with catastrophic results in the 2004 tsunami. Areas that had not been directed to remove natural barriers suffered dramatically fewer casualties (Bidwai 2005; Sharma 2005; Shiva 2005).

While tourism's structural inequalities and destructive impact are widely recognized (Browning and Ferraz de Oliviera 2017; Büscher and Fletcher 2017), many analysts and people in power continue to perpetuate a sunny mythology of its benefits (Niesing 2013; Echeverri et al. 2019). Conceits about economy, identity, culture, heritage, experience, and related capitalist tokens of the orange

FIGURE 2. Statue of Pedro de Heredia. (Source: Toby Miller.)

economy have become central to the growing discourse of nation branding (Aronczyk 2013). The evidence is certainly there for claims that the industry can produce economic growth (Brida et al. 2016), but to the benefit of the few rather than the many.

Tourism is also said to encourage tranquility. Giovanni Battista Enrico Antonio Maria Montini, trading as Pope Paul VI, called it "a passport to peace" (quoted in

Hiller 1976). He was echoing the European Tourism Commission in 1948 and the Marshall Plan's administrators in 1950. The UN nominated 1967 as International Tourist Year, using Montini's slogan. In 1980, the World Tourism Organization's Manila Declaration pronounced the industry "a vital force for world peace,"[6] as did Ronald Wilson Reagan and Karol Józef Wojtyla, passing as John Paul II, in 1988 (Bechmann Pedersen 2017). A meta-study analyzing the manifold claims about the nexus between tourism and peace across over a hundred countries relates international visitor statistics to the Global Peace Index.[7] It indicates that peace benefits tourism in middle- and high-income nations, but the trend is neither universal nor reciprocal (Pratt and Liu 2016).

International holidays to Brazil and the Southern Cone developed from the start of the twentieth century, and México and the Caribbean were included by midcentury (Colombia's consulates had started propagandizing from 1911) (Menchero Sánchez 2018). Domestic tourism in Colombia, much of it to places of origin or pilgrimages to holy sites such as Popayán and Santa Cruz de Mompox, has been a feature of national life for decades, but is rarely foregrounded in federal policies and programs (Escovar 2012). The foreigner is the desired subject.

From the 1950s to the 1980s, Colombia's tourism industry professionalized nationally, establishing peak bodies to negotiate with governments. There were massive fluctuations in the number of international visitors during this period and later. Annual growth across the 1970s was in the double digits, from 160,000 to over a million, but this was followed by chaos in the 1980s and '90s. Tourism shrank dramatically in some years, declining by 1999 to the level attained in 1976, and expanded in others. In the last three decades, the industry has accounted for between two and five percent of GDP rather than growing consistently, as a consequence of the conflict and the alternative appeal to investors of agriculture, extraction, manufacturing, and finance. But tourism numbers doubled between 2013 and 2016, reaching nearly three million in 2017 and almost seven million the following year. The industry's contribution to overseas revenue exceeded coal for the first time in 2015, at US$5.2 billion, thanks in part to propitious exchange rates. In 2017, the industry was responsible for more than half a million jobs (Brida et al. 2011, 2012; Medina 2016; Menchero Sánchez 2018; "Colombia—Travel" 2019; World Travel & Tourism Council 2018).[8] The government has piloted numerous schemes designed to construct and measure tourism's contribution to peace.

CARTAGENA AND TOURISM

Like much tourism around the world, Cartagena's appeal lies in commodifying a heritage of violence and war (Ojeda 2013; Lisle 2016). Fortifications built in the colonial period have been major attractions since the 1960s (Menchero Sánchez 2017). Named the Distrito Turístico y Cultural de Cartagena de Indias (Tourism and Culture District of Cartagena) in 1991, the city's World Heritage status derives from its place in the annals of military and religious history. At almost two hundred hectares, Cartagena's fortifications are the largest in South America and one of the most intact examples from the Spanish era. Its monuments pay remarkable testimony to faith and craft alike; various zones within the Old Town correspond to areas once occupied by slaves, merchants, artisans, and the occupying elite (Soloudre-La France 2015). UNESCO values these qualities both because they illuminate the history of maritime trade routes and because they are imperiled by visitors' impact on the natural and built environments.[9] Slave labor built the fortress. The prevailing mythology forgets that role, fetishizing away the city's conditions of existence in favor of a commodified "heritage." Ironically, by freezing culture in colonial times, or making it a streetwise but safely separate world that is visited en passant, a lengthy and valuable history of modern art is denied (Ramírez Botero 2010).

Some date the exploitation of the Cartagena population through tourism as far back as a century (Diz Caraballo 2014). From the 1920s, the U.S. government was calling on municipal administrators to attract Yanqui tourists via what is now a familiar formula: constructing luxury hotels, highlighting historic monuments, and forcing the popular classes to systematize trash disposal. That coincided with new mythologies among white people: in the nineteenth century, the sun had been regarded with caution, as something that would desiccate the skin and alter its pigmentation, while ocean immersion was for brief refreshment rather than serious exercise. By the 1920s, tanning was viewed as healthy, and swimming as a sport (Gmelch 2003: 5). Visitor numbers increased from 1933 with the advent of the Manga wharves and an airport. In December 1937, two dozen steamships dropped off and picked up two thousand European and U.S. visitors (Meisel Roca 1999). Eight years later, the city's first luxury tourist accommodation, the iconic Hotel Caribe, opened to wealthy customers.[10]

By the 1950s, Cartagena was designated as the nation's major tourist destination, combining its architecture, history, and myth with a reputation as a "ciudad turística con un ambiente alegre y múltiples diversiones para los turistas" (a tourist city with a relaxed environment and many pleasurable activities for visitors). The first National Conference on Tourism, held in Bogotá in 1952, recommended campaigns to attract visitors to Cartagena from the United States and western Europe and the construction of "un elegante casino internacional con todo el lujo posible, como hoteles con aire acondicionado, piscinas olímpicas, salones de bailes con shows internacionales, festivales, carreras de lanchas y de caballos" (an elegant international casino with every imaginable luxury, such as air-conditioned hotels, Olympic swimming pools, dance halls featuring international acts, festivals, marinas, and stables) (PCNT 1952: 20). In 1955, the government adopted numerous policies to stimulate tourism, including construction projects, zones reserved for visitors, wage subsidies, and consultancy plans (Carrillo Romero et al. 2013).

A World Bank economic commission studying Colombia in the 1970s proposed a strategy for generating foreign exchange and diversifying the economy through tourism. The Bank favored a Caribbean economic-development zone, drawing on the region's comparative advantages: proximity to the United States, reverse climatic seasons, and warm-water beaches (World Bank 1972: 4). Cartagena would convert itself into a paradise of *sol y playa* (sun and sand), a playground for North Americans. This was in keeping with what have been called the four *S*s sought by U.S. visitors: sea, sand, sun, and sex (Boyer 2002).

In response to the Bank's report, and various studies produced by the industry, the Centro de Investigación Económica y Social (Fedesarrollo) (Center for Economic and Social Research) argued that mass tourism would produce benefits following the provision of "exenciones e incentivos claros y atractivos" (clear and attractive tax exemptions and incentives). Fedesarrollo acknowledged that this would not necessarily be a boon for low-income segments of the population, and that an expanded industry could produce "una distorsión social de consecuencias imprevisibles" (social disruption through unforeseen consequences) (Fedesarrollo 1972: 140). The report expressed anxiety that a poor, and poorly treated, class of service workers might arise in order to meet the needs created by an influx of tourists, while ordinary people would be displaced from their traditional homes.

Those predictions proved prescient. Years of tax incentives roiled a luxury-hotel construction boom that has crowded locals out (Tyor 2013), for whom public services stagnate, violent crime increases, teen pregnancy crests, and education falters (Cartagena Comó Vamos 2017). The city prioritizes the interests of tourists above those of its own people.

The luxury real estate magazine *Mansion Global* merrily announces the impossibility of buying even a studio apartment in the historic center for under a million dollars, thanks to overseas and domestic demand (Cary 2019). In the cause of economic growth, a fresh national image, and strengthened relations with the United States, inter alios, the sector's growth has been accompanied by intense income and social inequality, social clearances, unemployment, underemployment, and sex tourism (Mosquera and Bozzi 2005; Bernal-Camargo et al. 2013; Londoño et al. 2014; Serrano-Amaya 2018: 48).[11] The selling of Cartagena as an ecological and historical wonderland belies the absence of effective policies and programs in the interests of residents. The persistent power of oligarchic interests sees resorts and high-rises for visitors and the wealthy—and flood-prone barrios with raw sewage for the poor. Climate mitigation efforts have focused on the former rather than the latter, especially as fancy hotels and apartments in the exclusive zone of Bocagrande are, madly, built on a sandbar and hence subject to flooding from off-shore swell (Andrade et al. 2013; Luna-Galván et al. 2017; see Stein and Moser 2014 for an optimistic account of true citizen participation in mitigating climate change in Cartagena). And tourism growth has come at the cost of the militarization and surveillance of everyday travel and various incentive schemes directed at investors (Medina 2016; Menchero Sánchez 2018).[12] As a consequence, residents have extremely negative views of the quality of their daily lives by contrast with most other Colombian city dwellers (Cartagena Comó Vamos 2017).[13]

There are two Cartagenas: one, a site burnished by its history and branding, a place of colonialism and revolution, preserved side by side, and a port of natural beauty; the other, a space of brutal modernity, characterized by the systematic exclusion and servitude of its majority-minority population, who are dispatched to the periphery to live, even when required in the core as workers. Black women in particular are massively overrepresented below the poverty line, while young people rarely proceed beyond primary schooling. Many live in swamps and shanty towns on the outskirts of town in disorganized settlements.

Lighter-skinned Cartagener@s assume this is by choice (Pérez Carrascal and Riccardi 2019). But the form of life is conditioned by the racial formation produced by slavery. International, national, and local shifts in social policy since the 1970s abandoned tentative attempts at regional equality, which had once been the ideal of countering uneven spatial living conditions. Poverty and underdevelopment were displaced as national issues by international competitiveness and the drive for comparative advantage. Marketing and image making became concerns at all levels of government, as cities turned their backs on social services to residents in search of attractions for visitors (Soja 2010: 65).

Tourism mavens around the world work assiduously with chorine academics to negate any negative news of prime destinations, lest potential visitors head elsewhere (Melián González et al. 2010; Xiang and Gretzel 2010; Pan et al. 2011). In Cartagena's case, sybaritic pleasure in sun and sand, allied to historical fragments of fortifications and slavery, are held up by boosters, both professorial and industrial, seemingly without regret or hesitation (Quintero and Bernal 2007). Little is said of Afro-Colombians' displacement from their points of historic arrival into slavery and ongoing struggles for freedom and the good life.

The United States provides more tourists to Colombia than any other country; about half a million a year. Most others come from the region, while approximately forty thousand British people visit annually. Cartagena is a major attraction (Oficina de Estudio Económicos 2017; Menchero Sánchez 2018).[14] The city hosts numerous conventions and conferences, where delegates gather with the real or imagined intention of doing work. The International Congress and Convention Association ranks it as the 76th busiest city worldwide and 17th in the Americas—ahead of Los Angeles, San Diego, San Francisco, and Miami, inter alia (2018).

Cruise ships represent world tourism's fastest-growing sphere, and Cartagena attracts over a quarter of a million disembarking visitors annually, two-thirds of them from the United States. They spend on average just five to six hours per day per person in the city. Although this is of no use to hotels and can produce seasonal street crowding, it benefits restaurants, bars, cafés, and those in the informal economy selling their wares in public spaces (Brida et al. 2011, 2012; Medina 2016; Menchero Sánchez 2018).

Bourgeois Anglo travel journalism paints a pretty picture of what awaits visitors. Media outlets from Berkeley's *Daily Californian* to London's *Telegraph* list Cartagena as the principal reason to visit Colombia. After all, "There was always live music, most likely a guitarist playing and singing nearby. When one of them was playing English-language songs, such as 'Hey Jude,' 'Hotel California,' and 'Let It Be,' everybody sitting outside the bar sang along, laughed and then cheered together for a beautiful night" (Yang 2018); better yet, apparently, the city "still sings of the Spanish Empire" (Leadbeater 2018). The *Guardian* applauds, insensitively, the fact that no one had the "genius for creating home from home as did the Spaniards" per Cartagena (Jenkins 2007) and the *New York Times*'s "starter kit for escaping into the world" describes Colombia as "eager to become the adventurous, cosmopolitan hot spot it deserves to be" thanks to the end of "a half-century of civil war" (Gill 2018).

Architectural Digest suggests that walking "the sultry streets of Cartagena" makes "a Gabriel García Márquez novel come to life." The city is full of "romance and mystery," like Cuba prior to the revolution: "you might run into Hemingway" (Barreneche 2016). The *Telegraph* avows that "every single street looks like something out of a García Márquez novel"; but caveat emptor: "taxi drivers are accustomed to tourists and will try to rip you off . . . [and] be aware of pickpockets" (Holland 2019). Damn locals spoiling the literary romance.

Assuming we've accounted for such difficulties, *GQ* magazine guarantees us "colorful . . . 16th-century mansions to ogle" and advice on where to go if "the DJ at Café Del Mar starts playing Ed Sheeran"[15] and one's girlfriend likes "to let loose" (Holland 2017). *Hello!* purrs that this is a "location for love" ("Cartagena de Indias" 2012). *Rough Guide* describes Cartagena as a "gorgeous mélange of narrow streets, blossom-smothered haciendas and Baroque churches." It promises visitors "romantic colonial architecture, gourmet dining, all-night partying and beaches." This is a place where "car horns blare constantly, *vallenato* and salsa beats boom out of every door, and shop assistants flirt with customers" (Jacobs and Keeling 2015: 5, 134, 132). How cute and adorable.

Condé Nast enthuses that "people working in the hospitality industry are not jaded by overtourism," so the city must be "your next destination" (Modak 2017). Its "Women Who Travel"[16] community sent a group of "trailblazers" on an "adventure" to Cartagena and Medellín—all of course "curated by our editors to be a once-in-a-lifetime experience," with the capacity to "take a displacement narrative and turn it on its head into a viable business option" (Spurrell 2019). *Gourmet Traveler* highly recommends this "jetsetter magnet" (Hill 2015).

CNN's modest "MyColombia" hashtag says that Cartagena's "underwater treasures" match and even surpass the "winding cobbled streets and colorful balconies" (Sherriff 2018). *Essence*, a style magazine for African American women, highlights the city among its 2019 "Black Travel Vibes" because "[s]unshine and smiles is what you'll find when you do a quick google search on Colombia" (Pointdujour 2019). *Fodor's Travel* celebrates "The Caribbean Destination That Looks Like a Disney Movie." Cartagena offers "a string of impossibly beautiful scenes that follow one after the next until you are so overwhelmed with beauty and music and happiness that you're reduced to the Disney version of yourself: wide-eyed, giggling and full of a warm, happy feeling that floats out of you in tiny cartoon hearts" (Butler 2018). The *Globe and Mail* says visitors will find "Cartagena's recent history blurry in the jetset's rearview" and enjoy artwork reminiscent of "Diego Rivera—minus the Marxism" (Mekhail 2018). Truly.

For its part, the *Wall Street Journal* says that "EVER SINCE COLOMBIA began shrugging off its don't-think-of-visiting status," the city has "emerged as glamorous" (Jones 2018). *Forbes* placed the country among "The 10 Coolest Places to Go in 2019" (Abel 2018), noting that Cartagena has "been drawing a fashionable crowd as of late . . . a must-visit for romance and culture alike" (Parker-Magyar 2019). *Vogue* avows that "Cartagena seduces" (Mendal 2018) and recommends it for a "Stylish, James Bond-Esque Wedding." As one New York bride put it to the magazine, "I had always envisioned a lot of greenery for my wedding with a bit of 1950s Cuba flair—kind of like a scene from an old James Bond movie" (Garcia 2017). We are told that one four-day wedding event for Angelinos:

> kicked off with a rehearsal dinner and welcome party on Thursday night. Aesthetically, these events embodied the tropical feel of the Colombian coast. The bride wore a Johanna Ortiz dress with ruffles and pops of color that matched the laid-back mood of the evening. She paired the dress with an Oscar de la Renta clutch that she carried throughout the weekend. (Macon 2017)

As one does. Warming to its task, the magazine explains that Cartagena and its environs "[a]re Practically Made for Instagram" (Mendal 2018). Somewhat further down the aesthetic list, Singapore's *Business Times* blithely observes that "You'll have plenty of practice fending off the touts (offering girls, cocaine and pizza—not necessarily in that order)" while recommending Cartagena to its readers precisely because of these attractions (Eu 2018). The *South China Morning Post* ranks the city at number four in its "top 10 cities for 'sexually suggestive' posts on Instagram for 2019" (Carter 2019).

Colombia is also a playground for international popular culture. In Warner Bros.' popular 2018 game *Hitman 2*, participants take on the role of vigilantes destroying drug cartels meeting in a remote village.[17] *Hollywood Reporter*'s review describes the country as a "richly detailed environment that acts as a deadly sandbox for the playable assassin," while its "jungle environments are beautifully rendered" (Shanley 2018). The stereotypes gleam through this glossy game, while Will Smith's video blog, shot during the making of *Gemini Man* (directed by Ang Lee in 2019) there, finds him telling us, "If I wasn't famous, I'd live in Cartagena."[18]

Amazon Prime's 2019 *Grand Tour* series saw its three Anglo petrol-head hosts driving around the country, with the alibi that they were filming animals (Sturges 2019), as part of the classic fetishes of the Global North: "Colombia is nature's treasure chest" they said, laden with "lazy rivers" and other attractions that drew them "far from the stain of humanity." The "Grand Tour" was, of course, a rite of passage for affluent white Europeans between the seventeenth and nineteenth centuries. This aristocratic education was predicated on the assumption that travel and exposure to the arts of the other would civilize the coming ruling class. Britain was the classic point of departure, Italy the classic destination (Burke 1997: 99).[19]

Interviewed prior to release of the series, the petrol heads described a "trip across Colombia where we have to try and get from one side of the country to another, without being eaten by any animals," adding "we went on this sub-challenge, which was to become the first programme in history to go to Colombia and not use the word cocaine" (quoted in Kasper 2019). At the season launch they announced: "We did a whole half-hour show and talked non-stop and didn't once mention cocaine. . . . The Colombians were thrilled" (quoted in Fletcher 2019).

In fact, there are constant oblique references to the drug throughout the two-part, two-hour special (Preston 2019). The first episode starts with the hosts driving three cars on a Cartagena beach, with no acknowledgment of the environmental impact. One of the vehicles floats onto the sand from the water, wrapped in tight polyethylene like a giant cocaine package. Then viewers are told that ships of the type that had dropped this car off in the water near the beach leave Colombia for the United States with "something" and return empty. "What are they shipping?" asks one presenter. The next question? "What does Colombia produce?" This is the first of many knowing, if sophomoric, references to cocaine.

While still on the beach, they drive cavalierly into cabanas, which is presented as humorous. Once in the walled city, the Anglos pilot a truck through its narrow vehicular entry, bumping into centuries-old brickwork and interrupting emergency services as well as colliding their jeep with a street fruit-seller's cart. As they leave Cartagena, driving past a glamorous marina, the chaps wonder how the simple agricultural industries they know of have made so many so wealthy. Again, the implication is cocaine—the *non dit* (unsaid) of the twin episodes.

NATIONAL IMAGERY AND GENDER

During their departure from the city, Amazon's *Grand Tour* films a local man having sex with a donkey in a field, and requests an unnamed female translator to ask Afro-Colombian men nearby whether this is a normal sight. One of the Anglos then asks "Why don't these Colombians just grow something? Surely, there must be something . . . that could be sold around the world . . . rather than interfering with animals." The program's hosts promoted this story via a column in Murdoch's *Sunday Times* entitled "Cheat, Love Bray—Let Me Put My Ass on the Line and Tell You That the Donkey Sex Scene Was Real" (Clarkson 2019).

Whether this, and their other experiences, were staged by Amazon's two-dozen film crew, security guards, and local fixers matters not. What does matter is the sense of the other as providing a playground in which straight white masculinity can cavort, pretending to criticize its own reference group through banter while using unnamed, mostly speechless locals as foils for a sense of humor that is as outmoded as it is unfunny. Such conduct perfectly captures both the arrogance of public figures toward the region, and the way that Colombia is portrayed in dominant discourse, as a place of violence, drugs, risk, regeneration—and sex.

Cartagena has a long history of heterosex demanded by conquistadores and *turistas* alike. In the colonial period, women allegedly used sex and magic to give themselves pleasure and power as well as to survive in the face of systematic rape (von Germeten 2013). And for almost a century, international tourism policy has been linked to stereotypical femininity: the creation of a Comité de Turismo (National Tourism Board) in 1931 virtually coincided with the first Concurso Nacional de Belleza de Colombia (Colombian National Beauty Pageant) in 1934 (Nasser De La Torre 2012).

The Concurso has played a crucial role ever since in constructing gender, articulating it to national identity, and promoting the nation. The competition captures the attention of the wider population in commemorating the city's status as the first area to free itself from the Spanish Crown. Tourism promotion highlights the contest as an emblematic event that brings the regions of the country together to admire the looks of Colombian women, linked in turn to natural resources (CO 2017).

The 1961 decision to hold the pageant annually was part of an attempt to construct a national popular in the wake of *La Violencia*. With the proliferation of TV sets over the next two decades, it became event television, not to be missed, and was swiftly articulated by local elites to tourist promotion through celebrity judges and invitations for Miss World/Miss Universe winners to attend (Streicker 1997: 113). The contest is not entirely hegemonic: there are now officially recognized *reinados transformistas* (drag-queen pageants) (Serrano-Amaya 2018: 51); but the *blanqueamiento* (whitening) of contestants over time is clear (Cepeda 2018). And the Concurso has drawn the inevitable Anglo *badinage* (banter): David Letterman distinguished himself on network television by saying that the 2001 queen, Cartagenera Andrea María Noceti Gómez, included among her special skills the capacity to swallow 50 kg of heroin ("Miss Colombia" 2001). The reality of female Colombian drug couriers, of whom there are many, is that they transport cocaine rather than heroin, and largely do so because they are impoverished single mothers (Fleetwood 2014).

As per the Concurso, the tourism industry highlights Colombian women. Promotional campaigns using them as decoration have included: "Turista satisfecho trae más turista" (A Satisfied Tourist Brings More Tourists) (1970), "Enamórese de su Colombia" (Fall in Love with Your Colombia) (1975), "Por las rutas de Colombia" (To the Pathways of Colombia) (1985), and "Colombia: Para amarla, hay que andarla" (Colombia: To Love Her, You Must Walk Her) (1994). Aimed at national and international visitors, these programs highlight the country's diverse regions and peoples as essential components of national identity, displaying women alongside products, places, and objects—fruit, landscape, and religious centers. The new century brought a reaction from the tourism establishment about reclaiming the nation: "Vive Colombia viaja por ella" (Colombia Lives; Walk with Her) (2001) (Criscione and Vignolo 2014). This may have been a cry of desperation from a nation dominated by armed conflict (Toro 2013), but it equally presaged a future that would coagulate nature with light-skinned femininity.

In keeping with the Uribe government's adoption of neoliberal models of development, the nation's 2005 branding exercise took "Colombia es Pasión" (Colombia is Passion) as its motto (Sanín 2016).[20] The campaign linked women to orchids, coffee, gems, and geography, feminizing the image of the nation as a country loaded with ardor in order to distance it from a male image of drug trafficking and violence. The official video of "Colombia es Pasión" stressed "the true face of the country," accompanied by the image of a beauty queen (Mejia 2007, minute 1:06). A signature feminine silhouette constructed women's bodies as visitor sites. Its heart logo, red color, floral design, and silhouette, designed by the U.S. firm Visual Marketing Associates, were alternately celebrated and denounced by public opinion. It is telling that the advisers on the "Colombia es pasión" campaign were Yanquis (Echeverri et al. 2010) charged with making Colombia and Cartagena attractive to outsiders.

Their mission was to configure the city as a place "that foreigners actually love and enjoy. Of color, festivity, vibrancy and more . . . its current realities embodied in the much softer imagery of Colombia is Passion" (Lightle 2017). Image .com International selected these elements for the government's tourism authority, ProColombia, to make the point: "flowers; flames; and a woman's curves."[21] Advocates saw this as an opportunity for sensual experience and emotional connection (Bolívar Ramírez 2007; Echeverri et al. 2010; Nasser De La Torre 2012, 2013). Critics likened the logo and its representation of passion to "a curvaceous woman's midsection" (Nasser De La Torre 2013: 7).

"El riesgo es que te quieras quedar" (The Only Risk Is Wanting to Stay) (2008) profiled the nation as a land girded by sea, with an image of a woman walking sensually from the ocean to the beach (Visitcolombia 2008, minute 0:47). The 2013 tourism slogan "Realismo Mágico" (Magical Realism) associated nature and femininity with García Márquez: ecology + beauty + male genius → tourists.[22] The type of woman celebrated was not representative of Colombia's racial and ethnic diversity, but rather of people connected to the country's historic and contemporary elite (Bolívar Ramírez 2007).

The 2014 brand, "¡La respuesta es Colombia!" (The Answer Is Colombia), focused on a broader economic and investment strategy ("¿Cartagena es Pasión?" 2012). It presented the nation as a modern, flexible country of unparalleled natural and cultural wealth, its people entrepreneurs "propelled into the future" (Wickcreativo 2012) and ready to be exploited by the international market. Passion and the color red remained present, human indices of that putative entrepreneurial resource: the NICL illuminated and highlighted.

The next campaign was "Colombia, la tierra de la sabrosura" (Colombia: Land of Sabrosura).[23] "Sabrosura" is akin to jouissance if one is in a Barthesian mood; something like "the sweet life" if one is feeling less sexy. Rather than being driven by feminizing the country, it relies on racialization, connecting blackness to rhythm; music is the glue that binds Colombia together in a unique amalgam with nature. The nation is depicted as a magical blend of colonial architecture, ecological beauty, and young, creative people who have almost inadvertently generated a mystic yet material playground available to the moneyed white or Asian cosmopolitan. No wonder Colombia comes third on the 140-strong "Happy Planet Index Score."[24] (Such a thing really does exist, a utilitarian metrication of environment, life expectancy, and neoliberal dreaming. It was produced by British creative-industries chorines at the New Economics Foundation.[25])

Despite being heralded by true believers as innovative, these campaigns are not so distant from their predecessors. Although the use of women as enticements has grown less prominent with the advent of minerals, music, and biodiversity as core actors, they continue to be protagonists. A recent example included the promotion of Cali, "city of salsa and fun," where "visitors will feel welcomed by the local charm and hospitality, by beautiful women and salsa music" (ProColombia 2015). ProColombia delightfully refers to "1,025 native rhythms" in its Sabrosura campaign's dozen music videos (quoted in Cabo 2018).

Again and again, Cartagena in particular is presented in the international bourgeois media and tourism promotion as an object of casual scopophilic pleasure for visitors, who are addressed in ways that obfuscate and fetishize history, race, gender, and beauty into just so many street names or topographic formations, viewed en passant and photographed or forgotten all too easily (Carbonell 2006; Cunin and Rinaudo 2008). And there is a gruesome underside.

SEXUAL TOURISM

Sexual tourism and trafficking are rife in many places, with Colombia both a source and a destination (George and Panko 2011; United Nations Office on Drugs and Crime 2018). Yet the Colombian establishment draws no connection between fetishistic tourism campaigns and the thousands of visitors arriving each year in search of the illegal sexual corollaries of such imagery (Torres 2011). The reality is known to all, but subtly recoded through informal strategies that sexualize young but avowedly legal-age women as part of the landscape, in much the same way as flora and fauna.

There is, of course, considerable feminist controversy over the issue of adult sex work, both locally and transnationally. For many, it represents, instantiates, and perpetuates the subordination of women to men, women's bodies as currency, and riskiness as a way of (an imposed) life. This abolitionist position originated in a mixture of nineteenth-century feminism, evangelical Christianity, and racialized concerns that young white women were being seized from the United States and trafficked to the Global South. There is little evidence in support of the contention that such slavery was widespread. The movement amounted to a moral panic about gendered modernity—women on the move, nationally and internationally, largely of their own accord. Today, advocates charge abolitionists with a moralistic rather than feminist agenda, driven by a displeasure with extramarital sex and lacking any commitment to improving women's financial, social, cultural, and political standing (Soderlund 2005, 2011; O'Brien et al. 2013).

The sex industry in general today involves millions of workers, mostly female, and customers, mostly male. Abolitionists regard this proliferation as evidence of a quasi-enslavement that should be eradicated, as per Alexandra Kollontai's lament that sex work "is an act of violence by the woman upon herself in the name of material gain" (1978: 275). The bourgeois Anglo media tend to constitute "good" versus "bad" classes of sex worker—the trafficked versus the voluntarist. Conversely, advocates regard sexual labor as a material reality of agency *as well as* a form of exploitation that must be managed, in the same way as the sale of human labor power via the body is governed in other sectors of the economy. For these advocates, the voices of women sex workers should be heard, their perils minimized, and global variations in their experiences taken into account (Nussbaum 1999; Agustín 2007; Della Giusta et al. 2008; O'Brien et al. 2013; Bennett 2016).

Several discussions of sexual tourism in Latin America emphasize that while the business is structured through monetary, gender, and racial domination, it is frequently characterized by assiduous female networking. Such perspectives argue that the industry's manifest and manifold inequalities need to be understood in the context of North–South relations and dependent underdevelopment, rather than rendered subject to sexual moralizing by people from wealthy countries with abundant occupational choices—and they note that Caribbean sex workers have organized and acted to protect their interests since the nineteenth century, a heritage continued in today's multinational Red de Mujeres Trabajadoras Sexuales de Latinoamérica y el Caribe (Network of Women Sex Workers in Latin America and the Caribbean). Colombia has a union that is recognized by the state, and some adult female sex workers voluntarily migrate as part of their careers (Brennan 2004; Kempadoo 2004; Cabezas 2009; Curtis 2009; Cabezas 2019; Chin 2013). Female sex tourism also proliferates in some sites (Gmelch 2003). These women are sometimes labeled "romance tourists" (Pruitt and LaFont 1995) by abolitionists, while feminists concerned with racial, international, and linguistic inequalities deem "sex tourism" the right moniker (Sanchez Taylor 2006).

Coercion and the statutory rape of those unable to give informed consent bring abolitionists and advocates closer. The issue they jointly confront is huge, because the exploitation of children is global and profitable. Unlike most trafficking, it generally involves mobility by offenders rather than victims (Bang et al. 2014). The UN's World Tourism Network on Child Protection[26] has been running under various names since 1997, stepping up its work each year in response to new intelligence. Colombian studies conducted by the Fundación Renacer (Reborn Foundation),[27] the Instituto Colombiano de Bienestar Familiar (Colombian Institute of Family Welfare),[28] and numerous academics demonstrate the enormity of child sexual exploitation (Mosquera and Bozzi 2005; Díaz Granados and Rodríguez Cruz 2006; Bernal-Camargo et al. 2013; Londoño et al. 2014).[29] Their research argues that between 30,000 and 40,000 Colombian children and adolescents have been victims since the expansion of tourism. Many young people also work in other poorly paid informal sectors, such as selling tchotchkes on beaches (Guerrero-Figueroa Guerrero 2016).

The *Guardian* suggests that "[s]exual exploitation and abuse is out of control" in Cartagena (Charles 2018). Current estimates are that the city has well over a thousand children and adolescents trafficked to tourists, 70 percent of them girls. Figures from 2018 suggest that thousands of children are involved in pornography and sex, but the statistics are widely regarded as understating the reality, due to the stigma involved and the fact that perhaps 90 percent of perpetrators act with impunity—many of them gangsters and illicit miners as well as tourists (Moloney 2018). The Fundación Renacer's research correlates increased child sexual exploitation in Cartagena with resources booms (2016):

> en Cartagena la ESCNNA está principalmente relacionada con la actividad turística, existe una red que trabaja en la negociación de los servicios sexuales de

> los menores, se encuentran vinculadas a esto personas que desempeñan labores relacionadas directa e indirectamente con el turismo, el valor de la oferta comercial de los NNA depende de la edad de éstos y del lugar de procedencia del turista. Las víctimas de ESC son generalmente de género femenino, entre los 14 y 17 años. Los factores propiciatorios descritos son: situación de pobreza y hambre, descuido o complicidad de familiares, y falta de acción de la comunidad inmediata que conoce la situación y no la denuncia.
>
> (In Cartagena, ESCNNA is profoundly linked to tourism. A network negotiates sexual services from minors. The price placed on children depends on age and the nationality of tourists. Victims are generally young women aged between 14 and 17. The key factors propelling their participation include poverty and hunger, the neglect or complicity of relatives, and lack of action by the immediate community, which may know of the situation but fail to report it.) (Arango Arias and Hurtado Díaz 2012: 92–93)

Although the core of the industry is foreign adult men seeking sex with female Colombian children, demand extends to male minors, some of whom enter prostitution following familial rejection of their sexuality (Castillo Murillejo and Rivera Reyes 2013). There is some evidence that Colombian children from desperately poor and violent homes find sex work to be an improvement on their daily lives and sense of agency (Camacho Ordoñez and Trujillo González 2009). But as in other countries with similar trends, there is a high incidence of coercion and sexually transmitted disease among the exploited; the Caribbean has the world's highest rate of HIV/AIDS after sub-Saharan Africa (Baral et al. 2012; Djellouli and Quevedo-Gómez 2015). As one sex worker put it, "[t]he Spanish built these walls to protect this city. But nobody protected me" (quoted in Charles 2018).

This sexual exploitation of minors relies on networks that are directly and indirectly related to the tourist industry. They operate in liminal contact zones: taxi rides, concierge desks, and plazas, inter alia, are frequent switching points between men's arrival and children's exploitation. These sites offer both information about the trade and articulation into it (Arango Arias and Hurtado Díaz 2012). The *Economist* notes that "[a]lmost any taxi driver will offer to hook male passengers up with prostitutes, and some of the city's major hotels are lax in allowing guests to bring guests to their rooms" ("Not the Kind of Press" 2012). Such things can also be arranged in advance; all-inclusive, avowedly adult, sex packages to Cartagena are offered by such services as Global Fantasies, Party Colombia, and Universal Fantasies. They sell "sex tours" for US$6,000, which supposedly purchases three days of "unlimited sex" with up to sixty people.[30] There are also informal networks providing online information to men seeking to visit the city for sex (Puello Sarabia and Ardila Palacio 2019).

FIGURE 3. Your vigilance can protect boys, girls, and adolescents from commercial sexual exploitation. (Source: Toby Miller.)

FIGURE 4. Protect children and adolescents from sexual exploitation by tourist travel. (Source: Toby Miller.)

Against such tendencies, advocates for children have collaborated with governments and the formal tourism industry to establish codes of conduct and lobby hotel owners, who have been powerful conduits for the trade (see figures 3 and 4) (Estella Nagle 2013):

SECRET SERVICES

Several examples from the region shed light on how outsiders regard sexuality in the Colombian Caribbean. The first occurred during the sixth Summit of the Americas meeting in Cartagena in 2012: the case of sex workers servicing numerous Drug Enforcement Agency officials (on repeat visits) and Barrack Hussein Obama II's Secret Service detail (who declined to pay) (Ryan 2012).[31]

The local press viewed the Obama scandal as an isolated event that did not do justice to the reality of the city and the efforts of local authorities and the national government to promote it. The potential to damage the image of Cartagena and Colombia was explained away as the character failings of a few foreigners ("¿Cartagena es Pasión?" 2012; Wickcreativo 2012).[32]

Despite diplomatic efforts to diminish the scandal, the episode went viral, illustrating the stark reality of the city's sex tourism. Spirit Airlines, a low-cost

U.S. carrier, immediately launched a "More Bang for Your Buck" commercial for flights to Cartagena, featuring a white man in Secret Service gear (earpiece, sunglasses, and dark suit) surrounded by pink-bikini-clad women.[33] It drew international attention, with major segments on CNN and Fox News. The incident signaled the image and marketing of Cartagena—stereotyped Colombian women as products for U.S. custom—in a shocking link between country branding, beauty queendom, statutory rape, and social inequality.

Other media scandals have involved webs of procurers who sell children to U.S. tourists for sexual purposes in the offshore Rosario islands, in one instance led by Kelly Johana Suárez Martínez Moyam, a 2013 Miss Cartagena contestant who featured in the video to the Juanez (Juan Esteban Aristizábal Vásquez) song, "La Luz" (The Light) (Bedoya 2014; Montaño 2018).[34] Liliana del Carmen Campos Puello, a renowned figure known locally as "Madame," spent much of the past decade in an alliance with Israelis and local officials, organizing hotel, beach, yacht, and island sex parties with 250 14- to 17-year-old female workers from Cartagena and Venezuela and shepherding children around the historic center of the city in search of tourists. Police were bribed and girls dispatched to the Bahamas and Miami. Hundreds of Israeli soldiers were regular customers. The link between the military and such activities is long-standing: the development of sex tourism for U.S. nationals, for instance, accelerated with participation by soldiers involved in the American war in Vietnam. "Madame" was eventually sentenced to eight years in jail (Charles 2018; Montaño 2018; "'La Madame'" 2019; Boyer 2002).

Such cases reference the centrality of the female body and the role of beauty queens and other conventionally attractive women working in the culture industries in the construction of gender in Colombia, and its articulation as an international calling card to the world's diplomatic underside and informal economy. They signal the casual arrogance and entitlement that peoples around the world experience from many U.S. and western European tourists, in contradistinction to the latter's banal, repetitive claims to a high moralism. These instances bring into question the creative industries as magic elixirs of development, cohesion, and all the other clichés.

We should not regard Obama's security detail, his drug interdictors, Madame, or the Israeli Defense Forces as aberrant. But the notion of an aberrant accident connects us to a plaque honoring British imperialism, an occasion when the contradictions of heritage-based tourism were brought into the white heat of Cartagena day.

THE BRITISH

The United Kingdom has been involved in extracting value from the Americas since Elizabethan times. With independence across Latin America, Britain became the most important foreign power. An economic core of world trade for much of the nineteenth century until the Great War, with the subsequent commercial and military assertion of U.S. power, the U.K. was long the principal destination for the region's mining and agricultural products, and exported cotton, wool, iron, and consumer goods (Funari 2019; Orser 2019). Today it does not have a powerful presence in Colombian discourse, despite the fact that thousands of expatriates live in London, generally fleeing urban violence to beaver away in blue-collar jobs without recognition of their minority status or interests (McIlwaine 2014; Miller 2018a).

But while the United States figures most centrally in the Colombian national imaginary of wealthy outsiders, daily flights from London to Bogotá, which had stopped when Britain required that Colombians obtain visas, recommenced right at the time of the plaque's unveiling; and since 2015, the U.K. has been the fastest-growing source of visitors to the region.[35] Britain is a particular target of expanded Colombian tourism, given its public's wealth, taste for travel to warm climes, and, ironically, avoidance of terrorism (Maslen 2014). So what is the history connecting London to Cartagena?

Because Cartagena was a slave port and a crucial outpost of naval and trade routes, it became a key site in the struggle between Spain and Britain for economic control of the Caribbean from the sixteenth century. Sir Francis Drake's forces blockaded the city in search of wealth stolen from the continent that was en route to Spain. His "privateering" is regarded as piracy by Cartagener@s. Admiral Vernon's similarly despicable—and ultimately failed—blockade attempted to starve the local population into submission and position the British empire to seize Spanish gold and territory in support of cross-imperial contraband trade. The blockade was part of what was once known as the War of Jenkins's Ear/*La Guerra de Asiento* (the Treaty War) but is now categorized as the War of Austrian Succession. The siege of Cartagena incarnated Britain's desire to assert its treaty right to deploy slaves in Spanish territory and engage in the "free" trade of goods (and people).

The attack on the port city took place between March 13 and May 20, 1741. Vernon oversaw an immense fleet: 186 ships, 2,620 pieces of artillery, and more than 27,000 men. By contrast, the defense comprised six ships, 4,000 soldiers, and 600 archers.[36] The latter were a mix of regular Spanish troops, militia made up of Creoles (as mestiz@s were then known), Native peoples, Africans, and their descendants (Robertson 1919; Lemaitre 1998; "Visita" 2014; Mazzotti 2016).

Bizarrely, illegal British supply chains provisioned the Spanish *guarda costa* (coast guard). That helped ensure the blockade's ultimate failure, along with chronic illness from tropical disease, which afflicted both sides (Earle 1996; Schmitt 2015). The chaos brought by fever and insect-borne death produced both the expression "Mosquito Empire" (McNeill 2010) and a nation of beef eaters, because that became the key ration for the Colombian military, prisoners, and slaves from the time of the siege (Van Ausdal 2008).

FIGURE 5. Statue of Bolivar. (Source: Toby Miller.)

Ironically, London has a statue of Bolívar that celebrates Britain as a beacon of freedom in the struggle against imperialism (figure 5). The Belgrave Square plaque (figure 6), not far from Colombia's consulate, quotes El Libertador (The Liberator) saying: "I am convinced that England alone is capable of protecting the world's precious rights as she is great, glorious and wise."

FIGURE 6. That contradiction continues. (Source: Toby Miller.)

THE OFFENDING PLAQUE

The 1741 triumph over the British quickly became, and has remained, a point of pride and central discourse in Cartagena's collective memory. Four decades after Vernon's assault, a Spanish blockade led by General Pablo Morillo y Morillo failed to undo Venezuelan-Colombian independence movements based in the city. Cartagena therefore incarnates high points of history for all Colombians. It is laden with symbolism: independence, festival life, the 2016 peace accord, sex, sand, and so on—and a marker of Spaniards occupying it against British invaders, and later freedom from those very Spanish.

But if we fast forward to today, many light-skinned, wealthy oligarchs take a different view. The 2013–2015 mayoral administration of Dionisio Fernando Vélez Trujillo sought to legitimize Cartagena's colonial past. It returned the city's logo (a celebration of the eradication of slavery and independence from Spain) to its old colonial emblem, and appealed to latter-day little-Englander imperialists by glorifying their country's eighteenth-century attempt to starve Cartagener@s into submission (Hernández-Mora 2014; Abello Vives 2016). A crucial part of this strategy was the construction of a plaque celebrating the gallant British and their heroic siege, and inviting the Prince of Wales and the Duchess of Cornwall[37] to unveil the following tribute:

FIGURE 7. Site of the offending plaque. (Source: Toby Miller.)

> Esta placa fue develada por sus altezas reales el Príncipe de Gales y la Duquesa de Cornualles en memoria al valor y sufrimiento de todos los que murieron en combate intentando tomar la ciudad y el fuerte de San Felipe, bajo el mando del almirante Edward Vernon en Cartagena de Indias en 1741.
>
> (This plaque was unveiled by their royal highnesses the Prince of Wales and the Duchess of Cornwall in memory of the valor and suffering of those who, under Admiral Vernon, died in combat attempting to take the city and the fort San Felipe in Cartagena de Indias in 1741.) (See figure 7.)

The event was timed by the Corporación Centro Histórico Cartagena de Indias (Corporation for the Historic Center of Cartagena de Indias) (a private institution with ties to elite politics and corporate business) to coincide with Charles and Camilla's 2014 visit to Colombia. This rather mysterious Corporación thought the plaque would bring honor and money via increased service-sector revenues from British visitors drawn to their warrior past. Sabas Pretelt de la Vega, a Corporación member and corrupt politician who was banned from holding public office for a decade and subsequently jailed, approved the plaque's wording. He planned to construct a cross in Tierra Bomba, an island off the coast, to remember the British dead, in the hope of luring additional tourists ("Cambiar" 2014).

De la Vega "argued that changing the text would cause offence, because it was approved by the British" (quoted in "Gobernador" 2014). But the plaque split the elite. Journalist Daniel Alfonso Coronell Castañeda tweeted "Placa que debe avergonzar a Cartagena. Por la lagartería de unos cuantos terminamos homenajeando a un verdugo" (The plaque should embarrass Cartagena. To satisfy the oleaginous self-interest of a few, we are paying homage to a killer) (2014). Governor Juan Carlos Gossaín Rognini stated:

> No quiero causar molestias incómodas por este tema, pero soy cartagenero y amo profundamente la historia de la ciudad. La batalla contra los ingleses fue el combate más importante de los que ha librado el país en su historia, y poner una placa en honor a los ingleses es como si un banco pusiera una placa en honor a los ladrones que se lo robaron. Lo que vino Vernon fue a robar, a saquear a Cartagena, pero no pudo.
>
> (I don't want to make things uncomfortable over this topic, but I am from Cartagena and love its history very deeply. The battle against the English was the most important conflict in our nation's history. Creating a plaque to honor them is like a bank erecting a plaque to honor thieves who stole from it. Vernon came to rob and plunder Cartagena, but failed to do so.) ("Citan a Alcaldía" 2014)

Chastened, Vélez Trujillo undertook to have the offending item removed. But before his apparatchiks could do so, Jaime Rendón Márquez, an engineer originally from Medellín but a long-term resident of Cartagena and self-anointed environmentalist who was to go on to be a mayoral candidate and implacable opponent of peace with the FARC, defaced the plaque and publicized his action. A day later, the offending item was officially excised. Rendón Márquez came to be known as "Mona Man" (Monkey Man) for the dexterity he supposedly showed to chisel his point (Taborda Herrera 2015; "Queman bandera" 2016).[38]

So just a few days after the old boy and his consort had landed in Cartagena and lifted the plaque's veil, it was gone (see figure 8) (Hernández-Mora 2014). A humiliated mayor Trujillo left office some time afterward, amid spiraling scandals about his love life and financial affairs, culminating with revelations in the *Panama Papers* ("Se investiga" 2016). Meanwhile, U.K. tourism flourished. The British, no doubt emboldened by their heroic decision to depart the European Union, flooded South America in search of cheaper cocaine than they could buy in their Home Counties idylls (Cottle 2018).

The incident can be read in various ways. Superficially, it marks the protection of popular historiography against a crude and reactionary elite revisionism that was driven by craven desires to promote Anglo tourism. For while no one could argue for the Spanish Empire as a beacon of endeavor and human rights by contrast with its similarly venal British equivalent, the fact is that the Cartagener@s'

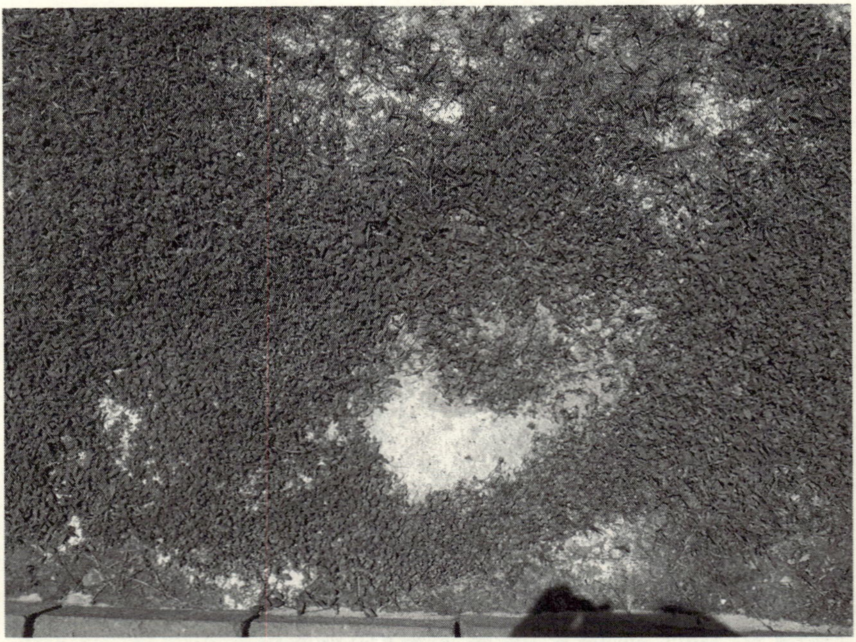

FIGURE 8. Remains of the plaque. (Source: Toby Miller.)

defense, in both the eighteenth and twenty-first centuries, represents a storied moment in local and national mythology, participating in, then commemorating, Blas de Lezo's victory.[39] The placement of the plaque a few meters from his statue, and its wording, were particularly problematic.[40]

The grandiloquent rhetoric of citizen empowerment, gatekeeper-free expression, and social-movement triumphs supposedly enabled by new technologies is largely overblown (Passy and Monsch 2014). But sometimes forms of surveillance capitalism, such as Twitter, can be sources of counter-power to hegemonic governments, whether embodied in small-minded mayors or small-minded heirs (Castells 2012; Lago Martínez 2012; Puyosa 2015). Commenting on the unveiling of the plaque and the resuscitation of this emblem, Alberto Salcedo Ramos tweeted "El alcalde de Cartagena es, tristemente, de esos cartageneros que presumen de virreinales y tienen nostaligia del látigo" (The mayor of Cartagena is, regrettably, one of those Cartageneros who love royalty and are nostalgic for the lash) (2014).

That said, few commentators protested the plaque's commemoration of the British Empire, or its neglect of the indigenous, Afro-descended, and Creole fighters who died in battle. Rather, critics highlighted the need to celebrate the Spanish armada in the new world, embodied by Blas de Lezo. And it is worth noting that some tweeters had more influence than others. For example, Rendón Márquez was inspired to destroy the plaque by a tweet from the ex-*guerrilla* Senator Antonio José Navarro Wolff, who threatened to deface the plaque, and other prominent social-media mavens ("Me les adelanté" 2014).

Neither side in the debate engaged a truly revisionist popular history, which would have focused on the roles of women, Afro-Caribbeans, and indigenous people in resisting the *conquista*, incarnated in figures such as Benkos Biohó, a king-become-slave who led a rebellion in 1599 (Urbina Joiro 2006). Nor was there a serious challenge to the corrupt traditions of the city's ruling elite. Instead, the incident became one more moment of forgetting native and Afro-descendant struggle against all imperialism.[41] Dominant historiography still heroizes the defense of what is euphemized as "el tráfico commercial español" (Spanish commercial traffic), that is, slaves (Sancho Gómez 2003). The perceived betrayal was not of the Colombian nation as an ethnic mosaic, but a country that still imagines itself as part of the Spanish Crown, albeit brokered through latter-day oligarchic nationalism (Arcieri 2014).

That said, vibrant reinterpretations of Cartagena's history abound, and the national conversation is opening up: the 2016 Bicentennial Law declared December 6 a civic celebration commemorating survival of the 1815 Spanish siege. It acknowledged the efforts of Cartagener@s in the struggle against Madrid. And new research stresses the cross-racial drive for liberty that propelled the 1811 declaration of independence (Cepeda Jiménez et al. 2011). Consider the case of General José Prudencio Padilla López. A fierce leader of the independence movement, he was falsely declared a traitor, executed by Bolívar, and erased from the record until very recently—but is taking his place in revisionist historiography (Helg 2012). Both he and Benkos Biohó are slowly gaining a presence in the imaginary of the city. And when Trujillo's administration returned the city's logo to the old emblem of the Spanish colony, significant debates ensued (Abello Vives 2016). In addition, popular art is a key site for resisting historic as well as contemporary racism and inequality (Rolston and Ospina 2017).

CONCLUSION

The international image of Cartagena is as a tourist's paradise. It offers spectacular views of the Caribbean from the old town, historic architecture, narrow streets, horse-drawn transportation, luxury hotels, street life, and a cornucopia of music and dance. That panoply hides the realities of extreme Afro-Colombian poverty, massive child and adult sexual exploitation, and oligarchic control of historiography and town planning alike.

Successive promotional campaigns designed to entice tourists are clearly not the sole cause of the rise in sex tourism—governmental policies aimed at visitors cannot be held entirely responsible for what has occurred. But in addition to attracting large numbers of people, these campaigns have focused on gender and sexuality. This is in keeping with the culturalist focus so beloved of development and creative-industry chorines. As a consequence, the industry incarnates and indexes a dark underside to Colombia: national branding has accidentally become a key component of sexual exploitation. Local citizenry and overseas visitors alike exploit the vulnerability of the young and the extremely young. It is clear that state interdiction and public-health campaigns coordinated across the globe are prerequisites to dealing with the problem. Some strides have been made in that direction, thanks to research and suasion from the third sector and academia.

But two governing fantasies stand in the way of resolving the basic problem. The first sees tourism as an unproblematic benefit to the Colombian economy that can be promoted with cavalier disregard for gender politics, when it is clearly the case that over half a century of drawing homologies between women, desire, nature, and tourism has had malign effects. The second fantasy is that the goodness at the heart of the average Anglo will ultimately express itself in untrammeled interaction with folks from other, albeit strange, lands, thereby connecting them to the other and finding an unlikely overlap of interests through their common humanity—as per *Grand Tour* masculinity, perhaps? How twee, when so many businesspeople, militarists, politicians, and officials are reared on doctrines of national, racial, class, and gender superiority and condescension.

The violence of contemporary child sexual exploitation and colonial contests over slave labor are just two instances of travel that instantiates and commemorates exploitation. Together, they reference both the continued transgression of human rights as routine elements of daily Colombian life, and the bathetic valuation of British imperial nostalgia. One form of popular culture is pseudo-clandestine, part of the informal economy dedicated to sex. The other is an overt celebration of defeated foes that exposed divisions within the Colombian ruling class. Together, they have been crucial to countless deaths over the past two centuries.

A serious shift in the rhetoric and imagery of development and nation must ensue, with Colombia revisiting its historiography, rewriting its tourism strategy, and rekindling its multicultural vision; and the rest of the world reeducating people about Colombia, sexual justice, and imperial history (Carrillo Romero et al. 2013). The nation must revise its views of the region's past and present, and the roles of age, masculinity, poverty, and race, which intertwine with economic inequality and industry policy.

3 • "I MYSELF HAD TO REMAIN SILENT WHEN THEY THREATENED MY CHILDREN"

Colombian Journalists Meet Prime-Time Narcos

WITH MARTA MILENA BARRIOS AND JESÚS ARROYAVE

We've seen how two aspects of popular culture and the orange economy embody and stimulate violence—football and tourism. This chapter looks at what many would regard as the core of the creative industries: the media. We examine both its purportedly democratic function—journalism—and its avowedly entertaining one, in drama. Putting them together disrespects classic divisions between factual and fictional media that one finds in both the media themselves and academic work. But the two genres are organically related in the impact of narco wealth and violence (on journalists) and how the spoils and struggles of cocaine cartels are represented in the popular (*narconovelas*).

Our methods mix political economy, interviews, and content analysis. In the first section, we'll uncover how violence distorts reportage by forcing journalists to censor themselves, as a consequence of the threats made to them by narco terrorists. The second section focuses on the appeal to the popular classes of some aspects of *narcocultura* that we encountered in football. Television drama's glamorization of mafiosi lifestyles and gender stereotypes of power, bling, and bodies are also not far distant from the misogynistic trappings of tourism.

THE JOURNALISTS

For democracies to function, current-affairs media must ply their trade without fear or favor. There needs to be regular press coverage of political affairs, with a focus on human rights, public policy, international relations, economy, society, culture, elections, lawmakers' deliberations, and judicial review. The idea is to draw citizens into the policy process, ensuring informed public comment and dissent as well as willing consent.

At its best, journalism connects people who would otherwise be out of touch with others' concerns, enables them to scrutinize private and public institutions, highlights social problems, informs debate over values, and animates the public power of reason (Sen 2009: 335–37). Such ideals have a venerable history. Milton avowed that "when complaints are freely heard, deeply considered, and speedily reformed, then is the utmost civil liberty attained" (1909–1914: 1). Bentham referred to journalism as the "check to arbitrary power . . . upon the conduct of the ruling few" (2012: 8, 13). Mill defended it "as one of the securities against corrupt or tyrannical government" (1859), and Bolívar called for "freedom of the press." He regarded an independent media as a cornerstone of autonomy from Spain—part of "all that is sublime in politics" (2003: 21, 42, 73). Camus's famous defense of press autonomy in Colombia against governmental "breach of faith" heralded the news medium as "better than intelligence or progress; it is the possibility of all that and of other things as well" (1961: 102). He cited approvingly Luxemburg's insistence that journalistic autonomy, along with freedom of association, were the "most important democratic guarantees of a healthy public life and of the political activity of the laboring masses" (1970: 389). Perhaps the most noteworthy proof of the point is the link established by Amartya Sen between a free press, multiparty democracy, and the avoidance of famine, in order to ensure the allocation of resources in terms of need via reportage of food shortages and action to alleviate them (2000). One can regard Marx's work as a journalist as both part of his intellectual formation and his financial occupation: "public criticism that he saw as political action *par excellence*" (Althusser 1969: 224).

Despite these heady claims made by political theory and welfare economics for the value of the news media to citizenship, reporters have long been regarded as disposable and unworthy, in ways that predate their supposed subordination to capitalism. If we go back to the origins of journalism in the seventeenth- and eighteenth-century European occupations of the gazetteer and newsman, we find they were derided as unreliable and given to sensationalizing. Such complaints indexed these writers' contradictory roles as spokespeople for traditional sources of ecclesiastical and state authority or rivalrous emergent bourgeoisies. The earliest journalists were passionate observers and partisan chroniclers of an urbanizing Europe, whether as roving anonymous reporters or sedentary philosopher-anthropologists named Kant (Foucault 2007: 48). They were describing the

Industrial Revolution as it deepened and spread (Briggs and Burke 2003). Inevitably, this attracted opprobrium. And there is self-censorship in newsrooms, for professional, procedural, organizational, reference-group, economic, and political reasons (Hanitzsch et al. 2010).[1] "[M]edia capture" jeopardizes independent reporting when journalists concentrate on satisfying oligarchs and oligopolists (Schiffrin 2017b; Dragomir 2018).

No wonder Trotsky referred dismissively to "adept bureaucrats of journalism whose writings bear no relation to actual events" (1970: 160); for Bukharin, they were amongst various "specialists" that "the capitalist State maintains . . . to stupefy and subdue the proletariat" (Buharin [*sic*] and Preobrazhensky 1922: 44). Lukács famously associated the press with

> subjectivity itself, knowledge, temperament and powers of expression that are reduced to an abstract mechanism functioning autonomously and divorced both from the personality of their "owner" and from the material and concrete nature of the subject matter in hand. The journalist's "lack of convictions," the prostitution of his experiences and beliefs is comprehensible only as the [outcome of] capitalist reification. (1972: 357–358)

Such mistrust is especially prevalent when protagonists in stories argue against the misrepresentations they encounter in the press. Consider A. J. Ayer's denunciation of "ignorant and irresponsible journalists" writing about logical positivism (1956: 72), Simone de Beauvoir confronting a senior editor at the *New York Times* who demeaned existentialism while knowing nothing of it (1999: 42), or Andrés Bello criticizing reports of the revolution against the Spanish as "ephemeral productions" written by reporters who were fated to "return to the bars where their authors learned their manners" (1997: 191).

Journalism's mission is far from simple: it requires research, interpretation, dissemination, and mobilization (Cassidy 2005). In addressing the profession's social standing, Weber found it was "always estimated by 'society' in terms of its ethically lowest representative." Conversely, he admired reporters, because of the extraordinary responsibility that came with their role and the factory-like discipline of the deadlines they faced, which both demanded and constrained creativity. This was especially true at times of war and new peace (Weber was writing in one such period, just after the Great War). Their ideal mission was very difficult to live up to, because journalists were "propertyless and hence professionally bound," their occupation "an absolute gamble in every respect and under conditions that test one's inner security." The sense of being obliged to employers was connected to the priority placed on advertising revenue over true independence and the absence of both "genuine leadership" and "the responsible management of politics" (1946: 96–98). In this context, Brecht suggested that journalistic labor is overdetermined by a "collective" way of working and thinking that "makes the individual's contribution unrecognizable" as a consequence of the "shared work of proletarianization and the shared fate of becoming the proletariat": reporters wrote in ways that urged workers to be obedient in just the same way that they themselves were subject to employers' control (2000: 180).

COLUMBIAN JOURNALISM

There is not a great deal of empirical research into Colombian journalism, but longitudinal content analyses of news and current-affairs television are revealing. What began in the 1960s as programming dedicated to transcendental ideas—love of country, democracy, republicanism, morality, progress, and development—was gradually displaced by material stories of violence, insurrection, insecurity, and a failed state (Narvaez Montoya and Romero Peña 2017). Hope-filled fantasy was eroded by hopeless resignation, mixed with shock. Something similar has happened to Colombian journalism more broadly.

The nation pioneered investigative or watchdog journalism in South America. But the stability of the polity, if not the country, meant that the long-standing partisan divide between Liberals and Conservatives produced coverage that usually aligned with one or the other political party, the state in general, and the interests of large conglomerates (Waisbord 2000: 9). And Colombia has not benefited from a wide variety of press opinion. In 1913, when it had three newspapers, Argentina boasted eighty-seven, Panamá fifty-three, Chile forty-four, and Costa Rica thirty-one (Bulmer-Thomas 2003: 85). The country's dynastic history finds many presidents linked directly to the media, as reporters, owners, or family legatees (Rathbone 2013). Unsurprisingly, newsrooms are particularly subject to media capture: failure to comply with the interests of oligarchic actors has significant consequences. We offer two instances.

The national daily *El Espectador* (*The Spectator*) reported extensively on white-collar crime in the 1980s, focusing in particular on Grupo Gran Colombiano, a corporation with interests across finance, manufacturing, and the media. It took a decade for the paper to recover from the resultant loss of advertising revenue—and having its offices blown up by gangsters (Duzán 1994; Rathbone 2013). Or consider Postobón, which we encountered in chapter 1 as a major football sponsor. In 2017, the company provided 3,130 children of Guajira, a 'forgotten' region in northern Colombia, with Kufu beverages in an experiment to evaluate the effects of their products. It did so without regard for health regulations. Despite concern from doctors, scientists, and some reporters for the possible harmful effects of the drinks on children's health, numerous journalists self-censored, failing to follow the story. As we saw earlier, Postobón owns two of Colombia's main media outlets: RCN Radio and Television. The story finally came out in *VICE*'s Colombian edition, thanks to funding from La Liga Contra el Silencio (The League Against Silence) (2018), an independent alliance of journalists linked to the nongovernmental organization (NGO) Fundación para la Libertad de Prensa (Foundation for Press Freedom) (FLIP).[2]

Further problems arise from journalism's labor process, such as the barrier that should exist between editorial and advertising work. Most print reporters in Colombia are initially hired through employment exchange centers. They are not formally tied to a paper or magazine, but work for subcontractors for between six months and a year. If the relevant media outlet considers their work valuable, these jobbing journalists are then directly employed. Even so, few receive a living wage or the social benefits that any Colombian worker should be guaranteed. It is therefore common for reporters to supplement their professional income by taking on another job within the same newspaper: selling advertising space and time to the very officials or business leeches who may also be their sources of information and targets of investigation. The outcome is that many journalists receive a small portion of their income directly from their occupation—often minimum wage—and the rest through these so-called advertising quotas, via a percentage of each sale or by directly charging clients. In other words, there is no wall between editorial content and advertising sales, as has traditionally been the case in the Global North.[3] This clearly challenges the right of Colombian citizens to scrutinize governments and corporations in a way unfettered by mammon.

In addition, the availability of political knowledge varies by region, in the context of the strength of the state vis-à-vis the *guerrilla* and *paramilitares* (Puig-i-Abril and Rojas 2018). FLIP estimates that eight million Colombians in five hundred municipalities effectively live in "zones of silence," without adequate access to information. Just ten percent of the population in those areas is connected to the Internet, and local radio is generally run by and for the military (FLIP 2018b, 2018c). FLIP's *Cartografías de la Información* (Information Maps), which track reportage across the country, refer to the "extinction of local journalism."[4] And in addition to these political-economic and infrastructural problems, there is persistent violence against reporters.

VIOLENCE AND JOURNALISM

Reporters

> often venture into the darkest corners to shed light on current events. A considerable number of them are subjected to intimidation, physical violence, kidnapping or illegal detention in direct relation to their work and, in extreme cases, they can be killed because of their professional activity. Some are killed in war or conflict zones or in situations of civil unrest, while others are the specific targets of homicidal violence—United Nations Office on Drugs and Crime (2013).

The "killing of a journalist is a sign of deteriorating respect for human rights," and frequently encourages repressive reactions from the state that further the rate and number of violent political crimes (Gohdes and Carey 2017; Freedom House 2017). Countries like Colombia, which lack a truly independent judiciary and separation of powers, easily lurch towards such violations (Whitten-Woodring 2009).

Given discrepancies in the collection of data, it is notoriously difficult to establish the global incidence of violence against journalists. But the Committee to Protect Journalists estimates that 1,842 reporters have been killed worldwide since 1992.[5] Although the deaths of war correspondents are often heavily reported as headline stories, local investigative reporters are more vulnerable: 93 percent of journalists murdered between 2002 and 2013 were working in their own countries, often executed by criminal gangs threatened by media exposure (González de Bustamante and Relly 2016; Gohdes and Carey 2017; International Federation of Journalists 2019). Such violence occurs both in overtly conflicted countries and putatively peaceful ones (González de Bustamante and Relly 2016; Jungblut and Hoxha 2016; von der Lippe and Ottosen 2016; Garcés-Prettel and Arroyave Cabrera 2017; Löfgren Nilsson and Örnebring 2017).

Assaults on journalistic integrity are not only physical. Verbal violence and the risk of physical harm alike affect reporters as individuals, and the practice of journalism more generally. The proliferation of online platforms means reporters "are more visible and accessible than ever, and audience members have an unprecedented opportunity to (anonymously) express whatever sentiments they wish to journalists, in particular in the online context" (Löfgren Nilsson and Örnebring 2016: 881; also see Yardy and Boyd 2010). Prevalent forms of harassment have expanded from physical attacks to swearing, defamation, calumny, trolling, stalking, and threats of sexual assault and murder. The pressures come not only from systematically violent groups or parties to particular disputes, but everyday citizens who dislike what they read (Cook and Heilmann 2013). Such aggression stimulates cultural and emotional differences; some reporters react to threats with greater resilience—or foolhardiness—than others (Høiby and Ottosen 2015). Across the globe, the frequently gendered nature of threats is clear (Ferrier 2019).

The Council of Europe rates press freedom across Europe as "more fragile than at any time since the end of the Cold War," because of violence and obstructiveness. Death threats doubled in 2018 on the previous year, as did impunity (2019: 5, 8, 16). Chema Suárez Serrano's meta-analysis concludes that "aggression against those who tell the truth does not discriminate between times of peace and war, professional journalists or citizens, not even the channel through which they send their messages" (2016: 27).

Hun Shik Kim notes that in Latin America, "political upheaval and turmoil not only force journalists to confront legal restrictions and political persecution, but also put the journalists at risk of physical intimidation and targeted killings" (2010: 485). Interviews across the region confirm the fact (Saldaña and Mourão 2018). Almost five hundred Latin American reporters disappeared or were assassinated between 2000 and mid-2017 (Díaz Nosty and de Frutos García 2017). Colombian figures suggest that over the last forty years, 154 journalists have been killed by *paramilitares*, the *guerrilla*, and narcos (FLIP 2017).

Despite touching academic faith from the Global North (Simon 2015: 451; Cottle et al. 2016: 187), peace with the FARC has not diminished violence against journalists (Hughes et al. 2017; Barrios et al. 2019), and reporters are also especially at risk of self-censorship at times of emergent peace, because "not all personal beliefs, opinions, and stereotypes disappear after a conflict ends" (Jungblut and Hoxha 2016: 223) and non-state actors frequently become key perpetrators of human-rights violations (Gohdes and Carey 2017).

Hundreds of Colombian social leaders, human-rights defenders, and trade unionists have been murdered over the last few years, with the perpetrators rarely brought to justice (United Nations Office on Drugs and Crime 2013, 2014, 2018a: 61–62). The victims are felled by two elements of cartel violence: first, the drive to control public life and break laws at will in certain areas; and second, rivalries between cartels that favor certain reporters and denounce others. Narcos are needy; they require "silence and submission" (Bergman 2018: 52).

FLIP reported 310 attacks on press freedom in 2017 suffered by 368 reporters, an increase of 43.5 percent on 2016. By the following year, one hundred and forty-four journalists were under guard contra the *paramilitares* by La Unidad Nacional de Protección (UNP) (the National Protection Unit), an agency of the Interior Ministry. Between 2016 and 2018, 188 legal proceedings went to trial, associated with threats to 277 journalists. The authorities identified those responsible as illegal groups or individuals working alone (FLIP 2018a; "Imputarán cargos" 2018). Various international organizations have been put on alert, and nineteen embassies publicly expressed their concern about the increase in threats, which went from 65 in 2017 to 89 in 2018 (FLIP 2018a; Office of High Commissioner of the United Nations in Colombia 2018).[6]

Around forty reporters were assassinated in 2018 (Naciones Unidas 2018).[7] The Colombian journalists most at risk are "men who work in radio stations, cover daily news as reporters, are professionals with 0 to 11 years of experience, and speak about social structural problems and the actions of political and economic elites of power in the country" (Garcés-Prettel and Arroyave Cabrera 2017: 14).[8]

The routine failure of governments to act against such crimes effectively endows those responsible with a sense of impunity and dampens press freedom (Harrison and Pukallus 2018). The result? Self-censorship among Colombian journalists is complex and widespread. The immediate post-conflict phase of the nation's history has not been the sole determining force: self-censorship existed before, and seems likely to continue as long as violence and oligarchy persist (Zuleta 2015).

A particular story lends spectacular contour to these trends. Three Ecuadorian reporters were abducted and murdered in 2018 by dissident FARC rebels, the Frente Oliver Sinisterra, on Colombia's southeastern border, "a region now considered the world's most deadly for journalists" (Giraudat 2018). Nineteen reporters from both countries investigated the crime. When the NGO Forbidden Stories[9] visited the area in search of what happened, it was accompanied by twenty Ecuadorian soldiers for immediate protection, and drones flying aloft in search of threats. The results of these investigations were published simultaneously in newspapers across the globe, from Brazil to Malta, Germany to Ecuador, Spain to the U.K., Belgium to Ghana, Switzerland to Italy, France to Senegal, Niger to Argentina, and Portugal to South Korea.[10]

Most incidents do not attract such international coverage. In the week of Colombia's annual Day of the Journalist in 2018, a newspaper editor and radio host were murdered and a hit list of reporters circulated. It emanated from the right-wing Bloque Central de Las Águilas Negras (the Central Bloc of the Black Eagles), which is notorious for leafleting marginal people with threats. It designated numerous journalists as *guerrilla* and hence "a military target" (Reporters Without Borders 2018; Serrano-Amaya 2018). There was also a Twitter threat against María Jimena Duzán of the *Semana* newspaper and an intimidatory phone call to the RCN Radio team led by Yolanda Ruiz Ceballos.[11]

In Antioquia and the Pacific region, numerous reporters have left their workplaces because of threats ("Presentadora Vanessa" 2018). FLIP details several critical cases where regionally based journalists have not received state protection ("FLIP alerta" 2018). The Foundation has reported these instances to UNP, but the Unit has not been fast enough to provide endangered reporters with security (FLIP 2018a). As a consequence, 2018 was the most fateful and fatal year of the decade for Colombian reporters, with assaults up 53 percent on 2017 and 120 percent from the year before (FLIP 2018d). In 2019, amid seemingly endless hortatory speeches by Duque calling for an end to violence against activists and journalists, his government expelled *New York Times* employees for revealing death quotas within the military, and supporters accused them of being tied to the *guerrilla* (Daniels 2019).

No wonder, then, that Colombia ranks 130th in the world on Reporters Without Borders' index of press freedom.[12] Numerous contending forces within society, from the conflict to cocaine to the state, from threats to corruption, create immense tensions for journalists, who find it challenging to remain attached to the values of their profession; to report without fear or favor (Garcés-Prettel et al. 2019).

Self-censorship has become as much a part of a Colombian reporter's makeup as courage, community service, resourcefulness, and hard work. Every journalist needs an underlying framework based not only on the fundamentals of the job but on understanding the political economy of the organization where he or she works, lest news stories conflict with other commercial investments of media proprietors. Along with the number of disappeared and murdered journalists and those under UNP protection, this helps explain the country's manifold silent zones and issues about which little is said in the media and public life more generally. A generalized fear seizes newsrooms.

OUR RESEARCH

Via in-depth face-to-face and telephone interviews with fourteen Colombian journalists based in numerous locales, we sought to learn which topics put them at risk and why, and how they combat self-censorship at a time where threats abound. Based on those discussions, this part of the chapter considers:

- The forms that self-censorship takes among journalists
- What produces it
- Available counterstrategies

Four of the reporters interviewed fled the country for security reasons but continued working for Colombian media; one left her hometown for self-protection, moving to Bogotá; two became well-known op-ed columnists and international professors of journalism; six continued working in local media, including danger zones; and one is a union leader.[13]

The expression "everyone owns their own fears" was often used by our interviewees to describe the difficulties they faced in deciding what to write and how to do so. One put it this way:

> In the department of Chocó, illegal armed groups converge. There are some issues that journalists must be silent about because they feel there is a gravestone next to them.... The direct influence of armed actors explains 70% of self-censorship, but some political leaders also have ties to them, which increases the danger ... several colleagues have been threatened, as have I; but one continues working for the benefit of the community. (Journalist 11, Quibdó)

Reporters employed by regional and local media feel especially isolated and vulnerable. Masked or ambiguous threats are as common as the murder of social leaders. Even when there are no direct threats, they self-monitor to avoid antagonizing others. Our informants argued the following:

> In a regional media context, one is very lonely. Self-censorship is greater in the regions; one senses danger, everyone knows where the journalist lives, everyone

> can reach your home; conversely, in large cities, a journalist is an anonymous citizen. (Journalist 14, Cartagena)

> There is a natural selection of news sources in regions with public-order problems. . . . Self-censorship occurs as a consequence of fear, but also due to particular interests. Everyone owns their own fear, but reporting in a place like Tumaco and other areas that used to be the epicenter of the armed conflict is different from working in cities. (Journalist 12, Bogotá)

> I experienced a climate of very strong threats in Córdoba. That meant we had to conduct research in silence. I myself had to remain silent when they threatened my children. The most difficult thing for a journalist is to remain silent from fear. . . . I was the editor-in-chief, and it was very difficult to find the right way to guide teams of reporters in the midst of this climate of violence. Many told me: I went to follow such and such a story, but the *paramilitares* were waiting for me. I couldn't do my job. (Journalist 9, Bogotá)

One Cartagener@ said,

> I had to leave my apartment when I mentioned in an op-ed piece a man who has a lot of power in Bolívar. First, he was looking for me, and after a while, somebody told me that this guy was not looking for me anymore. When I heard that, I worried all the more. I left all my possessions in my apartment and never returned. (Journalist 14, Cartagena)

These fears have created extreme self-censorship, to the point where presenters have closed down radio news programs in favor of music. On other occasions, the news has continued on air, but with coverage restricted to entertainment:

> In Tumaco, Buenaventura, and in some areas of Cauca, journalists are afraid of armed actors in the conflict. There are threats and murders of social leaders. Media workers are in a constant state of anxiety. . . . It is also a lot more complicated [to work as a reporter] in territory formerly under the control of the *guerrilla*, such as Chocó, Guaviare, Nariño, and the Montes de María region in Bolívar. There are very few media outlets, and those that exist depend to a large extent on official advertising . . . there are radio stations where you cannot transmit information, only music. (Journalist 4, Cali)

In sum, the environment militates against a free press. But this is not only due to the risk of violence. As noted earlier, the news media rely heavily on official and corporate sources for stories and revenue. That gives a powerful voice to the society's dominant ideology over alternative views seeking greater accountability. One reporter told us:

> Journalists use various sources in their news pieces, but if you look carefully, there is a strong chance that all of them are official sources. Our choice of sources excludes much of the story. (Journalist 12, Bogotá)

So threats against the flow of information come not only from armed actors but also due to this complex journalistic relationship with civilian and state authorities. Two of our informants put it this way:

> When reporters have daily relationships with their sources, they lose critical perspective . . . self-censorship is already present. (Journalist 3, France)

> When dependence between journalists and their sources is maintained, just as when slaves maintain their own chains, self-censorship becomes part of the biased or frightened language we use. (Journalist 10, Bogotá)

Reporters must take into account the recommendations of their employers' commercial departments:

> A lot of censorship derives from our advertising guidelines. The journalist receives direct mandates from the commercial section of the media on content. . . . There is a lot of pressure from the advertising companies that control the work of journalists. Corporate interests often prevail, to the detriment of journalistic principles. (Journalist 7, United States)

Several reporters noted that advertising is a particular problem in small outfits that depend entirely on such revenue. For their part, most large media companies belong to bigger conglomerates, with interests in various sectors of the economy. This keeps journalists in either context under constant pressure. When producing the news, they have to decide whether the interests of their proprietors in other industries or political parties will be affected by a story. One interviewee, who was employed by one of the largest newspapers in the country, put it like this:

> When I worked on the Bogotá section . . . and Gustavo Petro [Gustavo Francisco Petro Urrego, a leftist who stood for the Presidency in 2018] was mayor, we were free to criticize his administration, with minimal research to back it up. But we had to self-censor anything positive. In contrast, if criticism arose with regard to the next mayor's administration, Enrique Peñaloza [Londoño], I had to research a great deal, almost as much as a judge might do, to gain my editors' agreement to publish. (Journalist 3, France)

Many interviewees encountered this problem: their editors did not tell them directly to avoid certain topics, but demanded abnormally rigorous research before publishing material on sensitive subjects about favored corporate and governmental actors.

Senior reporters tend to work on 'hard' news. In the recent past, many have been fired due to budgetary problems and been replaced by novices experienced only in areas that stimulate few editorial conflicts, such as the international and entertainment sections. One journalist acknowledged the following:

> I used to work in a very important newspaper in the capital. . . . There was self-censorship over real estate and land ownership, infrastructure, cost of living, and many topics in the economy/business section that could produce a conflict of interest for the proprietor. Moreover, sometimes copy was subject to approval by the owner's private office. . . . Proprietors, people close to them, and advertisers were among the people named in the Panama Papers. Journalists were allowed to speak about the case in generalities but not to publish the list of those involved. We were troubled by these editorial constraints. None of the most important Colombian media reported freely on the Papers. (Journalist 3, Bogotá)

Reporters covering everyday topics or writing opinion columns experience significant editorial constraints. One journalist said her op-ed chief advised that "the best thing is that whenever you write, you ask me what you write and what you cannot" (Journalist 14, Cartagena). One interviewee commented,

> There is self-censorship when the newspaper or channel is not in solidarity with the journalist. Some issues must be handled with care, and on other occasions, journalists need to warn their bosses in advance that a particular person is implicated. (Journalist 2, Barranquilla)

Another reporter talked about how the media encourage self-censorship when editors emphasize certain topics while discarding others:

> Headlines and photographs of sports or entertainment news distract public attention from corruption, violence, and social injustice. (Journalist 10, Bogotá)

The journalists we interviewed felt that more effort should be made to investigate malfeasance in the private sector, where corporate corruption and bad practice equal or exceed that of the public sector and deepen the country's inequality:

> Eighty percent of what is investigated is official corruption: bribery, embezzlement, favoritism . . . only ten percent of research covers business. But there is a great deal of irregular management in banking, monopolies, and conglomerates. There is a huge research gap in business and private enterprise corruption in Colombia. This corruption is much more serious and has a greater impact than

> crooked public administration, through tax evasion and the concentration of power and wealth. (Journalist 8, United States)
>
> Powerful white-collar businessmen and some representatives of the private sector have a lot to hide; journalists can't say much about them. (Journalist 9, Bogotá)

One interviewee said:

> Facing the economic power of soft-drink producers and pharmaceutical companies that threaten and bribe, the common reaction of journalists is self-censorship. Reporters opt to ignore information, minimize it, or reiterate elaborate, fake explanations the companies hand out. (Journalist 10, Bogotá)

Powerful political leaders are also beneficiaries of journalistic self-censorship, often because of how official advertising is distributed:

> The way in which the previous government was covered was biased. Self-censorship was present in many decisions; people decided not to tell the whole story. (Journalist 12, Bogotá)
>
> Journalists have to make a living. The wages are so small—you cannot "kick the lunch box." When you write about certain topics, doors close. Journalists are not to be blamed for that. (Journalist 14, Cartagena)

Reporters want to investigate issues that were barely spoken of during the conflict, and of which little is said today, such as "forced displacement, illegal mining, and the murder of young people and social leaders" (Journalist 9, Bogotá). They become frustrated when, having dared to undertake detailed research into these misdeeds, and sent the evidence to the authorities, the outcome is nugatory. Two interviewees said,

> It's very exhausting to work hard on a news piece, get into a topic, and investigate it thoroughly, even send copy to the Government Accountability Offices or Oversight Committees, and find that those institutions do nothing. All officials in small cities have friendly ties or interests to defend, so investigations don't prosper. (Journalist 13, Bogotá)
>
> Journalists frequently denounce something courageously, but the authorities do nothing. This results in self-censorship. You ask: is it worth the effort? Is it worth the risk? (Journalist 2, Barranquilla)

Even graver frustrations arise when reporters are threatened with judicial processes because powerful people are discomforted by their investigations, and journalists frequently face civil lawsuits related to their coverage of corruption. In 2018, a reporter from Sabanalarga, a small town in the north, went to prison and was fined because he allegedly defamed an official. As one interviewee put it, "In outlying regions, some public servants who do not want to accept responsibility for their actions use their power to attack us. One has to be very careful when reporting, especially when telling ugly truths" (Journalist 15).

A reporter from a local outlet in Cartagena indicated that powerful social actors sometimes become upset when they are mentioned in the news and

> communicate with journalists in order to threaten them. Intimidation in reprisal against alleged injuries can include warning that you will be denounced for slander, judicial processes will be initiated, or formal claims sent to the newspaper. These tactics generate self-censorship. (Journalist 14, Cartagena)

Lawsuits are demanding and expensive. As a consequence, many reporters end up modifying or self-censoring coverage of certain topics:

> Judicial mechanisms are becoming means of intimidating the press. Powerful social actors use many legal tools to silence journalists, who receive minimum-wage salaries and are left alone to face the legal consequences of their work. In many regions, the judicial branch is corrupt. (Journalist 9, Bogotá)

> People no longer send threatening pamphlets to the newspapers; rather, they dispatch voluminous documents in legal language that question our stories. (Journalist 6, México)

This persecution comes not only from aggrieved individuals, but corrupt judges and other officials:

> Journalists often receive petitions to explain who provided the information they published; sometimes judges force them to do so. (Journalist 2, Barranquilla)

> In several emails, one prosecuting attorney told me he was going to denounce me; he even said he belongs to groups that operate outside the law. (Journalist 14, Cartagena)

Several journalists also mentioned that the virtual sphere has contributed to new kinds of harassment and attack: "Political groups behave like sects; there is a lot of passion online and social networks are full of hatred" (Journalist 2, Barranquilla).

Many reporters conclude that the legal system needs reform, because the public institutions that should shield them are sometimes the very ones that impede their work. The government must guarantee freedom of public information by improving their personal security, acting diligently when threats are reported, and denying criminals' impunity: "The only thing that really works is to support journalists institutionally. The law must be improved to make it much more protective of press freedom" (Journalist 7, United States).

Journalists see themselves at a crossroads. On the one hand, they feel a responsibility to fulfill their responsibilities to audiences/readers and democracy; on the other, they are conflicted over the difficulties and dangers that ensue. Many expressed doubts about continuing in the job. One said,

> I have a conflict with myself: I asked myself many times if I write my opinion pieces because I am very brave or very stupid. My work as an op-ed columnist oscillates: I veer between falling in love with my job and being disappointed by it. (Journalist 14, Cartagena)

In sum, our interviewees explained that the main obstacles they confront are widespread violence, a compromising dependency on official sources and corporate and state advertising, judicial and online harassment, and editorial constraints. Many have already experienced the consequences of lack of protection. They feel at risk and self-censor when covering corruption in the private and business sectors, forced displacement, illegal mining, the murder of activists, drug trafficking, and certain political topics. As a consequence, many have fled, leaving their families behind; obtained private security; or departed the profession.

Despite this bleak picture, Colombian journalism has found new ways to serve the citizenry. First, some reporters have asked newspaper editors for support to work independently when analyzing sensitive issues. One interviewee described "groups of investigative journalists who decide to share information with their colleagues through associations in Argentina, Brazil, Colombia, and Mexico" (Journalist 8, United States). Several reporters undertake projects with international sponsors in order to reveal stories that cannot easily be told in the traditional media, such as the Postobón revelations. Sometimes high-profile editors accompany journalists in their research (Journalist 5, Bogotá).

Journalists who work in the regions of Colombia, and believe there are stories they cannot publish without becoming vulnerable, may hand over their research to colleagues in the national media. They would prefer to lose the glory of a scoop than remain silent or risk their lives: "Many times, the information we produce comes out from the region's main city, and nobody knows its origin" (Journalist 13, Bogotá). On other occasions, they publish anonymously and in various media at the same time. As one put it, "The story should be in the hands of everyone" (Journalist 12, Bogotá).

Such strategies ally with the findings of Celeste González de Bustamante and Jeannine E. Relly (2016), who describe a tendency for Mexican journalists to share their research beyond the newsroom. That democratization of information can help fight self-censorship: when a story is in everyone's hands, it is harder for criminals to attack particular reporters in order to conceal the truth.[14]

These are valuable ripostes to self-censorship. Thanks to such teamwork, reporters from dangerous areas have found some relief from the pressures of everyday working life. One journalist recommended that his colleagues "try hard to work together, not be lone wolves" (Journalist 16, Manizales). "Networks must be strengthened: get together to get protected" (Journalist 9, Bogotá). Others said, "Whatever happens, we talk about it among our colleagues. That is how we protect ourselves; we shield ourselves" (Journalist 13, Bogotá).

In addition, the newer media can help disseminate research:

> Social networks have prevented the traditional media from neglecting some topics.... The media are power watchdogs, and social networks in turn provide media oversight. (Journalist 1, Bogotá)
>
> We rely on social networks to circulate information. There's a limit to this strategy, as not all municipalities have the Internet; but digital platforms like Twitter and WhatsApp have helped us communicate. (Journalist 11, Quibdó)[15]
>
> Social networks protect journalists.... [When] reporters position themselves in networks... they have many followers, their very own brand. (Journalist 3, France)

Innovative digital outlets such as Minuto30 (Minute30) and Las2ORILLAS (2Sides) have also been founded by outstanding journalists tired of low salaries and limitations placed on their work (Montaña 2014).[16]

Finally, journalists must organize to control their labor process. One reporter stated the following:

> Journalists do not have a strong union in Colombia, and therefore we do not support each other adequately in difficult times. Feeling alone isolates us and we stay quiet. (Journalist 9, Bogotá)

Reporters need to attach themselves to the ethical principles of their work, instead of serving particular interests:

> Colombian journalism sometimes works as a sniper's weapon. Some radio news programs denounce and harass a firm until it buys advertising. (Journalist 8, United States)

Our informants say the conflict is not truly over yet, especially for those in the regions who are harassed by illegal groups. Hence the appeal of peace journalism

(Prager and Hameleers 2018) despite criticisms of its supposed lack of objectivity and recognition of the realities of newsgathering and newsrooms—plus its cooptation by the previous administration to promote putative successes (Barajas 2016).

Reporters remain subject to fatal attacks by *guerrilla* and gangster alike, compromising their capacity to speak truth to power and their very physical safety. One example of fighting back is Proyecto Pitalito sin Censura (the Pitalito Project Against Censorship), which sought to bring to justice the assassin of community-radio reporter Flor Alba Núñez, part of a campaign to end journalists' killers acting with virtual impunity ("¡Pitalito sin censura" 2015). Resourcefulness in the face of such horrors is a reminder of the need for international solidarity and scrutiny to place state, corporate, militia, and narco criminals under notice. Keeping journalists secure—and relatively autonomous from proprietors—is equally crucial; in fact a sine qua non of a functioning democracy.

THE *NARCONOVELA*

We turn now to a very different account of Colombian mafiosi culture: the popular TV genre of the *narconovela*. It relates to the introduction's statistics on gendered violence, chapter 1's engagement with gangsters' infiltration of football, and the previous chapter's investigation of tourism campaigns stereotyping women. *Narconovelas* also touch on the appeal of glamorized violence to the nation's popular classes.

We illustrate here that:

- Novelas are largely written, directed, and produced by men
- They perpetuate negative representations of women
- Minority women are underrepresented
- These reactionary norms relate to the persistence of violence

We begin with contextual information about the social conditions under which *narconovelas* have emerged and thrived, including *narcocultura*'s impact on gender stereotypes and the objectification of women within society. Then we examine the history of *telenovelas* and address the genre in detail through content analysis.

The narcos and their apparatchiks seemingly embody upward mobility in a society where, as we have seen, the prospect of uplift via education and industriousness is minimal and life chances are dominated by birth and race; hence popular reason embracing the narcos' spectacular bling (Rincón 2015) as per *hecha la ley, hecha la trampa*. As per chapter 1, as a consequence of state interdiction and U.S. intervention, the principal site of spectacular, overt mafia violence has shifted west, to México. Today's Colombian narcos launder their money (as per football, inter alia) rather than parade it. Their infiltration of society has become less manifest, more embedded, and less terrifying. As this particular horror has migrated and transmogrified, its most potent and evident form—a televised, fictional representation of mafioso high life—has emerged: the *narconovela*.

Of all the stories that could be told about decades of conflict, the treatment of women, rural inequality, and racial discrimination, only the pro-capitalist violence of the narcos has been thoroughly dramatized on TV screens, glamorized in ways that play up both a rejection of traditional political-economic institutions and a reassertion of traditional identities, specifically machismo (with which readers may be familiar) and *Marianismo*, which is less-discussed outside the region.

Generations of Colombians have been raised with machismo and *Marianismo* as ways of life. These dual mythologies of masculinity and femininity restrict women's economic opportunities and daily conduct ("Wonder Women" 2015). Both ideologies are associated with Latin America, though some critics have traced their origins back to Latin Europe (Stevens 1973). They clearly derive from the sexual violence and forced marriages that were part of colonial experience (Strasser and Tinsman 2010) and the Roman Catholic family ideal of an unseen, judgmental father (God) and an ever-present, caring mother (Mary). Apart from the absent father, men are represented as eternal sons who need to be interpreted, spoilt, and cared for by their mothers. Because each man remains forever basically a child, his actions are beyond his own willpower to control. He cannot be held accountable or punished for aberrant conduct; instead, he must be understood and forgiven (Wills 2011).

Within this governing rhetoric, differences of course abound, notably a hypersexualized Colombian coastal narrative of the unruly, rapacious black man versus the businesslike, controlled white one (Viveros 2013). Both concepts permeate all levels of society, granting men a form of entitlement and the "right" to symbolic and physical violence that is a classic instantiation of hegemonic masculinity but goes beyond the norms of the Global North (Connell 2003; Pineda Duque 2003).

Marianismo sets up the Virgin Mary as the ideal for women, who are expected to uphold two key principles that she putatively embodied: chastity prior to motherhood, and motherhood itself. These precepts are designed not only as everyday guides but as the sole purposes of a woman's life, for which she is willing to sacrifice everything and anything, including her sense of self. The Concurso contestants we encountered in the previous chapter are expected to stand for conventional Colombian womanhood, as per *Marianismo*, albeit with a sexualized aspect (Nasser De La Torre 2013; Stanfield 2013).

Bolívar famously declared that his countrymen were blinded by liberty and pulchritude alike, with women offering a surfeit of pleasure and nature through their sexuality that had to be resisted, even as it was fetishized:

> Colombians! You have suffered greatly, sacrificed greatly and in vain, because you strayed from the healing path. You became infatuated with freedom, dazzled by her powerful allure; but because freedom is as dangerous as beauty in women, whom all seek to seduce out of love, or vanity, you failed to preserve her in her natural innocence and purity, just as she descended from heaven (2003: 102)

That contradiction helps inform *narcocultura* in general and the *narconovela* in particular.

THE *NOVELA*

Telenovelas derive most immediately from soap operas, but their full genealogy originates with the melodrama, a genre that was critically damned from its beginnings in eighteenth-century Europe because of a high-tensile emotionalism that contrasted with naturalism then realism. But the melodrama can also be read as a site for trying out new identities at a time of intense social disruption, when religious and monarchical power was being challenged by urbanizing capitalism and secular democracy (Merritt 1983).

The short form of melodrama, the soap opera, began on U.S. radio in the 1930s. It quickly migrated to television after the war and underwent local customization elsewhere as U.S. companies looked to sell the same cleaning products to women abroad as domestically (Straubhaar 2007: 9). The genre's revolutionary referent recurred in the 1940s and 1950s with the reestablishment of gender normativity after the war; Hollywood's melodramas and film noirs featured hysterical men, equally unsettled by the battlefield and their return from it (Cunningham 1981).

Latin America's *telenovela* has been the most notable localization, update, and export of the soap opera. It quickly became a regional then international genre of both symbolic consequence and monetary value (López 1995). The Observatorio Iberoamericano de Ficción Televisiva (Iberoamerican Television Fiction Observatory) reports that *novelas* attract the most sizeable financial investments of all genres in the region and usually draw the highest ratings (2014). México's *Las Tontas no Van al Cielo* (2008) (*Stupid Girls Don't Go to Heaven*) and Colombia's *Sin Tetas no Hay Paraíso* (2006) (*There's No Paradise without Breasts*) have been among the most popular programs on the U.S. Spanish-language network Univision (Morgan 2013). *Sin Tetas* set the trend: a young woman becomes a sex worker for leading mafiosi in order to pay for the cosmetic surgery she desires. Adapted from a novel, it was sold abroad both in its original version and as a format, and became a celebrated feature film (underwritten by state subvention) (Muñoz Rodríguez 2016).

Novelas always feature melodramatic romantic and social relationships (Mazziotti 1996). They can offer testing grounds for new subjectivities in an era of apparent choice but also widening inequality, articulating women's constraints and freedoms, albeit in a sometimes explicitly antifeminist, and rarely overtly feminist, form (Acosta-Alzuru 2003; Abu-Lughod 2005). In many parts of the world, the genre has addressed complex social issues, such as extramarital sexual pleasure, same-sex relationships, public health, and progressive gender politics. It has even been likened to a "nineteenth-century weekly sermon to a packed congregation," minus some of the moralism (Graham 2000: 7).

Jesús Martín-Barbero posits that *novelas* portray a "drama of recognition . . . fighting for an identity that would be recognized in the society" (1993: 58). These are sites of dreams made tangible, of worlds where something not real can be made so, or something uncomfortably close refracted as fiction (Orozco 2014: 4). One can cry along with the heroine of a *telenovela* without feeling silly or guilty, or identify with a *capo* in a *narconovela* without fearing arrest and incarceration. *Novelas* embody and stimulate an abundance of desires and identifications at the intersection of reality and the screen.

What do audiences make of *telenovelas*? They appear to give spectators the opportunity to invent histories, imagine selves, seek liberation, engage in personal reflection and reinterpretation, encourage innovative personal encounters, and seek new forms of communication. The symbiosis between *novelas* and their viewers endures well beyond the moment of watching on a screen; it gains expression in private and public life, with families, neighbors, and coworkers (Martín-Barbero and Muñoz 1992).

The early Peruvian *novela Simplemente María* (*Simply María*) (1969) encouraged thousands of women to pursue educational goals, as the main character had done, in order to change their economic and social lives (Singhal et al. 1994). Several 1970s Mexican successes were stories with a message: "telenovelas de refuerzo social" (social reinforcement) (Garnica 2011). The issues covered included, inter alia, literacy and birth control. Of the ten million adult Mexicans who were analphabetic at the time, a million registered to take literacy classes after watching *Ven Conmigo* (*Come with Me*) (1975). And following *Acompáñame* (*Accompany Me*) (1977), 562,464 people started using contraceptives, almost one-third more than before it was screened (Garnica 2011). Colombia's *Café, con Aroma de Mujer* (*Coffee with the Scent of a Woman*) (1994–1995) portrayed female characters as assertive and ambitious (the female lead had won the Concurso a decade earlier; her character suffered sexual trafficking during the series). It did not conform to the *Marianismo* stereotype of the pure and virginal damsel, which had dominated Latin American melodrama. Instead, *Café, con Aroma* featured scheming businesswomen, supposedly inspiring viewers to further their careers and change their lives—and was sold to eighty countries.[17] Not all social reinforcement is progressive: a week prior to the 2006 Mexican presidential elections, the most popular *novela* saw one character say, "Who are you going to vote for? I will vote for Felipe Calderón" (a conservative candidate, who won) (quoted in Padilla et al. 2011). The 2012 elections saw US$205 million spent on product placement of policies in favor of political parties in *novelas*—more than the budget for campaign advertising (Fundar Centro de Análisis e Investigación 2015).

Viewers are more likely to chat about soaps and draw on them to think about everyday life than is the case with other genres, whether the subject matter is diurnal marital frustration versus diurnal televisual romance, glamour versus suburbia, or a raft of social issues (Ang 1982; Brown 1990). The *novela* is not only a site where social tensions are articulated and made manifest, but also a "communicative bridge that links viewers across national, expanded regional, and global realms of transmission and reception, working to shape new cultural and intercultural communities" (Benamou 2009: 152).

Ethnographic research has shown that Mexican women living in the United States enjoy watching imported Mexican *telenovelas* because they actualize affective and symbolic ties, but many men there dislike the genre's sensationalized representation of their homeland. For other Latin American audiences, what matters is not geopolitics but a mixture of exoticism and repetition, a blend of new scenery with familiar sexual relationships. There are further differences between urban and rural spectators. Indigent young female viewers' social imaginaries in particular may be expanded by the ideas of pleasure and autonomy that abound in the genre, as they compare their lives with *novela* representations (Concept Media, n.d.; La Pastina 2004; Uribe 2009; Beljuli Brown 2011; Mayora Ronsini 2014; Sifuentes 2014).

When Colombia's hugely popular *Yo soy Betty, la Fea* (1999–2001)—which was sold as a format and became the global phenomenon *Ugly Betty*—was first broadcast, it challenged beauty as a sufficient attribute for success in life, contributing to a national then international debate on the social, professional, and personal lives of women (Miller 2010; MacCabe and Akass 2013). But how far can this progressiveness go? Yeidy Rivero maintains that many female characters in the show (apart from Betty herself) appeared "unconcerned about other people's opinions of their bodies." But the ability to become beautiful, and thus ensure upward mobility, depended on conforming to class-based gender norms and relations: "despite the presence of some forms of counter-hegemonic discourses, Betty's narrative normalized Latin American gender constructions and the power inequalities between women and men" (2003: 72–74).

Julee Anne Tate (2007) suggests that the restrictive social norms and values that define womanhood in Latin American societies are embodied in *telenovelas'* binary opposition of "good" versus "bad" women. As per *Marianismo,* the foundational principle is that women belong in the domestic sphere. Their lives revolve around the care of the household and the perpetual sacrifice of personal aspirations in order to prioritize their husbands' and children's needs. Leading ladies are usually mothers willing to give anything up for their children, including their own wishes and well-being. And women's sexuality is restricted to finding a steady male partner and meeting his needs. They can never be subjects of desire—only its objects. Those women who embrace sexual drives, and pursue their satisfaction, are branded with epithets.

This conservatism also relates to the political economy of the media. Since the privatization of television two decades ago, commercial TV in Colombia has moved closer and closer to the desired minima and maxima of factory life—small amounts of innovation and large amounts of replication. When ratings remain stable, the networks are content. *Narconovelas* disturb that pattern with their spectacular success and subsequent pressure to maintain quality and quantity at high, and therefore expensive, levels. The success of these series has propelled a change to the genre: *telenovelas* have become much shorter, action-driven, and internationally themed. The narco theme continues, so well does it blend sex, violence, and upward mobility (de Pablos 2019).

Colombian productions have succeeded in international markets because they blend the traditional emotional intensity of melodrama with the violence and high production values of action adventure, providing broadcast television with an answer to its newer audiovisual competitors and attracting key audiences for advertising (Piñon 2019). In addition to huge overseas sales, *narconovelas* are among the most-pirated TV programs on YouTube, which has led to titanic legal battles (Goodwin 2009; James 2009; Wentz 2009).

Renowned Colombian *Narconovelas* from 2001–2014 include the following:

- *Pandillas, Guerra y Paz* (*Gangs, War, and Peace*) (2001–2004 and 2007–2008)
- *Pasión de Gavilanes* (*The Passion of Hawks*) (2003)
- *La Viuda de la Mafia* (*The Mafia Widow*) (2004)
- *Sin Tetas no hay Paraíso* (*There's No Paradise without Breasts*) (2006)
- *Soñar no Cuesta Nada* (*Dreaming is Free*) (2007)
- *Los Protegidos* (2008) (*The Protected*)
- *El Cártel* (2008) (*The Cartel*) and *El Cártel 2* (2010)
- *El Capo 1, 2,* and *3* (2009, 2012, and 2014)
- *Las Muñecas de la Mafia* (*Mafia Dolls*) (2009)
- *Escobar: El Patrón del Mal* (*Escobar the Drug Lord*) (2009–2012)
- *Rosario Tijeras* (*Rosario Scissors*) (2010)
- *La Bruja* (*The Witch*) (2011)
- *La Mariposa* (*The Butterfly*) (2012)
- *La Ruta Blanca* (*The White Route*) (2012)
- *La Prepago* (*The Escort*) (2012)
- *Los 3 Caínes* (*The Three Cains*) (2013)
- *El Mexicano* (*The Mexican*) (2013)
- *La Viuda Negra* (*The Black Widow*) (2014)

Colombia's *narconovelas* entered the international mainstream with *Escobar: El Patrón del Mal*. It turned the genre into a bountiful biopic about the most infamous

FIGURE 9. Advertisement promotion for Netflix series *Narcos* (2015–). (Source: Toby Miller.)

narco of all, drew critiques for its fetishization of luxury, drugs, and violence—and was sold to thirty countries (Barreras et al. 2016; Caselli 2016; Amaya Trujillo and Charlois Allende 2018). The related Netflix series *Narcos* (2015–) was as guilty of historical inaccuracy as it was insistent on having diligently recorded reality—and successful in satisfying lazy, distant eyes, as per those looking on listlessly from a British commuter train. The company says over sixty million people have devoured this ode to rivers of blood (figure 9) (Britto 2016; Marcos 2018). Some celebrate such successes as signs of contra-flow in the television market, especially given exports to the United States and México (Rincón 2018).

Narconovelas have generated political controversy among audiences and critics, as well as garnering devoted followers, including academic acolytes (Morgan 2013. The critique is due to their cocktail of violence, in which women are often abused and humiliated, and sexual desire, illicit money, unwarranted assault, and cavalier killing glamorized. The state is either absent or corrupt.

Critics deem the genre nothing to be proud of unless one admires the logic of capital, as it brings together the extraordinary violence of primary accumulation with the acquisitive brutality of secondary accumulation (Martín-Barbero 2004; Rincón 2018). In 2014, the Venezuelan and Panamanian establishments (Chavistas [followers of Hugo Rafael Chávez Frías] in Caracas and conservatives in Panama City) sought to ban *narconovelas* for glorifying cruelty and drugs; Left and Right were equally appalled (Rincón 2015; Caselli 2016).

For those millions affected in real life by the violence these programs depict, it is not always easy to embrace the genre and its use of *Marianismo*. Yet series such as *Sin Tetas* can be said to criticize the violent misogyny they portray even as they offer audiences the risky pleasures of narco luxury and taboo-breaking (Cabañas 2012), while fiction in general has arguably documented Colombian violence more effectively than news and current affairs (Rincón 2019). The genre has the potential to question inequality and display, much as Warner Bros. gangster films might be said to have done for the United States in the 1930s. One moment responds to the mass unemployment of the Depression and the prohibition of alcohol with the heroization of gangsters; the other reacts to the destabilization of globalization and the prohibition of cocaine with the heroization of gangsters (Sklar 1992; Giraldo 2015).

THE RESEARCH

There has been minimal content analysis of gender and Colombian TV fiction; the sparse record shows that women are generally represented in commercials as performing either sexual or domestic roles, and as dependants (Velandia-Morales and Rincón 2014). We aim to add to that knowledge, studying 532 programs over 585 hours, broadcast between 16 and 30 October 2009 during prime time (1900 to 2230) on Colombia's national networks (Caracol TV, RCN TV, Canal A, and Canal Uno) and regional open-access channels (Telecaribe, Telepacífico, TeleOccidente, and TeleAntioquia). The ratings were dominated by national commercial stations.

Our numbers reflect all prime-time genres. *Narconovelas* took up 26.8 percent of time on national stations and 4.9 percent on regional ones, for an average of 14.3 percent. As mentioned earlier, we analyzed their gendered perspectives off and on screen, starting with the relative presence of men and women as scriptwriters and directors in Colombian television, then assessing on-screen indices:

- The distribution of roles between sexes
- Racial and ethnic difference among characters
- The visibility of men and women in positions of authority
- Methods used to gain power
- The prevalence and nature of violence[18]

The data reveal that men directed four out of every five *novelas* at regional and national levels and wrote three-quarters of the scripts (see figure 10).[19] Their vision dominated content as well as production: there were more male than female characters per program across all genres (see figure 11). This finding held true for protagonists, antagonists, and secondary characters, on both national and regional channels. Such figures instantiate a well-established *narconovela*

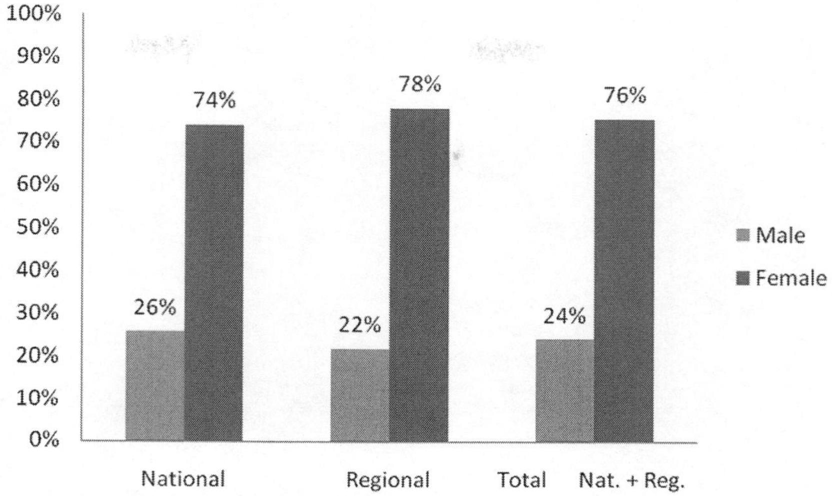

FIGURE 10. Scriptwriters by gender.

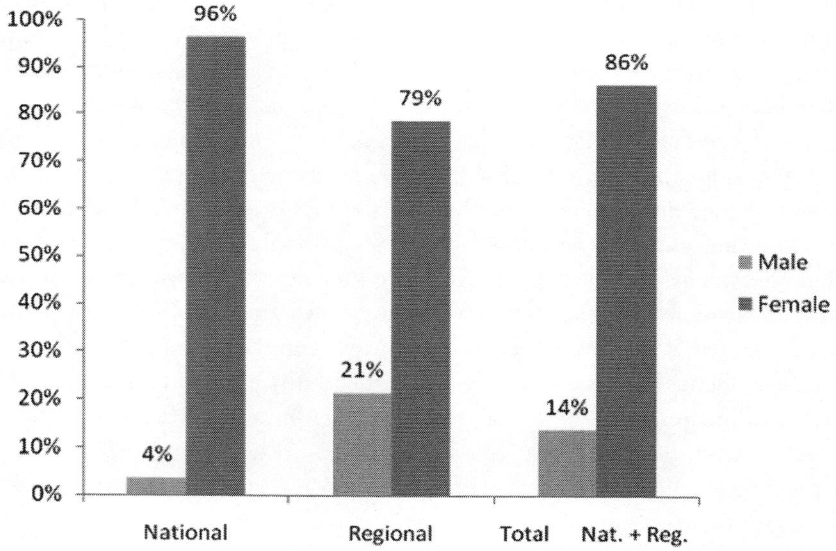

FIGURE 11. Directors by gender.

formula: immensely wealthy *capos*, adolescent assassins, beautiful young sex workers, ambitious police officers, corrupt politicians, and bloody *paramilitares* (the latter sometimes seen as heroic by contrast with mafiosi and corrupt government agents) (Laroussi 2014–2015; Casey 2018). This male numerical domination even occurs in stories told from women's perspectives, such as *Las Muñecas de la Mafia*, where gendered violence dominates the plot (see table 1).

TABLE 1. Characters by gender and type

	Characters	Averages per program National	Regional
Men	Protagonists	2	3
	Secondary	8	4
	Antagonists	2	2
	Total	12	9
Women	Protagonists	1	2
	Secondary	6	3
	Antagonists	1	1
	Total	8	6

Women are not only unequally unrepresented on- and off-screen; when they *do* appear, they are represented as weaker than men. In our sample, 12 percent of male characters and 7 percent of female ones were closely connected to social power or exercised it themselves. This difference is more evident when looking at main characters only: male 26 percent, female 18 percent. We found a strong tendency to portray women as victims or in need of men's assistance. The difference between male and female characters' political influence was huge (nearly 50 points). We also noticed a strong association of women's success with men's support, influential family connections, or links to powerful third parties, and to a lesser degree with qualifications or productivity. This is in keeping with a latter-day trend in Colombian *novelas*: women are increasingly represented beyond the domestic sphere of daily chores and looking after all living things, but in a world of clientelism, where they must rely on the favored eye of influential men and their own mastery of corruption (Ramírez Murcia 2016).

Other cultural stereotypes were also evident. There was little space in *narconovelas* for non-traditional relationships. Heteronormative family structures predominated in over half the programs analyzed, and there was minimal minority representation. For female characters, the ethnic averages on national channels were mestiza 66.83 percent, white 27.8 percent, black 2.2 percent, and indigenous 3.13 percent; on regional channels, mestizas accounted for 56.93 percent, whites 36.77 percent, blacks 3.2 percent, and indigenous 3.03 percent. Among male and female characters, for every forty people, one was black. The same ratio applied to indigenous female characters and one man in every fifty was indigenous. In sum, one in twenty main characters were from ethnic minorities, generally playing the roles of maids, servants, or slaves. There was no image of a professional minority woman or of one occupying an important narrative position (see figure 12).

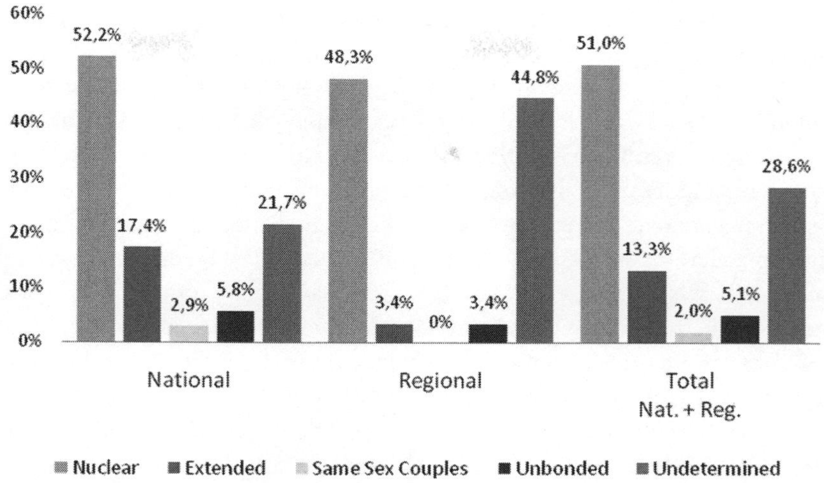

FIGURE 12. Type of family.

Verbal aggression toward women was present in 15 percent of the content analyzed, and physical aggression in 13 percent. In one of *Las Muñecas de la Mafia*'s most memorable moments, a mafioso tattoos his girlfriend's bottom with his name, resembling the way in which cattle are branded. In a scene from *El Capo 1* (2009), a drug lord yells at his wife, telling her he has had sex with more than three hundred women, just because he can. And throughout, the desirable female body is surgically sculpted, light-skinned, voluptuous, thin, and sexually available (Laroussi 2014–2015).

INTERPRETATION

García Márquez viewed the success of narco genres in both literature and television as indicative of an ongoing popular fascination with the abject, the cruel, and the spectacular, embodied in a male rule-breaking that no amount of positive stereotypes could wish away. He provides a hinge connecting political-economic and content analysis to the popularity of this destructive genre: it takes the seemingly inevitable, inexorable violence that characterizes national history and fixes the population between desire and futility, passion and resignation, celebration and denial (Vásquez 2013).

The *novela* has been used for half a century to test out new relations of authority, not least the grotesqueries of the narco era (Ramírez Murcia 2016). It is significant that many men publicly defend the narco variety as embodying popular values: support for the church, family, loyalty, and friendship. They argue that narco excess and violence are products of a society that excludes them and people like them—many of the people watching—from power, comfort, and pleasure (Rincón 2015).

The fact that *narconovelas'* hypermasculine violence relates so clearly to Colombia's social world is itself a sign that a nation consumed by a virtual civil war for decades still needs critical catharsis to transcend its history. The genre offers a cosmically ambivalent transformation of this limiting story—a site where women may pursue power, autonomy, riches, and pleasure through sex and clientelism, but in ways that draw a textual and social condemnation that harks back to the still-present past via *Marianismo* and machismo's contradictory placements within tradition and modernity, continuity and transcendence, family and singularity (Ramírez Murcia 2016). The popularity, past and present, of *narconovelas,* is neither an index of, nor a stimulus to, a progressive national popular. As Gabo said, they dramatize contests between the values and anti-values that persist in Colombian life more generally (Villasmil Faría 2015).

Colombian women's struggle for equality has had a long and hard road to hoe. It is of the utmost importance that the media become aware of the constructive role they could play in destabilizing machismo and *Marianismo* and campaigning to stop gendered violence. This is especially crucial in the putatively "cool" genre of the *narconovela,* so lovingly lapped up at home and abroad, and so laden with misogyny at its very core.

Popular knowledge of Pablo Escobar and his kind is stronger and deeper than familiarity with human rights, feminism, and democracy (Rincón 2015). The way forward, borrowing from the many opponents of machismo and *Marianismo,* should be the construction of new gender relations (Hurtado and Sinha 2016). A corporate television system built on minimal difference and maximal repetition cannot play a part in changing that, unless it offers a multiplicity of perspectives on narco violence and commits to a feminist gaze among a variety of ways of seeing that place passion, self-determination, security, and care at their center. Similar changes are needed to protect the lives but also the work of journalists, whose experiences and evocations of *narcocultura* are of such value in alerting the citizenry to the realities of the informal sector. That value is circumscribed by both the very violence they seek to describe and the labor process that constitutes their work.

4 • GREEN PASSION AFLOAT

The Magdalena River

WITH MARTA MILENA BARRIOS

In addition to cocaine, the conflict, football, and sex, Colombia is also renowned as one of the world's most extraordinary natural environments. From animals to flowers, insects to fruits, gorges to mountains, and rivers to oceans, a cornucopia spreads across its continental and tropical climates. We saw the appeal this has to tourism marketers in chapter 2.

But the nation's natural environment has been subjected to ruinous exploitation and repeated human-rights violations. The conquistadores relished telling heroic tales detailing their destruction of indigenous life. That devastation was also ecological—their sixteenth-century arrival brought new diseases and land use, disrupting an environment that had long sustained human and other life (Colmenares 1996).

Since that time, Colombia has been in thrall to the extractive industries, industrial farming, and the use of biopower to control populations and jeopardize the environment, all in the name of government, development, tourism—and sometimes even sustainability (Asher and Ojeda 2009; Anguelovski and Alier 2014; Rochlin 2015). Most recent armed violence has occurred in "biodiversity hotspots" rather than cities, in keeping with the tendency for post-conflict periods across the history of capitalism to see rapid and brutal economic development. With corporations itching to exploit minerals and farmland in jungle areas formerly occupied by the FARC, deforestation shot up by almost half in 2016, when the peace accord was signed (Salazar et al. 2018). Environmental defenders are assassinated in the interests of legal and illegal miners at rates beyond, for example, the deaths of British and Australian soldiers serving in wars over the same period (Butt et al. 2019). Global Witness estimates that Colombia has the second-highest number of such murders, behind the Philippines (2019: 8).

The country's extraordinary ecosystem is also under massive population pressure, with a quadrupling of residents to almost fifty million over the last three decades (Salazar et al. 2018). The rate is faster than the regional average, with precious mangrove swamps progressively lost (Bolívar-Anillo et al. 2019). Most of Colombia's people live in the elevated Andes. With a changing climate, water shortages and unstable land plague their lives. On the coasts, higher sea levels and increased flooding are becoming a norm (Escobar 1998; Oslender 2004; Vergara et al. 2016).[1]

In reaction to developmental exploitation of the kind that produced this coming catastrophe, the nation has a significant and growing informal recycling sector and environmental movement. The particular environmental challenges faced by *campesino*, indigenous, and Afro-Colombians have seen social movements organize around collective versus individual and corporate rights over everything from biotechnology to river banks (Nemogá 2014; Velasco 2016). Protesting traditional landowners experienced firsthand the devastation thirty years earlier when a dam was built to redirect the Río. Now they face many more such interventions, as well as fracking. Two hundred thousand residents have been displaced by dams, and forced departures are accompanied by military and private-security occupation of public areas once used for sustainable fishing and relaxation (Caycedo and Aguas 2015). When the venerable yet still quaintly adolescent research and agitprop multinational Greenpeace set up shop there in 2009, rather than simply channelling global corporate campaigns, it sensitively focused on issues of particular pertinence to the nation, notably the *páramos* (moors) of the Sierra Nevadas and Andes, which produce three quarters of the water for Colombia's major cities, and are under dire threat from climate change (Ruiz et al. 2012).[2]

Our focus here, the Río Magdalena (Magdalena River), is 1,500 kilometers long. It passes through eleven of Colombia's thirty-two departments to its mouth in the Caribbean Sea, draining most of the Colombian Andes along the way. The Río "covers 22% of the surface of the national territory, is home to 80% of the population and produces 85% of GDP" (Escobar Ramírez and Barg 1990). Some call it "the homeland river" (Castro 2013). The entire area has long been subject to intense anthropocentric change: in the thirty years from 1970, more than 230,000 hectares of forest were destroyed annually in a restless search for precious metals, arable land, and grazing for cattle. By 2000, 80 percent of the tropical Andes's natural vegetation had been lost, most of it in the Magdalena's basin (Restrepo et al. 2015).

The Río already has the largest sediment yield of all South American rivers, and the tenth-highest worldwide. That sedimentation has negatively influenced fishing and the transport of goods for import and export (Peña et al. 2015; Restrepo et al. 2018). In addition, deforestation through agriculture and urbanization has produced dramatic erosion and pollution, endangering water supplies not only along the coast but in the central region as well. Climate change and volcanism have also transmogrified the river. Its wildlife has been particularly affected by human economic exploitation, with a unique turtle threatened, fishes suffering high concentrations of mercury due to gold mining, and coral reefs and sea-grass beds imperiled. Even the OECD notes that environmental imperatives have been overrun by state-capitalist ones, because governmental institutions supposedly dedicated to preservation and sustainability have grown weak by contrast with more developmentalist agencies (Restrepo et al. 2006; Vargas 2009; López-Castaño and Cano-Echeverri 2011; Hammond et al. 2013; Organisation for Economic Co-operation and Development 2014; Restrepo 2015). Yet the same OECD laments the fact that delays in "navigation projects" devised for the Río held back national economic growth in 2018 (Organisation for Economic Co-operation and Development 2018: 97)!

The Corporación Autónoma Regional del Río Grande de la Magdalena (Autonomous Regional Corporation of the Great River Magdalena) is responsible for managing the river in terms of energy, land use, port facilities, transportation, and sustainability. Its slogan reads: "The energy of a river that drives a country."[3] But a Chinese state multinational, Hydrochina, produced a key vision of the Magdalena's future. Embraced by the Colombian government, this model satisfies all the current clichés of privatization and power generation while in fact being promulgated by Chinese Communist Party cadres dressed as businesspeople, alongside Spanish and Italian firms ("El futuro" 2014; Ramírez and Santiago 2015). The record of PRC investment in Colombia's extractive sector is not promising when it comes to environmental responsibility (Wu 2019).

The physical terrain of the region has long been a stimulus to aesthetic and political celebration and lamentation as well as exploitation. Landscape narratives of conquest and control were important to the Spaniards and to the consolidation of Colombia as an independent nation during the nineteenth century (Acosta Peñaloza 2014). The Magdalena in particular has animated contestation, comfort, fear, beauty, horror, and cultural expression. Some conquistadores believed they had found the original Garden of Eden, watered by the Magdalena (Galeano 1997: 14). The river's eighteenth- and nineteenth-century indigenous and African rowers shouted, prayed, and stomped in order to mark out their labor and connect with one another, annoying and obsessing their white chroniclers in equal measure (Ochoa Gautier 2014: 35–42).[4]

We demonstrate in this chapter that a vibrant green passion is evident in Colombian popular culture, specifically in letters to the editor covering environmental matters, notably the river. Our analysis shows that it has provoked a wide array of emotions that flow through—and sometimes flood—daily life. As per the previous chapter, we use political economy and content analysis. Prior to doing so, it is necessary to engage the nature of our current ecological crisis and its links to anti- and pro-environmental thought.

WHAT ON EARTH IS GREEN?

The world's climate is changing in ways that imperil us, our fellow animals, other forms of life, and the Earth itself. Past and present industrial processes have exposed the planet to potentially irrevocable harm as we enter what the scientific community announced in 2016 as the Anthropocene—an epoch characterized by major geological and ecological changes brought about by human activity (Subcommission on Quaternary Stratigraphy 2016).

Climate science leaves little doubt that humans have made the Earth an inhospitable place for life to flourish. The UN's Intergovernmental Panel on Climate Change warns that we have about twelve years to make radical changes to our carbon-emitting ways, or disaster awaits (Watts 2018). The U.S. National Climate Assessment, a project of thirteen federal departments and agencies, reports that the country faces imminent risks from rising sea levels, wildfires, drought, floods, atmospheric warming, and a weakening of its ecosystems' ability to absorb carbon emissions and other greenhouse gases (U.S. Global Change Research Program 2018). Ninety-seven percent of scientists say humans are responsible for global warming and we must radically change our behavior to save the planet's biosphere, ecosystems, and inhabitants (Marlon et al. 2018). The message has gotten through in Colombia. Well over three-quarters of the population regard climate change as a critical challenge (Evans and Zechmeister 2018). What is the history to this growing awareness?

In the late 1960s and early '70s, the word *pollution* was in vogue to explain environmental hazards. Both a ubiquitous and a local sign, it seemed to be everywhere, yet isolable. The problems it described occurred when particular waterways, neighborhoods, or fields suffered negative externalities from mining, farming, and manufacturing. The issue was how to restore these places to their prior state: pristine, unspoiled, enduring. Pollution was about corporate malfeasance, governmental neglect, public ignorance, and how to remedy their malign impact. It could be cleaned up if governments compelled companies to do so—and would soon be over, once those involved understood the problem.

But when greenhouse gases, environmental racism, global warming, occupational health, and environmental imperialism appeared on the agenda, pollution reached beyond national boundaries and became ontological, threatening the very Earth that gives and sustains life, and doing so in demographically unequal ways.

A word was found to describe the values and forms of life that encompassed a planetary consciousness to counter this disaster, as per the utopias of world government that had animated transnational imaginations for decades: *green* emerged to displace the more negative and limited *pollution*, signifying both new possibilities and a greater and more global sense of urgency. Its purview expanded from waterways and work places to populations and the planet.

Today, *green* can refer to local, devolved, non-corporate empowerment, or international consciousness and institutional action. The term is invoked by both conservatives, who emphasize maintaining the world for future generations, and radicals, who stress anti-capitalist, postcolonial, feminist perspectives. *Green* may highlight the disadvantages of technology as a primary cause of environmental difficulties or hail such innovations as future saviors, via devices and processes yet to be invented that will alleviate global warming. It can favor state and international regulation, or be skeptical of public policy. It may encourage individual consumer responsibility, or question localism by contrast with collective action. It can reflect left–right axes of politics, or argue that they should be transcended, because neither statism nor individualism can fix the dangers we confront.

This massive, conflictual expansion in meaning has generated a wide array of instrumental uses. So green environments are promoted as exercise incentives (Gladwell et al. 2013), encouragements for consumers to use quick-response codes (Atkinson 2013), ways of studying whether plants communicate through music (Gagliano 2013), attempts to push criminology toward interrogating planetary harm (Lynch et al. 2013), gimmicks for recruiting desirable employees (Renwick et al. 2013), and techniques for increasing labor productivity (Woo et al. 2014).

In short, *green* has come to signify the good life—not merely our own, but that of our fellow animals and collective descendants yet to be born. It stands for a new solidarity that takes off from climate science to seek a better, more secure future, transcending the usual homilies and shibboleths of individual agency or investor returns.

There is a spirited and growing green youth movement around the world protesting political inaction over the eco-crisis, standing up to billionaires and politicians, insisting that they act on the science (Wearden and Carrington 2019). A generation born in an era of peak disaster from global warming will not tolerate the craven politics of world leaders beholden to barons of industry and finance, fossil-fuel giants, and technology moguls. Tens of thousands of western European school pupils went on strike in the winter of 2019 with the slogans #FridaysForFuture and "There's no Planet B" ("Children's Climate" 2019), attracting major Latin American coverage.[5] Hence also women deciding to #BirthStrike because they feel unable to guarantee climate security to future generations (Doherty 2019), and the efforts of Extinction Rebellion.[6] Their task is huge—UN secretary-general Antonio Guterres warns that the political will to combat climate change is "fading" (quoted in "Political Will" 2019). Public support for action to stem our eco-crisis remains a work in progress, building slowly as people come to grasp the urgency of a planetary problem. But there are signs of a new citizenry ready to act on their environmental commitments. *Nature* and the *British Medical Journal* alike drew inspiration from #FridaysForFuture (Fisher 2019; Stott et al. 2019).

Like scientists in general, climate scholars emphasize the need for patience in undertaking and understanding their work, which relies on the steady accumulation of data. Climate is history: the average of weather (Chakrabarty 2014). These researchers face a special difficulty: the willful distortion of climate science by the bourgeois Anglo media. Corporate and state polluters and their acolytes in strategic communications and pseudo-academia feast on mundane but sensible scholarly disagreements among climate experts, which are mendaciously misconstrued as evidence that climate change is an invention (Lewandowsky et al. 2015; Maxwell and Miller 2016). Public discourse is dominated by such coin-operated ideologues, while climate-change scientists struggle to be heard.[7]

How did we arrive at this state of affairs? Latour proposes that "it is as though a significant segment of the ruling classes . . . had concluded that the earth no longer had room for them and for everyone else" (2018: 15–16). But that way of thinking has a longer history than his otherwise correct analysis might suggest.

A complex heritage underpins worldviews that focus on the interests of human beings (anthropocentrism) versus the planet as a whole (eco-centrism). Hobbes argued that as part of "the war of all against all," it is right for people to domesticate or destroy nature (1998: 105–106), their brute state legitimized via the physiocratic transformation or destruction of subjects and objects. For Bacon, "commerce between the mind of man and the nature of things . . . is more precious than anything on earth" (1620). Descartes maintained that "reason or good sense . . . exists whole and complete in each of us, . . . the only thing that makes us men and distinguishes us from the lower animals" (2007: 1). Kant deemed humans uniquely important: "through rank and dignity [they were] an entirely different being from things, such as irrational animals, with which one can do as one likes" (2006: 15). No vegan or animal-rights guy he.

A century later, Hegel celebrated human mastery of nature; it is because one can put one's "will into everything" that a place or object "becomes *mine*." People were purportedly unique in their desire and capacity to conserve objects and represent them via semiosis, and such willpower was independent of simple survival. It set humanity apart from other living things. As per Kant, the capacity to transcend "spontaneity and natural constitution" supposedly distinguished us from other animals. Semiotic abilities legitimized the destructive use of power; Hegel termed this "the right of absolute proprietorship." The corollary of this right was that "unused land cannot be guaranteed." The necessary relationship between people and nature asserted itself at the core of human consciousness as a struggle to achieve freedom from risk and want (Hegel 1954: 242–243, 248–250).

These thinkers reasoned that because people are unique in their desire and capacity to conserve objects and represent them via semiosis, a strange dialectical process affords humanity a special right of destruction. Willpower is independent of simple survival and sets humanity apart from other living things. When semiotic abilities were mobilized by civilizations intent on transformation rather than stasis, they licensed colonial and imperial adventurism over indigenous rights: "sacred respect for . . . unused land cannot be guaranteed," argued Hegel. Nature's "tedious chronicle," where there is "nothing new under the sun," is rightly and righteously disrespected and disobeyed by colonialism's drive toward progress (Hegel 1988: 50, 154, 61).

These originary contradictions of development included a heartfelt desire for transformation of enslaved nations, whether for religious or liberal reasons. The cultural policies of Spain's *conquista de América*, Portugal's *missão civilizadora*, and France's *mission civilisatrice* mentioned in the introduction informed the dogma of *terra nullius* (empty space), which denied land title to native people, imagining their ideological and pragmatic lives to be harmonized with nature and hence incapable of transforming and marking it.[8] When efforts directed at rural development failed, this was because "peoples of low social efficiency" predominated (Kidd 2009: 311). The equivalent to *terra nullius* in Colombia was the vast swath of land known in the colonial period as *baldíos* (useless or empty territories), areas largely occupied by indigenous people living beyond the hacienda system. This terrain was understood as essentially eminent domain, property of the state awaiting disposal. By the 1930s, the government recognized the right of rural workers to unionize, but declared that any land not used would be resumed (Celis González 2018: 33, 35–36). Hegelian discourse suits just such applied philosophizing: economic growth as a creed. Henry Ford argued that "unused forces of nature [must be] put into action . . . to make them mankind's slaves" (1929: 71), while Vannevar Bush celebrated the drive to release humanity "from the bondage of bare existence" (1945).

That ideology of growth has served to undo nature, with unimagined consequences. Its mythology of innovation and adoption mixes the sublime—the awesome, the ineffable, the uncontrollable, the powerful—with the beautiful—the approachable, the attractive, the pliant, the soothing. In philosophical aesthetics, the sublime and the beautiful are generally regarded as opposites. But they have blended in the "technological sublime," a totemic, quasi-sacred quality that industrial societies cathectically ascribe to modern machinery, engineering, design, and marketing, as simultaneously powerful and pretty (Nye 1994, 2006). The emergence of the technological sublime has been attributed to Japanese, western European, and U.S. industrial achievements of the post–Second World War period, when the successful provision of food, power, communications, and water allied with the emergence of new consumer products to supplant nature's capacity to inspire fear and astonishment.

ALTERNATIVES

Within the traditions that birthed anthropocentrism, wiser views have always flourished, given the reality that "we have only ever managed to philosophize with the help of things: the turning stars, apples which fall, turtles and hares, rivers and gods" (Muecke 2008: 95). Intergenerational care has long been a centerpiece of African American environmental thought (Smith 2007), and indigenous cosmologies deny a bifurcation between humanity and the Earth (Escobar 2012).

Within Western philosophy, Plato referred to the power of natural disasters to undo social and technological advances, which he called "crafty devices." When these "tools were destroyed," new inventions and a pacific society, based on restraint rather than excess, could emerge (1972: 119–122). Even Bacon recognized that we must "wait upon nature instead of vainly affecting to overrule her" (1620). Burke acknowledged each generation as "temporary possessors and life-renters" of the natural and social world. People must maintain "chain and continuity" rather than act ephemerally as if they were "flies of a summer," thus ensuring "a partnership not only between those who are living, but between those who are living, those who are dead, and those who are to be born." This would sustain "the great primeval contract of eternal society" (1986: 192–195).

Hume maintained that animals, like people, "learn many things from experience," developing "knowledge of the nature of fire, water, earth, stones, heights, depths, etc." in addition to processing instructions as part of their domestication (1955: 112–113). Rather than being merely sensate, some of our fellow creatures apply logic through inference—what he called "the reason of animals" (1739). Bentham enquired of our duty of care to them: "the question is not, Can they *reason*? nor, Can they *talk*? but, Can they *suffer*?" (1970). Alexander von Humboldt was horrified by Hegel's anthropocentric method as much as his theory: "To a man like me,—spellbound, insect-fashion, to earth and the endless variety of natural phenomena which it contains,—a dry theoretical assertion of utterly false facts and views about America and the Indian world is enslaving and oppressive" (2009: 34).

Even Kant acknowledged our fellow animals' capacity for reflection (2000: 15). He wrote vivid descriptions of the natural world as simultaneously beautiful and sublime, aesthetic and awesome—a terrifying place where "the shadows of the boundless void into the abyss before me." This horrifying specter risked an apocalyptic vision that one day we may realize there is nothing left, nothing else, nothing beyond (2011: 17)—akin to William James noting that "nature is but a name for excess" (1909: 63). Such anxieties obliged Kant to recognize that the objects of natural science had a history; and hence, perhaps, a limited future. But he remained anthropocentric, convinced that "to know the human being . . . deserves to be called *knowledge of the world*, even though he constitutes only one part of the creatures on earth" (2006: 3).

Horkheimer dolefully regarded "man" [*sic*] as a "rapacious race, more brutal than any previous beasts of prey; he preserves himself at the expense of the rest of nature, since he is so poorly outfitted by nature in many respects" and must survive through violence (1996: 32).[9] Schopenhauer saw himself "as a mere temporal product of nature that has come into being and is destined for total destruction" (2015: 16); Spinoza understood that "men, like all other things, are only a part of nature" (de Spinoza 2016: 14); and Charles Babbage, the mythic founder of programmable computation, noted in 1832 the partial and ultimately limited ability of humanity to bend and control natural forces without unforeseen consequences:

> The operations of man . . . are diminutive, but energetic during the short period of their existence: whilst those of nature, acting over vast spaces, and unlimited by time, are ever pursuing their silent and resistless career.

It took Engels to recognize the fundamental truth of environmentalism: that "nature does not just exist, but *comes into being* and passes *away*" (1946: 9). He noted anthropocentrism's peculiar faith in "the *absolute immutability of nature*. In whatever way nature itself might have come into being, once present it remained as it was as long as it continued to exist . . . everything would remain as it had been since the beginning" (1946: 6). In that context, Luxemburg criticized "bankrupt politicians" who "seek refuge and repose in nature" without observing that its very existence was compromised and shortened by industrial capital (1970: 335). And Marcuse realized that

> the demands of ever more intense exploitation come into conflict with nature itself, since nature is the source and locus of the life-instincts which struggle against the instincts of aggression and destruction. And the demands of exploitation progressively reduce and exhaust resources: the more capitalist productivity increases, the more destructive it becomes. This is one sign of the internal contradictions of capitalism. . . .
>
> [Nature] is a dimension *beyond* labor, a symbol of beauty, of tranquility, of a nonrepressive order. Thanks to these values, nature was the very negation of the market society. (1972: 11)

In Engels's words, the appearance of human beings marked the evolutionary point where "nature attains consciousness of itself" (1946: 17). Despite this debt to Hegel, he realized that people therefore had the ability and responsibility to observe and speak for those without voices, and protect those without power. For while our fellow animals can transform their living conditions, they do so without an evident, deliberate, and elaborated codification of what that achieves or means. The distinction does not make us and our interests superordinate; with special abilities come special responsibilities.

William Morris's call for the art world to recognize its links to everyday life insisted on the need to re-create beautiful surroundings as a precondition for beautiful creations following the devastation of the Industrial Revolution: "Of all the things that is likely to give us back popular art in England, the cleaning of England is the first and most necessary. Those who are to make beautiful things must live in a beautiful place." Put another way, the semiosis so prized by Hegel is only sustainable in a state of nature, so humans must "abstain from willfully destroying that beauty" (Morris 1884).

Heidegger argued that technology makes "the unreasonable demand" that nature "supply energy which can be extracted and stored," bending seasonal rhythms to the demands of work, growth, and competition (1977: 288, 296, 299). For Baudrillard, "the human race is beginning to produce itself as waste-product, to carry out this work of waste disposal on itself" (1994: 78). Latour says that "while we emancipated ourselves, each day we also more tightly entangled ourselves in the fabric of nature" (2015: 221). Here again, the impact of technology is not merely a human problem, but one shared by all inhabitants of Earth. There is a duty of care to the weak on the part of the strong as denizens of shared space—and a recognition that the ultimate technological fix to counter ecologically destructive conduct may not be found.

The lesson is clear. Nature's duality—that it is simultaneously self-generating and sustaining, yet its survival is contingent on human rhetoric and despoliation—makes it vulnerable. But nature will strike back, sooner or later, in mutually assured destruction. Without it, there can be no humanity, as changes in the material world caused by people and their tools compromise the survival of the planet's most skillful and willful, productive and destructive, inhabitant (Marx 2008). Latour explains:

> From the time the term "politics" was invented, every type of politics has been defined by its relation to nature, whose every feature, property, and function depends on the polemical will to limit, reform, establish, short-circuit, or enlighten public life. (2004: 1)

Beneath this lofty philosophy, more mundane social-science accounts of the environment proliferate. They are dominated by three discursive formations:

- Economics, to assess exchange value
- Psychology, to evaluate individuals
- Sociology and anthropology, to comprehend societies

Environmental economics focuses on climate change as a consequence of the supposed absence of pure market forces (Ostrom 2000). Dutifully obeying the *données* (set beliefs) of reactionary fans of an imaginary capitalism, it argues that once prices are placed on such negative externalities as pollution, everything can be put to rights through the operation of supply and demand (Hardin 1968).

Ecological economists dissent from their monotheistic parent discipline, calling for restraints on growth via governments limiting unbridled impacts on our future and the use of varied forms of thought to comprehend and counter climate change. They evaluate the technologies and materials that can support human populations and nature, with the goal of avoiding undue stress on all participants. Their "Ecological Footprint" instrument measures environmental value rather than monetary exchange, and prioritizes sustainable life over productivity and profit. It calculates global environmental capacity by hectare and judges numerical sustainability (Martínez-Alier 2012).

Feminist economists have also called for a reconsideration of elements not generally assumed relevant by neoclassicists, because they transcend market pricing. These critics seek to bring the body as a sensate entity into analyses of environmental impact (Perkins and Kuiper 2005; Nelson 2009). As part of an ongoing dispute with binaristic divisions between nature and culture, feminist theory more generally has interrogated the notion of progress as productivist and accumulationist (Soper 1995; Conley 1997). Some strands posit an essential distinction between men and women that finds the former responsible for the theory and practice of environmental destruction, and the latter conversely blessed and cursed with unshakeable connections to the Earth, due to their enhanced experience of reproduction and caregiving (Sandilands 1999; Thompson 2006). Others look at the gendered politics of labor and differences between the Global North and South, with religion, class, and indigeneity important factors (Goldman and Schurman 2000: 571–574).

For their part, environmental anthropology and sociology struggle against both extrapolations from the magical mechanics of supply and demand and the latest incarnations of the "Human Exceptionalism Paradigm" that emerged from Kant and Hegel. As we have seen, that regrettably influential declaration allocates to us and us alone the right and the capacity to exercise sovereignty over the Earth (Catton and Dunlap 1978).

It is under challenge. For while early modernity was dedicated to establishing national power and producing and distributing goods and revenue in a struggle for the most effective and efficient forms of industrialization, with devil take the hindmost and no thought for the environment, today's risk society involves enumerating, euphemizing, and managing those dangers (Beck 1999). It is now clear that developed modernity produces new, trans-territorial risks, beyond the scope of traditional governmental guarantees of collective security and affluence (Goldman and Schurman 2000). Populations face crises brought on by deliberate policies, for example, nuclear energy, genocidal weaponry, biotechnology, and industrial pollution—"professional miscalculations and scientific discoveries hurtling out of control" (Kitzinger and Reilly 1997: 320). Despite their chauvinism, feelings of national patrimony can persuade people to transcend consuming desires and think about heritage and legacy, as citizens who think backward and forward rather than just contemporaneously (de-Shalit 2006: 76).

Environmental Marxism ties nature to capital and labor. It favors the regulation of business and work to comply with ecological principles (Benton 1996; O'Connor 1998), while deep ecology presents the most venerable and severe challenge to social-science and public-policy anthropomorphism. Arne Naess summed up his basic eco-centric precepts like this:

1. The well-being and flourishing of human and non-human life on Earth have value in themselves (synonyms: intrinsic value, inherent worth). These values are independent of the usefulness of the non-human world for human purposes.
2. Richness and diversity of life forms contribute to the realization of these values and are also values in themselves.
3. Humans have no right to reduce this richness and diversity except to satisfy vital needs.
4. The flourishing of human life and cultures is compatible with a substantially smaller human population. The flourishing of non-human life requires a smaller human population.
5. Present human interference with the non-human world is excessive, and the situation is rapidly worsening.
6. Policies must therefore be changed. These policies affect basic economic, technological, and ideological structures. The resulting state of affairs will be deeply different from the present.
7. The ideological change will be mainly that of appreciating life quality (dwelling in situations of inherent value) rather than adhering to an increasingly higher standard of living. There will be a profound awareness of the difference between bigness and greatness.
8. Those who subscribe to the foregoing points have an obligation directly or indirectly to try to implement the necessary changes. (1995: 68)

There are problems with this perspective, notably the insistence on restricted population growth and zero pleasurable consumption, and its assumption of a capacity to sidestep propaganda. Deep ecology requires a mixture of millenarianism, hope, and activism that sometimes veers closer to religious mind control than democratic science.

Sen proposes a compromise between anthropocentrism and eco-centrism:

> The impact of the environment on human lives must be among the principal considerations in assessing the value of the environment. To take an extreme example, in understanding why the eradication of smallpox is not viewed as an

> impoverishment of nature (we do not tend to lament: "the environment is poorer since the smallpox virus has disappeared"). (2009: 248)

As noted earlier, human beings are the most powerful and destructive creatures on Earth, and we have a special responsibility to speak for and defend others; to support a world given to us that may hold unthought-of benefits to our descendants, if only it is maintained for them (Sen 2009: 251–252).

Most of these philosophers and social scientists remain shy of phrasing the real question, the one that haunts both neoclassical chorines and dutiful Marxists, who are equally dedicated to the triumphant march of development—namely, the requirement to limit consumption, restrict the generation of need and the exploitation of scarcity, and hence bind the twin arms of capitalism in a controlling embrace. How can this be achieved, given the growth evangelism of state, capital, and the bourgeois media?

Social psychology and neuropsychology indicate that people who do not regard themselves as directly affected by climate change may adopt environmental values when stimulated to think beyond their own lives and consider, albeit anthropocentrically as per Burke, the lives of those yet to be born (Zavall et al. 2015). Longitudinal studies suggest that people familiar with climate-change evidence are confirmed in their beliefs by personal experience, while those with less knowledge can be stirred to commitment when directly confronted by environmental events (Myers et al. 2013). Such strategies align with research on environmental frames, ideology, and political partisanship (Lakoff 2010).

Media coverage and public-service announcements usually frame environmental risk via moral arguments about social harm and care, especially following disasters of epic proportions (Pantti et al. 2012). Such stories resonate with progressive readers. When pro-environmental approaches evoke purity and disgust, they resonate with conservatives (Feinberg and Willer 2013). Progressives can be appealed to by social- and self-awareness, conservatives through risks and rewards (Schreiber et al. 2013). Conservatives react to repellent imagery of environmental disaster in pro-environmental ways when it elicits horror or poses threats to bodily purity, such as contaminated water from the Magdalena.

Emotion discourse has also proven effective in educational settings for stimulating environmental awareness (Reis and Roth 2009). The Canadian Centre for Policy Alternatives notes that "people are more likely to engage with stories about people and ecosystems (and polluters) that are close to where they are" (Cross et al. 2015: 40). So green persuasion should include a liberal emphasis on the aesthetic and moral values derived from nature, in combination with frightening photos of habitat destruction and oil-slimed waterways. As we shall see, a spectrum of the Colombian population is deeply committed to "their" river—a suitable and necessary case for environmental commitment and activism—and express their concern as vividly as one can imagine.

THE MEANING OF THE MAGDALENA

Orlando Fals Borda's analysis of the people who inhabit the Río's banks found "communities immersed in a world that seemed to have stopped in isolation, but which suffered from . . . the tensions of the great modern society to which they belonged" (1986: 16a). Their amphibious culture presented a "complex of behaviors, beliefs, and practices related to the management of the natural environment," replete with "ideological elements . . . prejudices, superstitions, and legends" (1986: 21b). One of the most famous legends, which has also appeared in music, concerns the alligator man. It tells the story of a fisherman from Plato Magdalena who becomes an alligator with the help of a magic formula so he can spy on women bathing in the river without being discovered. One day, the white liquid that enables him to return to his natural shape disappears in the water. A few drops fall on his face and he is permanently transformed into half man, half alligator—a hybrid beast that women fear and men hunt (1986: 26b).

The sense of a spirit incarnate in the Magdalena has influenced artists, writers, filmmakers, curators, and composers alike,[10] often identified with the very nation itself, as in Marco Aurelio Álvarez and Óscar García's song "Puente Pumarejo."[11] J.A.M. Gómez counts sixteen Colombian and four foreign feature films, three videos, fifty-six short movies, and four television series about the river (n.d.).[12] For example, the video artist Carolina Caycedo works with anti-extraction groups to record the destruction wrought by damming (Gómez-Barris 2017).

It can be no surprise that the country's astonishing variety of wildlife, scenery, and tragedy went on to stimulate the celebrated and passionate literary genre, *realismo mágico*. Its most noted rhapsodist was of course García Márquez. Because most Colombians have lived in the basin formed by the river, Gabo could not think of a more fitting background to the magical lives of his characters than the natural scenery and human welfare it provided (Salazar et al. 2018). He based his description of the region's exuberant fauna and flora on observation; knowledge of untold numbers of adventurers, migrants, traders, and romantics; and an interpretation of nineteenth-century artworks that represented zones which were already subject to malevolent ecological transformation at the time he wrote (Williams 2013; Anda 2015).

In contrast to García Márquez's imagined village of Macondo, the river was real. The protagonists of *Love in the Time of Cholera* (1988) travel it to heal the pain in their hearts. *The General in His Labyrinth* (2015) explains the meaning of the river in detail for the people who lived on its shores, and the suffering they and other creatures experienced as a consequence of its deterioration: "fish will have to learn to walk on land because the water will end." Gabo described how "alligators ate the last butterfly, and gone are the maternal manatees, parrots, monkeys, peoples" (1988: 55, 185). Elsewhere, however, the Magdalena is reborn through the power of love; life is always stronger than death. Gabo's fantasy of returning to his youth was about living in a boat on the river, because he learned more on it than he had in school, and more profoundly. He thought of it as dead yet capable of renewal—but it would take a century of reforestation from the disasters of private ownership and pollution, both to restore the river itself and to make life palatable for those who relied on its supply of water, long contaminated (García Márquez 1981).

In response to the Magdalena's evident decay, citizens' letters to newspaper editors in Colombia have told stories, made appeals, and launched critiques of those responsible for the great river. Their imaginative prose and passionate concern index both the legends summarized by Fals Borda and Gabo's *realismo mágico*. We look next at the lineaments of that genre and its place alongside the cultural meaning of the river, inquiring into organically emergent audience emotions, rather than those sought by advocates and social scientists. Popular responses to the horrendous contamination of the Río Magdalena show a passionate rejection of hyper-consumption—and the persistence of violence.

LETTERS TO THE EDITOR

It is easy to write off, so to speak, letters to the editor as of minimal significance—venues for slightly dotty retired British army officers to claim sightings of spring's first cuckoo (Gregory 1976) or places where readers with too much time and newsprint on their hands offer pedantic corrections to stories. Journalists are notoriously dismissive of these letters, regarding them as little more than minor sources of market intelligence (Wahl-Jorgensen 2002; Raeymaeckers 2005; da Silva 2013; Craft et al. 2016). The letters-to-the-editor section can also be rarefied. It appeals to minorities of the population and can stimulate conspiracy theories, while its results in terms of science are ambivalent, with anti-evolutionary ideology prominent (Karlsson et al. 2015; Silva and Lowe 2015; Slavtcheva-Petkova 2016). And under authoritarian regimes, such letters can be sources of problematic legitimation (Fielder and Meyen 2015).

In addition, they tend to exclude the least powerful in societies. Even though the technology gap in urban Colombia is not huge—most citizens have access to cellphones and a significant percentage participate in social media—racial and class barriers in everyday life translate to the virtual world, which is generally used by the popular classes to meet and express feelings interpersonally rather than collectively. It is not seen as a route to political participation or expression. This is due to the exhaustion that racial minorities experience in a fundamentally unequal, segregated society where civic participation has been systematically denied them (Barrios 2016; Salcedo 2016). We saw in chapter 2 how an online campaign was essentially an intra-elite dispute at play.

But letters to the editor, albeit unrepresentative of societies, do form part of the democratic process. Consider the serious, sensuous, fascinating debates between readers and journalists that occur in, for example, the *Economist*'s letters page: this venerable genre might be a guide to the participatory ethos of so-called social media. For what was once the only way of replying to a newspaper's reports and claims is also a model for Twitter, comment strings, and other forms of popular gossip and critique (Ihlebæk and Krumsvik 2015). Rasmus Kleis Nielsen describes letters to the editor as

> a fragmented contentious zone between politics, the media, and the private life of the limited number of citizens who get a chance to express themselves through the concrete operations of one of the institutions that gives the abstraction "the public debate" whatever reality it has. (2010: 21)

He identifies three tendencies: "storytelling, criticism, and appeal." Together, they enable letters to the editor to help constitute a potentially vigorous environmental counter–public sphere, especially when coverage of activism and critique are loaded toward anthropocentrism, as is the case in South America (Pinto et al. 2017).

The depth of feeling experienced and expressed by letter writers incarnates their potential commitment, sometimes in response to disasters that are sudden and prominent, sometimes as reactions to more subtle stories beyond the headlines. We examined their language in highly charged discussions of the difficulties confronting the Magdalena and its inhabitants, via content analysis of 5,425 letters to the editor between 1999 and 2008 in the *El Tiempo* and *El Heraldo* newspapers. In accordance with their respective circulation figures, 90 percent of the data came from *El Tiempo*.

Our unit of analysis was the paragraph, because the letters frequently referred to more than one theme. Using QDA Miner software, we put keywords associated with the environment in context and carried out simultaneous searches focused on climate change. Categories emerged organically from the data (Ryan and Bernard 2003; Guest et al. 2012). Over 650 paragraphs were organized in a database. They mentioned risks, accidents, collapses, rainy seasons, floods, rivers, creeks, water, badlands, mountains, disasters, the natural environment, emergencies, the Red Cross, civil defense, and relief.[13]

The letters had four main political-economic themes: citizenship, domestic policy, international policy, and the production of newspapers (Barrios 2013, 2017). Many writers were very emotive in their accounts of the conflict, and a number focused with equivalent passion on the environment and climate change—595 letters expressed views on sensitive ecological issues to do with the Magdalena.

The research discloses a mixture of emotions and expectations about the river, indicating its salience and importance to readers—a nostalgia for its original condition and an embrace of its national significance. The "great river

TABLE 2. Percentage of key words in paragraphs, 1999–2008

	El Tiempo		*El Heraldo*		Total	
Keywords	Paragraphs	%	Paragraphs	%	Paragraphs	%
Water	93	14.3	64	9.8	157	24.1
River	89	13.7	39	6	128	19.6
Risk	52	8	17	3	69	11
Natural Environment	40	6.1	13	2	53	8.1
Accident	40	6.1	9	1.4	49	7.5
Emergency	25	3.8	6	0.9	31	4.8
Rainy season	19	2.9	8	1.2	27	4.1
Rain	12	1.8	14	2.1	26	4.0
Magdalena River	6	0.9	17	2.6	23	3.5
Bogotá River	16	2.5	0	0	16	2.5
Creek	1	0.15	14	2.1	15	2.3
Mountains	10	1.5	5	0.8	15	2.3
Disaster	9	1.4	3	0.5	12	1.8
Sierra Nevada	6	0.9	0	0	6	0.9
Red Cross	3	0.5	3	0.5	6	0.9
Relief	2	0.3	3	0.5	5	0.8
Collapse	4	0.61	0	0.0	4	0.61
Badlands	4	0.6	0	0	4	0.6
Civil defense	1	0.2	2	0.3	3	0.5
Flood	3	0.46	0	0	3	0.46
Total	435	67	217	34	652	100

Magdalena" was a prominent saying, along with frequent expressions of sadness and disappointment at the negligence of the authorities and the apathy of citizens—and joy at projects that gave the Río the importance it deserves. Consider this text:

> A letter from our incomparable poet José Asunción Silva to his relatives in Bogotá says, "I'm on a train from Calamar to Cartagena. . . . I think of Cartagena as Colombia's golden gates and Calamar as the nation's lobby, because everything that comes into the country enters through Cartagena, then by train to Calamar before being transported along the Río Magdalena for all of Colombia to enjoy, including Barranquilla," as there were no highways in those days. (*El Heraldo*, November 20, 1999)

Another letter, a decade later, said:

> One Sunday in December 1966 . . . [,] peeking through a small window, I spotted a large flamingo in the Caño de la Auyama, a tributary to the River Magdalena. It

> had long legs, a long neck, a downturned beak, and pink plumage.... Today, forty years later, I no longer see these beautiful birds—just rotten waters full of excrement. (*El Heraldo*, June 2, 2008)

These texts have a literary tone that describes the river as a spoiled but still creative force; it has clearly inspired ordinary writers as well as Gabo. Hope for recovery of the river awakens joy in readers, who express approval for initiatives that seek to solve the problems besetting it:

> Barranquilla and the Caribbean coast in general welcomed the River Avenue project.[14] It met a yearning across generations of people who did not think of the area as a national tourist attraction. It is a great pleasure to watch the sunset and the dawn between the murmur of waves and currents, to bear witness to the ephemeral idyll noted by the poet Julio Flórez, and the perennial kiss that the river shares with the sea.... [C]leaning up the river is primordial: the morning glory and the hyacinths that form on its banks are cleaned or sanitized to avoid unpleasant odors.... God willing, we shall see the realization of desires that course through our beloved Barranquilla. (*El Heraldo*, July 7, 2006)

> The Great Pact for the Recuperation of the Río Grande de la Magdalena must become part of our national purpose, with the full backing of political leaders. This is the only way to return the River Magdalena to its glory as the engine of development in the region and a place where Colombia unites. *El Heraldo*'s participation in this noble campaign to create citizen culture and consciousness about the river is a significant contribution that further embellishes this important publishing house. (*El Heraldo*, November 29, 1999)

> If Bogotá could control the river that bears its name so that its rubbish only contaminated Sabana [de Bogotá], we could say that this was a problem for the capital and the province. But because these effluents flow into the Magdalena and adversely affect other regions, they become a national issue, originating in the capital. It's a great pity that resources that could improve the state of the Magdalena have been cut. (*El Tiempo*, February 18, 2008)

Letter writers lament the lack of potable water and basic infrastructure in towns on the banks of the Magdalena and other tributaries:

> I congratulate our Governor for including in his plans a particular priority. As he put it, "I'll give special treatment to the water problem." It is inconceivable—inexplicable—that the inhabitants of the banks of the generous River Magdalena must endure grievous water scarcity when they live so close to this precious, sacred liquid. (*El Heraldo*, May 19, 2004)

People living by other major rivers, such as the Amazon, report similar deficiencies in the supply of drinking water:

> I had the wonderful experience of spending a year in Puerto Nariño, the principal municipality in Amazonas province, and I dare to denounce the neglect of this place and its people: they do not have drinking water, and they line up both to drink from and to pollute the river, with all the health problems that entails. They have three phone booths, which only function during office hours, and weather permitting (a rarity in Amazonas). But what concerns me most is electricity; they have only one plant, and in addition to making monstrous noises, it only works for a few hours in the afternoon—when the Mayor's office has the money to buy fuel, and when it's not damaged (which is the case several times a year). In the afternoon, with the temperature above 40 degrees and 80 percent humidity, you can't eat, work, or even rest. I hope the Government takes action to counter this abandonment of its people, given there is sufficient infrastructure to export energy to other countries. (*El Tiempo*, July 10, 2004)

This recurrent problem is addressed in the following letter:

> How can it be that we have an abundance of water through two oceans, the Magdalena, Amazonas, and underground currents, but half our inhabitants lack access to this vital and irreplaceable resource? Twenty-five million of our countrymen consume poor-quality water. The remainder enjoy pure, uncontaminated water, much of which they waste. (*El Tiempo*, January 15, 2000)

Numerous letters appeal to the government to find permanent solutions to the environmental problems affecting vulnerable populations, especially those living on the river's banks:

> I do not know whether hidden interests have constructed our forestry legislation. It certainly assists multinationals. When laws are passed without great scrutiny or analysis of their costs and benefits, that inevitably excites suspicion. It makes one sad to think that the nation's leaders do not concentrate on the need to protect its future. Why is there such a lack of environmental consciousness when the rest of the world acts to protect its ecosystems and water resources? Without a credible opposition, politicians just do what they want. Now they are looking to privatize water. (*El Tiempo*, December 19, 2005)
>
> The lack of official solidarity with coastal peoples who must deal with a harsh winter season is amazing. Poor people have always lived there. Their difficulties are not of their making: we have invested in massive development that has

> polluted the River. Again and again, we fail to apply the resources necessary to solve, once and for all, problems with rivers and dykes that arise every year. (*El Tiempo*, March 20, 2008)
>
> If we do not end deforestation . . . if we fail to reform our land use, starting with the highlands where our rivers begin, we will be left with regular, devastating flooding. Putting levees in lower Cauca is useless. I hope that next year I shall not feel obliged to write these words yet again. (*El Tiempo*, January 5, 2000)

The Magdalena and other waterways have been casualties of the conflict as well as industrialization, because the *guerrilla* used them as battlefields and weapons to pressure the government. They bombed sections of the country's oil pipelines, such as Transandino, causing major environmental disasters—massive oil spills that killed uncountable numbers of species. Letters to the editor indicate readers' anger and grief. They call for the exclusion of natural resources and underprivileged communities from armed conflict:

> How can we say everyone should respect everything, when we have birds without forests? Rivers without fish? Land without crops? Crops without water? Pets with brutal owners? Riverbeds without rivers? People who must use oxygen masks to breathe? Where children have no fathers, no brothers—no family at all? What will become of the children without friends? Should we have freedom without order? God said about the world: I welcome you all; you can live in peace. (*El Tiempo*, December 17, 2005)
>
> The ELN, with all the arrogance that characterizes it, has made a very unclear proposal. They speak of a bilateral truce. Is this a real cease-fire, where they release hostages and end kidnapping, extortion, laying mines, burning vehicles, destroying pipelines, and poisoning rivers? Or is it a truce so that our Army will leave them alone so they can continue their war against the Colombian people? (*El Tiempo*, July 13, 2004)
>
> It would be good to compile all the atrocities committed by the terrorists of the FARC over the past 40 years. . . . Likewise, the number of gas cylinders launched to destroy barracks, schools and health centers; the amount of spilled oil that has polluted our rivers and fields; the tons of exported drugs. (*El Tiempo*, May 31, 2014)

CONCLUSION

As Martha Nussbaum says, "Emotions directed at the geographical features of a nation are ways of channeling emotions towards its key commitments—to inclusiveness, equality, the relief of misery, the end of slavery" (2013: 2). In this case, readers' letters aim to push their compatriots and decision makers to preserve natural resources in general, and rivers in particular. Veritable rivers of emotions surround these citizens' criticisms and appeals for drinking water and sewage services for populations on the banks of the Magdalena. Many letters call for urgent action to stop the contamination caused by mining, industrial waste, and the conflict. The expressions of emotion amount to a local yet telling instance of how Colombians relate to "their" river.

The kind of environmental mobilization needed across conservative and progressive thinking alike is exemplified in these passionate engagements. Given global-warming forecasts, and absent major mitigation, the likely future for Colombia is for a hotter and more arid country (Salazar et al. 2018). That is the responsibility of countries far beyond the Magdalena, of course; but local efforts to halt untrammelled development are crucial—hence the violence done to traditional owners of Colombian territory by enforcers hired by multinationals that seek maximal mining and agricultural opportunities and minimal democratic regulation.

The degradation of land by farming and mineral extraction must be stemmed. Ideas of ethical consumption pale beside such crucial interventions:

> We were able to think we were modern only as long as the various ecological crises could be denied or delayed. . . . When the first tremors of the Apocalypse are heard, it would seem that preparations for the end should require something more than simply using a different kind of lightbulb . . . a timid appeal to buy new garbage cans. (Latour 2009: 462)

The Magdalena River has triggered popular writers' affection for the nation, reaffirming some core social values and collective goals. We see great value in such commentaries, alongside other ways in which the discourse of emotions is applied to ecological crises. Given the significance of such commitments for developing and maintaining environmental consciousness, letters to the editor even model readers communicating with media outlets via newer platforms.

Perhaps none of these writers has produced imagery of the quality of Gabo, but they express a commitment as great as his to a precious world under threat from the violence of capital, the state, and the *guerrilla* alike. If their commitments can blend with those of scientists and traditional owners, a new, post-development force may mobilize to protect the Magdalena and other natural resources against the attacks of development and conflict.

CONCLUSION

The Persistence of Violence has been haunted by Colombia's scarred and scarring coming-into-being, the strange, ongoing dialectic of a state that is either too present or too absent—able to coerce/unable to serve—and prevailing economic, racial, and sexual dogmas. My coauthors and I have engaged these issues at a different angle from the norms of the human sciences, by focusing on the popular.

I began with García Márquez's oppositions about the Colombian people:

- A proclivity for making laws and ignoring them
- Prevalent cathexes onto paperwork amid contempt for bureaucratic norms
- A dedicated work ethic and love of get-rich-quick schemes
- A taste for creating icons, then ridiculing and bringing them down
- An obsession with sporting triumph and failure, greater than any identification with human suffering
- Love of life mixed with murderous tendencies
- Adoration of animals but neglect of the loss of species and the environment in general, alongside imperilment of one of the world's great rivers
- Loathing for negative international stereotypes of Colombia, matched by a failure to admit that the reality may be worse

Those binaries remain useful ways of understanding a profound duality over violence in Colombian life that is both evident in, and sustained by, popular culture. And his list gave me the book's topics. That said, although such oppositions are good to think with, they are frequently logocentrically interdependent, rather than truly opposed to one another. One can see them more as paradoxes than contradictions—which is of course in the spirit of Gabo's original book.

The evidence of diverse yet interconnected sites of the popular is that the tendency toward violence is never far from the surface; but nor are alternatives. For alongside the horrors of everyday life—as well as those of the spectacular—we must also consider equally Colombian tendencies: pacific and welcoming daily conduct, vibrant social movements, dogged news gathering, cultural critique, and scientific endeavor. They are just as persistent as the violence they oppose. And it is possible to see the nation's history not only as successive waves of horror punctuated by perilous peace, but as a series of settlements that expand the definition and exercise of citizenship in terms of belonging and rights (Carranza-Franco 2019).

So what are the prospects for peace—by which I mean not only with the *guerrilla*, but in terms of narcos, *paramilitares*, sexual trafficking, historiography, a free press, and ecological sustainability—the spheres we have addressed?

At a macrolevel, it is clear that there needs to be an end to corruption, a dismantling of cartels, the prohibition of forced clearances by governments and corporations, land reform, return to their homes for the millions who have been violently displaced, and compensation paid to those kidnapped, injured, threatened, or bereaved by state, *guerrilla*, narco, or *paramilitar* action. But there must also be action to remake the national popular, at economic, cultural, and social levels. And this has to be done with an eye to those original explanations for the persistence of violence, with which we also began:

- A topography that militates against the effective government of numerous regions (Cauca, Antioquia, the Andes, and the north coast) with people left to fight for terrain and power in the absence of a functioning state
- Machismo
- Systematic inequality
- A racial formation discriminating against indigenous and Afro-Colombians
- Marxism
- The role of the United States, from the creation of the Panama Canal to Plan Colombia and Peace Colombia, today's military policies
- The World Bank making Colombia a template for development via the exploitation of natural resources and antisocialist strategies
- The Janus face of neoliberalism, as a blend of economic deregulation and statist reformation of citizens
- Cross-generational oligarchy
- The media dominated by clientelist and familial ties to politics
- Paramilitary, guerrilla, and mafioso forces
- Kidnapping, drug dealing, and the informal economy
- A state riddled with corruption
- Public distrust of the police, the judiciary, and politics

What are the resources of hope before us?

In addition to the counter-power evident in the topics analyzed in the last four chapters, I take inspiration from the images shown here. The first is from a group of artworks on display in Cartagena in 2015 by Afro-Colombian women who survived violence (see figure 13). Their work avows that one must acknowledge, accept, and transcend suffering, in order to emerge stronger than before.

FIGURE 13. Know yourself, accept yourself, and move on. (Source: Toby Miller.)

The next two images are from the Spanish Library Park in Medellín, an initiative in a popular sector that is dogged by extreme poverty, violence, addiction, and the exploitation of children (figures 14 and 15). When I visited the park in 2011 with my coauthor Anamaria Tamayo-Duque and her children, I was struck by the vibrant thematization of violence and its resistance; injury and its survival; and loss and its commemoration. The murals show a determination never to forget those who have been killed, displaced, disabled, or raped, and to seek a better life for all.

There are equally powerful reactions from groups such as Cartagena's Corporación Cultural Atabaques (named for Yoruba drums) (see figures 16, 17, and 18).

Gabo's paradoxes are encapsulated in the art of Wilfran Barrios Paz, one of the region's leading choreographers, and other participants in the Corporación. They focus on youth empowerment and black traditions of motion that refuse insular nationalism in favor of diasporic connections, highlighting mise-en-scène as well as phenomenological approaches to culture. Their dances incarnate both a peaceful form of life and a vibrant, physical, dance-driven alternative to passivity. The body is shown to move in wrought, fraught, human settings rather than as a pure, unchanging essence (Barrios 2016; Tatis Guerra 2017).[1]

Alongside Barrios's peaceful, graceful, powerful, assertive bodies in motion—akin to football at is best—are brave reporters withstanding intimidation, and letter writers insisting on the need to preserve the Magdalena. They give a sense

FIGURE 14. We are all the Spanish Library Park. (Source: Toby Miller.)

FIGURE 15. Homage to community victims of the conflict. Displaced below the water. Change the mines for hope. No more sexual violence. (Source: Toby Miller.)

FIGURE 16. No more violence against women. (Source: Toby Miller.)

FIGURE 17. WARNING—Machismo kills. (Source: Toby Miller.)

FIGURE 18. We neither tolerate nor practice sexual violence against children here. (Source: Toby Miller.)

of hope. How could that materialize across the spheres discussed in *The Persistence of Violence*?

An extraordinary linkage of the issues discussed here emerged with the massive mobilization of Colombian civil society in November and December 2019 against the classic mix of neoliberal economics and authoritarian policing that characterizes the government of Uribe's creature, currently trading as Duque. The brave new world of creative industries had come to look problematic next to further transfers of money upwards, targeted killing of social leaders, ecological devastation, willful misconduct of the peace process, and the usual litany of oligarchic and oligopolistic self-satisfaction and parthenogenesis.

Hundreds of thousands of people from across territories, classes, ages, and races had had enough. They took to the streets against persistent violence—knowing, rightly, that some of their number would suffer further brutality as a consequence. As I write these words, in the first days of 2020, it is impossible to say what the outcome of this powerful but pacific unrest will be. The oligarchs are powerful, the state vicious, and fear of progressive politics palpable.

But it may be that this moment signifies that many people who are equally opposed to the *guerrilla*, the narcos, the *paramilitares*, ecological destruction, and inequality have severed the powerful connection between direct action and fear of the FARC or becoming a new site of *Chavismo*. The peace, however fragile

FIGURE 19. Popular protests and armed responses in Cartagena in November 2019. (Source: Nicholas Ford Woodward.)

and incomplete, has revealed how much prejudice and bastardry thrive in mainstream society, and that those tendencies are products of a history prior to the *guerrilla*. Figures 19 and 20 illustrate both the power and intimidating solemnity of the state in all its monochromatic uniformity versus the color and verve of a protesting public.

FIGURE 20. Popular protests and armed responses in Cartagena in November 2019. (Source: Nicholas Ford Woodward.)

There must be a focus from the left on creating a new national popular that embraces cultural difference and rejects class difference. Creative-industries discourse needs to be challenged, given its manifold, manifest prejudices and problems, but also used in order to forward a new kind of development, as opposed to clearing areas for mining, building freeways, and refurbishing airports.

Football must remove the powerful narcos who still populate it and end money laundering. Clubs must support their more peaceful *hinchas* and insist on safe seating and transportation for women and children, provide education regarding hateful speech, and expel for life anyone indulging in linguistic or physical violence. The notion that words are without adverse material consequences does not hold when they promote harm done to others.

Grassroots organizations dedicated to minorities need not only more support but serious state consideration and media coverage as more than niceties—the mainstream must give room, time, and hearing to indigenous, *campesino*, and Afro activists and cultural producers and children living in poverty. Tourism must be rethought to support the formalization of the industry, but without wholesale corporatization. New construction must be done in the material interests of all classes, including long-term minority residents, who along with their forebears have created and sustained the very culture that encourages such investment.

Cocaine should be legalized rather than glamorized. Prohibition in Europe and the United States has failed—it cannot turn people away from making, transporting, or using the drug. Decriminalization in the Global North must be the quid pro quo of Bogotá accepting money and interdiction from Washington as per Plan Colombia. That will in turn diminish the power and rivalry of the cartels and their impact on good government.

Journalists should be properly protected by the state apparatus, and legislation passed to require media proprietors to disinvest from other business interests and create serious boundaries between themselves and editors and between reportage and advertising. Corrupt officials must be identified and punished, whether in the police, the courts, or municipal administration. In addition, some precepts from peace journalism need to be adopted, such as focusing on the victims of violence—their stories, their needs—and acknowledging that the distinction between criminal and political violence is a comforting but false one, in this case as many others (Ottosen 2010, 2017). The bourgeois media should feature writing by rural social leaders, journalists, and commentators, and work with governments to protect them, while respecting their desire for autonomy. Newsrooms more generally must provide more room to move and breathe.

The country needs a major national public TV broadcaster to break up the commercial duopoly and offer high production-value drama from home and abroad that can rival the bling of *narconovelas*, drawing on the cultural talent available to tell other stories. What might those themes encompass? Resistance to the *conquista* and piracy, sustainable ways of life in the light of tourism, footballers' lives, women as high flyers, and so on. That is not a recipe for dull, worthy, 'positive' television; rather, it can make for a telling encounter with key areas of the popular to dramatize Colombia's history of violence, from colonialism and slavery to Conservatives versus Liberals, *guerrilla* contra *paramilitares*, and narcos against everyone—along with peaceful and joyous tendencies, be they sporting triumphs or street singing.

The environment must be made an absolute priority, for with it comes protection of indigenous, *campesino*, and Afro-life in the face of degradation under the sign of development. Building on the warm and sometimes fiery spirit of popular reason expressed over the Magdalena, "emotional communities" must be cultivated that can reflect on violence, activate kinship networks, forge peaceful political alliances, and embark on dialogues across society (Jimeno et al. 2018).

Tension over collective memory and history is prevalent throughout Colombia. There is a schizophrenic identification with both a lost past of order and even a supposed grandeur associated with European domination, and pride in having thrown it over. This bizarre contradiction is animated by racial difference and inequality and a sense of the country constantly being re-forged through horrific violence and a struggle over the definition and curation of national narratives. With the right interventions, the Colombian state can improve its reputation with the population, stimulate a new national popular, and engage the past to prevent its agonizing recurrence. Then there might be persistent peace.

ACKNOWLEDGMENTS

I was fortunate enough to work at the Universidad del Norte, Tulane University, the Universidad Tecnológica de Bolívar, and the Universidad Autónoma Metropolitana—Cuajimalpa while writing this volume. I am immensely grateful for those opportunities.

Personal gratitude is due above all to my coauthors—Jesús Arroyave, Marta Milena Barrios, Alfredo Sabbagh Fajardo, Olga Lucia Sorzano, and Anamaria Tamayo-Duque.

I also wish to thank those who have encouraged and enabled aspects of this work: Alberto Abello Vives, Akuavi Adonon Viveros, Pal Ahluwalia, Daniela Alvarez, Jorge Luis Alvis Arrieta, Paulina Aroch-Fugellie, Claudia Arroyo Quiroz, Idelber Avelar, Adolfo Baltar Moreno, Eva Baaren, Mario Barbosa, Wilfran Barrios, Michael Butterworth, Haroldo Calvo Stevenson, Emily Capdeville, Alejandra Castaño Echeverri, Burçe Celik, Mayra Alejandra Cogollo Gutierrez, Joselyne Contreras Cerda, André Dorcé Ramos, Chris Dunn, Aarón Eduardo Espinosa Espinosa, Natalie Fenton, Bob Franklin, Des Freedman, Jorge Galindo, Néstor García Canclini, Kimberly Giunta, Bill Grantham, Suyapa Inglés, James Jacobs, Micah Kleit, Amalia Leguizamón, Justin Lewis, Karin Ljuslinder, Ana López, Casey Love, Yennifer María Martin Cabarcas, Daniel Mato, Richard Maxwell, Vicki Mayer, Benjamín Mayer Foulkes, Graham Meikle, Gabriela Méndez Cota, Caitlin Kataryna Miller, Lainey Paloma Miller, Anamaria Ochoa Gautier, Rune Ottosen, James Pamment, Mauro Porto, Cielo Patricia Puello Sarabia, Isabel Cristina Ramírez Botero, Tom Reese, Luis Reygadas Robles Gil, Ana Rosas Mantecón, Jorge Saavedra Utman, Federico Guillermo Serrano López, Ingrid Silva Arroyo, Annika Egan Sjölander, David Smilde, Gretchen Soderlund, Imre Szeman, Dominic Thomas, Daniel Toro Gonzalez, Lisette del Rosario Urquijo Burgos, Enrique Uribe Jongbloed, Aimée Vega Montiel, Berit von der Lippe, Karin Wilkins, Rosalía Winocur Iparraguirre, Nicholas Ford Woodward, Shinjoung Yeo, Myke Yest, George Yúdice, and Susan Zieger.

NOTES

INTRODUCTION

1. I italicize "guerrilla" when using it as a collective noun with the definite article, as this is the form used in Spanish. I do not do so when using it as an adjective, as per English.
2. My thanks to Dominic Thomas, who helped in my search for the origin of the line attributed to Hugo.
3. The word "activist" soothes the balm of Anglo readers. The more common terms in Colombia are *lidera/lider social* (social leader) or *defensor* (defender) of rights.
4. An indicative contemporary list of writers on the topic might include Orlando Fals Borda et al. (1962), Herbert Braun (1994), Arturo Escobar (1995), Marco Palacios (2003), Steven Dudley (2004), Winifred Tate (2007), Ingrid Betancourt (2010), Michael Taussig (2010), Nazih Richani (2013), Grupo de Memoria Histórica (2013), Jasmin Hristov (2014), Stella Sacipa-Rodriguez and Maritza Montero (2014), Jairo Estrada Álvarez (2015), Estanislao Zuleta (2015), Lesley Gill (2016), and Angélica Durán-Martínez (2018).
5. http://www.himnonacionaldecolombia.com/letra/.
6. That formulation transcends sovereign-state actors to include more complex collectives, albeit ones that seek hegemony over terrain as per states.
7. http://www.rgs.org/OurWork/Schools/Teaching+resources/Key+Stage+3+resources/The+geography+of+conflict/The+causes+of+conflict.htm; http://www.hiik.de/en/konfliktbarometer/pdf/ConflictBarometer_2014.pdf.
8. I owe this explanation to Federico Guillermo Serrano López, whose insights into the Conservative–Liberal binarism of Colombian politics have also proven invaluable.
9. https://www.youtube.com/watch?v=IYfgvSoFA7U&t=194s.
10. http://colombiadiversa.org/base-datos/nacional/.
11. This claim is also made by the vast majority of Colombian Catholics, who are disciples of the "prosperity gospel" (Pew Research Center 2014: 68).
12. July 2019. https://www.youtube.com/channel/UCm4BXaCpgI7exZ_Nu3dkXcQ.
13. https://www.netflix.com/title/80141259; https://www.youtube.com/watch?v=GB3qQJKLlVw.
14. https://rtd.rt.com/films/escobars-hitman/.

CHAPTER 1 THE ABSENCE AND PRESENCE OF STATE MILITARISM

1. We are writing about football (as it is known to 96 percent of the world's population) or soccer (to 4 percent of the world's population). The 4 percent's use of the term has produced one thing of awe in Raymond Chandler's great sentence: "The smell of old dust hung in the air as flat and stale as a football interview" (1949).
2. https://www.youtube.com/watch?v=o6O_8RohRrI.
3. https://www.youtube.com/watch?v=HM-E2H1ChJM.
4. https://www.youtube.com/watch?v=tWwkU-CWy9o.
5. https://www.youtube.com/watch?v=pYFTYanZXiE.
6. Holmes may have been referring to rugby union, given the polysemic usage of his day.
7. Pop philosopher Simon Critchley rather touchingly claims this expression as his own (2014).

8. https://www.youtube.com/watch?v=I-5xyqvlirY.
9. Now known as La Corporación Deportiva Once Caldas S. A.
10. https://www.youtube.com/watch?v=mOO3hTaH5tw.
11. https://www.youtube.com/watch?v=V2UTERPg9GU.
12. https://www.youtube.com/watch?v=VPDxWcLaLHo.
13. https://www.youtube.com/watch?v=2QpdtsP79w4.
14. https://www.youtube.com/watch?v=EqQxvthwia4&app=desktop.
15. https://www.youtube.com/watch?v=7JdGNyX2_r0; https://www.youtube.com/watch?v=enJuQBNyazc.
16. https://www.youtube.com/watch?v=z7myTM35OLU.
17. https://www.youtube.com/watch?v=RFlHVpvMYH0; https://www.youtube.com/user/FuerzasMilCol.
18. https://palimpalem.com/1/cdlmillonarios/index.html?body5.html.
19. https://www.youtube.com/watch?v=TRj3dKKp9tI.
20. https://www.youtube.com/watch?v=DKEFvLn-VWs.
21. http://www.juanjosebellini.com/.
22. http://tmz.vo.llnwd.net/o28/newsdesk/tmz_documents/0705_Pablo%20Escobar%20Letter.pdf.
23. This cheeky adolescent xenophobia/tabloid imperialism is typical of Murdoch's media when they target the white, monolingual working class. Pride in Britain's vicious enslaving past characterizes the paper.
24. https://www.youtube.com/watch?v=EOifeBLL2ho.

CHAPTER 2 INDUSTRY POLICY AND SEX TOURISM MEET THE CASE OF THE DESTROYED PLAQUE

1. The Ministry of Industry and Tourism has a site dedicated to educational classes and other resources that seek to counter child sexual exploitation: http://escnna.mincit.gov.co/.
2. Thanks to Aarón Espinosa Espinosa for helping me locate the site of the plaque.
3. The troops included Lawrence Washington, George's older brother, who named their slave-built and slave-worked Virginia property Mount Vernon after the Admiral.
4. http://www.himnonacionaldecolombia.com/letra/.
5. http://www.dane.gov.co/files/censo2005/PERFIL_PDF_CG2005/13001T7T000.PDF.
6. https://www.univeur.org/cuebc/downloads/PDF%20carte/65.%20Manila.PDF.
7. http://economicsandpeace.org/.
8. As with tourist numbers in general, Colombian data need to be approached with caution. For example, the government sometimes treats all international visitors as 'tourists' http://www.citur.gov.co/estadisticas/df_viajeros/all/4.
9. http://whc.unesco.org/en/list/285.
10. https://www.hotelcaribe.com/.
11. http://www.icbf.gov.co/portal/page/portal/PortalICBF/macroprocesos/misionales/restablecimiento/2/LM11.MPM5.P1%20Poblacion%20Especial%20Violencia%20Sexual%20v1.pdf.
12. As a minor example, I have sometimes struggled while on the road between Barranquilla and Cartagena to prove to the army that I am neither a kidnap victim nor a gunrunner.
13. http://www.cartagenacomovamos.org/cartagena-entre-las-ciudades-con-menor-satisfaccion-con-su-calidad-de-vida/.
14. http://www.citur.gov.co/estadisticas/df_lleg_pax_inter/all/48. The numbers for 2018 are unusual because they include millions of Venezuelan refugees.

15. One opinion from travel journalism that resonates.
16. https://www.cntraveler.com/package/women-who-travel.
17. https://www.hitman.com/locations#&gid=3&pid=1.
18. https://www.youtube.com/watch?v=t2sJpeL-Ars.
19. Thanks to Susan Zieger for this point.
20. https://www.youtube.com/watch?v=XEuYunbf8Ww.
21. http://www.icimarcom.com/COLO.html.
22. http://www.procolombia.co/noticias/colombia-realismo-magico; http://colombia.travel/realismomagico.
23. http://www.colombia.travel/feel-the-rhythm/es.
24. http://happyplanetindex.org/.
25. https://neweconomics.org/.
26. http://ethics.unwto.org/content/world-tourism-network-child-protection.
27. https://fundacionrenacer.org/.
28. https://www.icbf.gov.co/.
29. http://www.icbf.gov.co/portal/page/portal/PortalICBF/macroprocesos/misionales/restablecimiento/2/LM11.MPM5.P1%20Poblacion%20Especial%20Violencia%20Sexual%20v1.pdf.
30. https://www.globalfantasies.com/cartagena.htm; http://www.partycolombia.com/; https://www.universalfantasies.com/cartagena-packages.htm. I do not know whether these services use children.
31. https://www.youtube.com/watch?v=EaCaIPKbkf8.
32. https://www.youtube.com/watch?v=RiNVP2tOXuo; https://www.youtube.com/watch?v=TJEJ2JLOGh8.
33. https://www.youtube.com/watch?v=PHS5KdLwbmk.
34. https://www.youtube.com/watch?v=fuvMQAYhf48; https://www.youtube.com/watch?v=fw8kQxMQ6uc.
35. http://www.mincit.gov.co/loader.php?lServicio=Documentos&lFuncion=verPdf&id=77374&name=OEE_DO_WA_Turismo_Diciembre_05-02-2015.pdf&prefijo=file.
36. The historical literature varies in its estimates.
37. To give them their full titles: Charles Philip Arthur Windsor/Duke of Rothesay/Prince of Wales/Duke of Cornwall/Baron of Renfrew/Earl of Carrick/Prince and Great Steward of Scotland/Lord of the Isles/Earl Chester, or whatever his current aliases are (you know the one—baptized with water from the Jordan River?—we've left out all the military ranks because we love brevity) and his wife, Camilla Shand/Parker Bowles/Windsor/the Duchess of Cornwall/the Duchess of Rothesay/a 1965 debutante (Clarke 2007). Had Vernon taken Cartagena, Charles might boast a further title.
38. The story received significant TV news coverage. See https://www.youtube.com/watch?v=sZPSSCbT7L8.
39. As an ironic footnote, in the same year as the action against the plaque in Cartagena, Catalan nationalists in Spain militated for the removal of a statue of Blas de Lezo in Madrid, because he, too, had run a starvation blockade (of Barcelona) (Medialdea 2014).
40. A splendid expression is attributed to Blas de Lezo: "One must always piss facing England."
41. Today, leading Afro-Caribbeans are routinely deployed to justify neoliberalism as supposed signs that anyone with talent can succeed (Sierra Becerra 2017).

CHAPTER 3 "I MYSELF HAD TO REMAIN SILENT WHEN THEY THREATENED MY CHILDREN"

1. This is discernible through numerous methods, from the ethnographic to the textual (Tao et al. 2017).

2. http://ligacontraelsilencio.com/; https://www.flip.org.co/index.php/es/.

3. Although even there it is increasingly permeable (Bærug and Harro-Loit 2012; Artemas et al. 2018) as disclosed most outrageously in the *New York Times*'s *Innovation* report of 2014.

4. https://flip.org.co/cartografias-informacion/.

5. https://cpj.org/data/killed/?status=Killed&type%5B%5D=Journalist&start_year=1992&end_year=2018&group_by=year.

6. This is part of a developing international trend to mobilize universalist doctrines of human rights in order to protect journalists (Relly and González de Bustamante 2017).

7. In the case of indigenous groups, distinctions between these occupational categories are problematic—all may be deemed indigenous subjects engaged in collective struggle (Caballero Fula 2016).

8. This may underplay the specific risks faced by indigenous journalists (Krøvel 2017).

9. https://forbiddenstories.org/.

10. https://forbiddenstories.org/case/deadly-border/.

11. https://twitter.com/mjduzan/status/1018534439176024064?lang=en; https://twitter.com/rcnradio/status/1018880051918639105.

12. https://rsf.org/en/ranking?#.

13. The interviews were recorded and transcribed. The results have been encoded to conceal the identities of the journalists, especially those who spoke about sensitive issues, such as crimes against colleagues, or acted as witnesses in murder and graft investigations. The reporters had the opportunity to edit the transcriptions.

14. That said, relying on external foundations of course risks becoming subject to their agendas and precepts (Schiffrin 2017a).

15. This is very much as per the work of Monica Löfgren Nilsson and Henrik Örnebring (2016), who found that violence against journalists changed from physical to strong language, trolling, and defamation; Sallie Hughes et al. (2017), who encountered many journalists afraid to cover political elites and conflicts; and Thomas Hanitzsch et al. (2010) on occupational pressures.

16. https://www.minuto30.com/; https://www.las2orillas.co/.

17. https://www.canalrcn.com/rse/articulo-noticia/educacion-agropecuaria-en-cafe-con-aroma-de-mujer-responsabilidad-social-118.

18. Coding was performed by MA students and recent graduates of the Social Communication Program at UniNorte. All coders had previous experience undertaking content analysis. The instrument designed for our study was applied independently to a subsample (6 percent of the hours analyzed) to ensure coder reliability. We achieved 77.32 percent intercoder agreement. We used the statistical measure Cronbach Alpha for all categories to establish the instrument's internal consistency, resulting in a value of 0.8.

19. For international perspectives see Conor (2014) and Banks (2015).

CHAPTER 4 GREEN PASSION AFLOAT

1. http://intercambioclimatico.com/es/itemlist/tag/Colombia.htm.

2. https://www.greenpeace.org/archive-colombia/es/campanas/paramos-en-peligro/. Admirable work, though the multinational's stern warning that it only wants intercourse with

journalists, not the public or researchers, is as arch as it is telling. https://www.greenpeace.org/colombia/prensa/.

3. http://www.cormagdalena.com.co/.

4. An othering of black music goes back to colonial terrors at the sound of slaves drumming. Former slaves and their descendants have used music to organize and celebrate groups that address social issues, while the latter-day emergence of *champeta* (a form of music and dance) challenges whitening and clearance, blending African and black diasporic music with local rhythms and themes (Streicker 1997; Andrews 2004; Martínez Miranda 2011; McGraw 2014; Paschel 2010, 2016; Birenbaum Quintero 2018).

5. https://elpais.com/tag/greta_thunberg_ernman/a/; https://sostenibilidad.semana.com/noticias/greta-thunberg/1928.

6. https://rebellion.earth.

7. https://www.youtube.com/watch?v=LiYZxOlCN1o.

8. http://www.migrationheritage.nsw.gov.au/exhibition/objectsthroughtime/bourketerra/.

9. This chapter's astute copyeditor (Diane Ersepke) helpfully points out that Horkheimer's take is reminiscent of the Garden of Eden story, but the scribe who penned the Eden story added that further development of the human brain (i.e., "eating from the tree of knowledge") was the undoing of the species and its link to nature (excluded from the "garden" and forced to live by killing and subduing other life forms).

10. http://www.museoscolombianos.gov.co/fortalecimiento/comunicaciones/noticias/Paginas/La-nueva-propuesta-museogr%C3%A1fica-del-Museo-del-R%C3%ADo-Magdalena.aspx. Consider the variety of these exhibitions: http://www.arteinformado.com/agenda/f/el-rio-magdalena-109949; http://www.citytv.com.co/videos/340548/exposicion-en-museo-de-arte-del-quindio-rindo-homenaje-al-rio-magdalena; http://www.vkgaleria.com/es/exposicion/el-rio-magdalena.

11. https://www.musixmatch.com/lyrics/Los-Melodicos/Puente-Pumarejo-with-Ramon-Alberto.

12. A selection of films is excerpted in Calderón (2015).

13. We created a virtual file for each thematic area and pasted articles into the corresponding documents. Two graduate students read the texts several times, along with the authors. Each reviewer grouped quotations from letters with similar issues to form categories and establish possible connections between themes. We discussed each coder's categories. Final categories were agreed upon, merged, and reorganized, providing topical diversity (Van Mannen 1990). A selection was translated by the coauthors and is quoted here. Words that derived from indigenous languages were associated with themes and emotions in Spanish then English.

14. A beautification project that gave renewed pedestrian access to the Magdalena.

CONCLUSION

1. http://videomovimiento.com/wilfran-barrios/.

REFERENCES

Abel, Ann. 2018. "The 10 Coolest Places to Go in 2019." *Forbes*, December 12, 2019. https://www.forbes.com/sites/annabel/2018/12/12/the-10-coolest-places-to-go-in-2019/#575f6f281fdc.

Abello Vives, Alberto. 2016. Interview with Anamaria Tamayo-Duque and Toby Miller, December 2016.

Abu-Lughod, Lila. 2005. *Dramas of Nationhood: The Politics of Television in Egypt*. Chicago: University of Chicago Press.

Acemoglu, Daron, James A. Robinson, and Rafael J. Santos. 2013. "The Monopoly of Violence: Evidence from Colombia." *Journal of the European Economic Association* 11, no. S1: 5–44.

Ackerly, Brooke A., Maria Stern, and Jacqui True, eds. 2006. *Feminist Methodologies for International Relations*. Cambridge: Cambridge University Press.

Acosa Ordoñez, Karina. 2013. "Cartagena: Entre el progreso industrial y el rezago social." *Economía & Región* 7, no. 1: 5–66.

Acosta-Alzuru, Carolina. 2003. "'I'm Not a Feminist . . . I Only Defend Women as Human Beings': The Production, Representation, and Consumption of Feminism in a *Telenovela*." *Critical Studies in Media Communication* 20, no. 3: 269–294.

Acosta Peñaloza, Carmen Elisa. 2014. "'Remá, remá': Las literaturas del río Magdalena." *Credencial Historia* 292 (April). http://www.banrepcultural.org/blaavirtual/revistas/credencial/abril-2014/rema-rema.

Adorno, Theodor W. 1945. "A Social Critique of Radio Music." *Kenyon Review* 7, no. 2: 208–217.

———. 2005. *Critical Models: Interventions and Catchwords*. Translated by Henry W. Pickford. New York: Columbia University Press.

———. 2009. "*Kultur* and Culture." Translated by Mark Kalbus. *Social Text* 99: 145–58.

Adorno, Theodor W., and Max Horkheimer. 1977. "The Culture Industry: Enlightenment as Mass Deception." In *Mass Communication and Society*, edited by James Curran, Michael Gurevitch, and Janet Woollacott, 349–383. London: Edward Arnold.

———. 1979. *Dialectic of the Enlightenment*. Translated by John Cumming. London: Verso.

Aguilera Díaz, María M., and Adolfo Meisel Roca. 2009. "¿La isla que se repite? Cartagena en el censo de población de 2005." *Documentos de Trabajo Sobre Economía Regional* 109: 15–55.

Aguilera Peña, Mario. 1999. "Caida de Rojas Pinilla: 10 de Mayo de 1957." *Credencial Historia* 117 (September). http://www.banrepcultural.org/blaavirtual/revistas/credencial/septiembre1999/117caida.htm.

Aguirre Acuña, Ahmed. 2003. *Junior: Una historia de diamantes*. Barranquilla: Milenio.

Agustín, Laura Maria. 2007. *Sex at the Margins: Migration, Labour Markets and the Rescue Industry*. London: Zed.

"Alarma y repudio en Colombia por ataques con ácido." 2014. BBC Mundo, April 4, 2014. http://www.bbc.com/mundo/noticias/2014/04/140404_colombia_ataques_acido_wbm.

Allen, Jamie. 2015. "Pablo Escobar and the Narco-Fútbol Years." *These Football Times*, May 30, 2015. http://thesefootballtimes.co/2015/05/30/pablo-escobar-narco-futbol/.

"Alocución del Presidente Juan Manuel Santos de agradecimiento a la Selección Colombia de Fútbol." 2014. July 5, 2014. http://wsp.presidencia.gov.co/Prensa/2014/Julio/Paginas

/20140705_04-Palabras-Alocucion-Presidente-Santos-agradecimiento-la-Seleccion-Colombia-Futbol.aspx.

Althusser, Louis. 1969. *For Marx*. Translated by Ben Brewster. Harmondsworth: Penguin.

———. 1971. *Lenin and Philosophy and Other Essays*. Translated by Ben Brewster. New York: Monthly Review Press.

Altman, Daniel. 2015. "The Strategist's Curse: A Theory of False Optimism as a Cause of War." *Security Studies* 24, no. 2: 284–315.

Alvarado, Arturo. 2012. "Violencia y democracia: Balance de los estudios sobre violencia." *Estudios Sociológicos* 30: 29–57.

Amaya Trujillo, Janny, and Adrien José Charlois Allende. 2018. "Memoria cultural y ficción audiovisual en la era de la televisión en streaming. Una exploración en torno a la serie *Narcos* como relato de memoria transnacional." *Comunicación y Sociedad* 31: 15–44.

Anda, Mónica Perea. 2015. "Homenaje: Del río Magdalena, al río de aguas diáfanas: Aracataca." *Revista Estudios* 30: 280–303.

Anderson, John Lee. 2018. "The Afterlife of Pablo Escobar." *New Yorker*, March 5, 2018. https://www.newyorker.com/magazine/2018/03/05/the-afterlife-of-pablo-escobar.

Andrade, Carlos Alberto, Yves François Thomas, Alexandre Nicolae Lerma, and Brice Anselme. 2013. "Coastal Flooding Hazard Related to Swell Events in Cartagena de Indias, Colombia." *Journal of Coastal Research* 29, no. 5: 1126–1136.

Andrade de Melo, Victor, and Mauricio Drumond. 2014. "Globo, the Brazilian Military Dictatorship and the 1970 FIFA Football World Cup: Ambiguous Relations." *Television & New Media* 15, no. 8: 703–710.

Andress, David. 2018. "The Song That Once Unified France Is Tearing It Apart." *Quartz*, July 3, 2018. https://qz.com/1320059/la-marseillaise-frances-national-anthem-is-causing-tension-once-again/.

Andrews, George Reid. 2004. *Afro-Latin America, 1800–2000*. Oxford: Oxford University Press.

Ang, Ien. 1982. *Het Geval Dallas*. Amsterdam: Uitgeverij SUA.

Anguelovski, Isabelle, and Joan Martínez Alier. 2014. "The 'Environmentalism of the Poor Revisited': Territory and Place in Disconnected Global Struggles." *Ecological Economics* 102, no. C: 167–176.

Aponte, David, Diana Carolina Pinzón Paz, Diego Rodríguez, and Andrés R. Vargas. 2009. *Las barras de fútbol en Colombia: Balance de Producción académica y algunas reflexiones sobre su cubrimiento periodístico, programas y normatividad (2000–2008)*. American Friends Service Committee/Centro de Recursos para el Análisis de Conflictos. http://www.cerac.org.co/assets/pdf/Other%20publications/Estado_del_Arte_BarrasDeFutbol.pdf.

Arango Arias, Ana Lucía, and Carlos Andrés Hurtado Díaz. 2012. "Especificaciones sobre la explotación sexual comercial de niños, niñas y adolescentes (ESCNNA), el turismo sexual y sus relaciones con el discurso capitalista." *Textos y Sentidos* 6: 79–101.

Aranguren Romero, Juan Pablo. 2017. *Managing Testimony and Administrating Victims: Colombia's Transitional Scenario Under the Peace and Justice Act*. Translated by Laura Pérez. New York: Palgrave Macmillan.

Arcieri, Vicente. 2014. "'Estaba indignado por el irrespeto a los héroes de Cartagena y por eso le di con una mona'": Ingeniero Rendón." *El Heraldo*, November 5, 2014. https://www.elheraldo.co/bolivar/ingeniero-partio-la-polemica-placa-en-cartagena-en-homenaje-los-ingleses-caidos-172770.

Arendt, Hannah. 1970. *On Violence*. New York: Houghton Mifflin Harcourt.

Arias, Oscar, Enrique Uribe, and Toby Miller. 2018. "Colombia y el dilema clásico del apoyo cinematográfico." *Revista Internacional de Comunicación y Desarrollo* 2, no. 9: 115–128.

Armstrong, Gary. 1998. *Football Hooligans: Knowing the Score*. Oxford: Berg.

Armstrong, Gary, and Malcolm Young. 1997. "Legislators and Interpreters: The Law and 'Football Hooligans.'" In *Entering the Field: New Perspectives on World Football*, edited by Gary Armstrong and Richard Giulianotti, 175–191. Oxford: Berg.

Arnold, Matthew. 1875. *Essays in Criticism*, 3rd ed. London: Macmillan.

———. 2003. *Culture and Anarchy*. Project Gutenberg. http://www.gutenberg.org/dirs/etext03/7cltn10.txt.

Aronczyk, Melissa. 2013. *Branding the Nation: The Global Business of National Identity*. New York: Oxford University Press.

Artemas, Katie, Tim P. Vos, and Margaret Duffy. 2018. "Journalism Hits a Wall." *Journalism Studies* 19, no. 7: 1004–1120.

Asher, Kiran, and Diana Ojeda. 2009. "Producing Nature and Making the State: Ordenamiento Territorial in the Pacific Lowlands of Colombia." *Geoforum* 40, no. 3: 292–302.

Atehortúa Cruz, Adolfo León, and Diana Marcela Rojas Rivera. 2008. "El nacrotráfico en Colombia. Pioneros y capos." *Revista Historia y Espacio* 31. http://historiayespacio.univalle.edu.co/index.php/historiayespacio/article/view/2743.

Atkinson, Lucy. 2013. "Smart Shoppers? Using QR Codes and 'Green' Smartphone Apps to Mobilize Sustainable Consumption in the Retail Environment." *International Journal of Consumer Studies* 37, no. 4: 387–393.

Attali, Jacques. 2001. *Bruits: Essais sur l'économie politique de la musique*, 2nd ed. Paris: Librairie Arthème Fayard/Presses Universitaires de France.

Avelar, Idelber. 2004. *The Letter of Violence: Essays on Narrative, Ethics, and Politics*. New York: Palgrave Macmillan.

Ávila, Ariel. 2019. "El tráfico de armas en Colombia." *El País*, July 9, 2019. https://elpais.com/internacional/2019/07/09/colombia/1562689881_492148.html.

Ayer, A. J. 1956. "The Vienna Circle." In A. J. Ayer, G. A. Paul, D. F. Pears, P. F. Strawson, G. J. Warnock, R. A. Wollheim, and Gilbert Ryle. *The Revolution in Philosophy*, 70–87. London: Macmillan.

Babbage, Charles. 1832. *On the Economy of Machinery and Manufactures*. http://www.gutenberg.org/ebooks/4238.

Bacon, Francis. 1620. *The Great Instauration*. http://www.constitution.org/bacon/instauration.ht.

Badiou, Alain. 2007. *The Century*. Translated by Alberto Toscano. Cambridge: Polity Press.

Bærug, Jan Richard, and Halliki Harro-Loit. 2012. "Journalism Embracing Advertising as Traditional Journalism Discourse Becomes Marginal." *Journalism Practice* 6, no. 2: 172–186.

Bang, Brandy, Paige L. Baker, Alexis Carpinteri, and Vincent B. Van Hasselt. 2014. *Commercial Sexual Exploitation of Children*. New York: Springer.

Banks, Miranda. 2015. *The Writers: A History of American Screenwriters and Their Guild*. New Brunswick, NJ: Rutgers University Press.

Barajas, Héctor. 2016. "Peace Journalism—a Panacea for Post-Conflict Colombia?" *Panorama* 10, no. 18: 121–135.

Baral Stefan, Chris Beyrer, Kathryn Muessig, Tonia Potect, Andrea L. Wirtz, Michaele R. Decker, Susan G. Sherman, and Deanna Kerrigan. 2012. "Burden of HIV among Female Sex Workers in Low-Income and Middle-Income Countries: A Systematic Review and Meta-Analysis." *Lancet Infectious Diseases* 12, no. 7: 538–549.

Barranquero Carretero, Alejandro, Carlos Arcila Calderón, and Jesús Arroyave Cabrera. 2017. *Manual de teoría de la comunicación: II. Pensamientos Latinoamericanos*. Barranquilla: Editorial Universidad del Norte; Bogotá: Ediciones de la U.

Barreneche, Raul. 2016. "*AD*'s Guide to Cartagena, Colombia." *Architectural Digest*, March 16, 2016. https://www.architecturaldigest.com/story/travel-guide-cartagena-colombia.

Barreras, Luis, Miguel Menza Padilla, and Paula Pedelaborde. 2016. "La Narcotelenovela: ¿irrupción de un nuevo género?" *Actas de Periodismo y Comunicación* 2, no. 1. http://sedici.unlp.edu.ar/handle/10915/71043.

Barrios, Marta Milena. 2013. "Las cartas a los editores de lta prensa en Colombia: Escenario de solidaridad y acción ciudadana." PhD diss., Universidad del Norte.

———. 2017. "Colombian Cries: Internal Armed Conflict and Emotions in Letters to the Editor." *Journalism* 18, no. 2: 159–75.

Barrios, Marta Milena, Lina María Vega Estarita, and Luis M. Gil. 2019. "When Online Commentary Turns into Violence: The Role of Twitter in Slander against Journalists in Colombia." *conflict & communication online* 18, no. 1. http://www.cco.regener-online.de/2019_1/pdf/barrios-et-al2019.pdf.

Barrios Paz, Wilfran. 2016. Interview with Anamaria Tamayo-Duque and Toby Miller, December 2016.

Barthes, Roland. 1994. *Roland Barthes*. Translated by Richard Howard. Berkeley: University of California Press.

Bassols, Narcís. 2019. "Evolving Iconization and Destination Building: The Example of Cartagena, Colombia." *Tourism Planning & Development* 16, no. 3: 334–352.

Baudrillard, Jean. 1988. *Selected Writings*. Edited by Mark Poster. Stanford: Stanford University Press.

———. 1994. *The Illusion of the End*. Translated by Chris Turner. Oxford: Polity Press.

Baudrillard, Jean, and Edgar Morin. 2004. *La violencia del mundo*. Translated by Charles Roche. Barcelona: Paidós.

"Bavaria y Colfútbol extendieron su vinculación." 2015. *El Espectador*, January 13, 2015. http://www.elespectador.com/deportes/futbolcolombiano/bavaria-y-colfutbol-extendieron-su-vinculacion-articulo-537610; https://www.youtube.com/watch?v=xcns89HFr6A.

Bechmann Pedersen, Sune. 2017. "Peace through Tourism: A Brief History of a Popular Catchphrase." In *Cultural Borders and European Integration*, edited by Mats Andrén, 29–37. Göteborg: Centrum för Europafroskning vid Göteborgs universitet.

Beck, Ulrich. 1999. *World Risk Society*. Cambridge: Polity Press.

———. 2002. "The Cosmopolitan Society and Its Enemies." *Theory Culture & Society* 19, nos. 1–2: 17–44.

Bedoya, Nicolas. 2014. "Cartagena Beauty Queen Arrested in Child Sex Tourism Ring Bust." *Colombia Reports*, October 14, 2014. https://colombiareports.com/beauty-queen-among-five-arrested-cartagena-child-sex-tourism-ring-bust/.

Beljuli Brown, Lisa. 2011. *Body Parts on Planet Slum: Women and Telenovelas in Brazil*. London: Anthem.

Bello, Andrés. 1997. *Selected Writings of Andrés Bello*. Translated by Frances M. López-Morillas. Edited by Iván Jaksi. New York: Oxford University Press.

Bello-Urrego, Alejandra del Rocío. 2013. "Sexo/género, violencias y derechos humanos: Perspectivas conceptuales para el abordaje de la violencia basada en género contra las mujeres desde el sector salud." *Revista Colombiana de Psiquiatría* 42, no. 1: 108–119.

Beltrán, Luis Ramiro, and Elizabeth Fox de Cardona. 1980. *Communicacíon dominada: Estados Unidos en los medios de América Latina*. Mexico City: Instituto Latinoamericano de Estudios Transnacionales/Editorial Nueva Imagen.

Beltrán, William Mauricio. 2012. "Descripción cuantitativa de la pluralización religiosa en Colombia." *Universitas Humanística* 73: 201–237.

Beltrán Villegas, Miguel Angel. 2018. *La vorágine del conflicto colombiano: Una mirada desde las cárceles*. Buenos Aires: Consejo Latinoamericano de Ciencias Sociales/Instituto de Estudios y Capitación.

Benamou, Catherine L. 2009. "Televisual Melodrama in an Era of Transnational Migration: Exporting the Folkloric Nation, Harvesting the Melancholic-Sublime." In *Passion, Pathos and Entertainment: Latin American Melodrama,* edited by Darlene J. Sadlier, 139–171. Chicago: University of Illinois Press.

Benhabib, Seyla. 2002. *The Claims of Culture: Equality and Diversity in the Global Era.* Princeton: Princeton University Press.

Benjamin, Walter. 2016. *One-Way Street.* Translated by Edmund Jephcott. Edited by Michael W. Jennings. Cambridge, MA.: Belknap Press of Harvard University Press.

Bennett, Barbara. 2016. "Dividing Women: The Framing of Trafficking for Sexual Exploitation in Magazines." *Feminist Media Studies* 16, no. 2: 205–222.

Bentham, Jeremy. 1970. *The Principles of Morals and Legislation.* Darien: Hafner.

———. 2012. *The Collected Works of Jeremy Bentham: On the Liberty of the Press, and Public Discussion, and Other Legal and Political Writings for Spain and Portugal.* Edited by Philip Schofield and Catherine Pease-Watkin. Oxford: Oxford University Press.

Benton, Ted, ed. 1996. *The Greening of Marxism.* New York: Guilford.

Bergman, Marcelo. 2018. *Illegal Drugs, Drug Trafficking and Violence in Latin America.* New York: Springer.

Bergquist, Charles. 1991. "Introduction: Colombian Violence in Historical Perspective." In *Violence in Colombia: The Contemporary Crisis in Historical Perspective,* edited by Charles Bergquist, Ricardo Peñaranda, and Gonzalo Sánchez, 1–8. Wilmington: Scholarly Resources.

Bernal-Camargo, Diana Rocío, Antonio Varón-Mejía, Adriana Becerra-Barbosa, Kelly Chaib-De Mares, Enrique Seco-Martín, and Lorena Archila-Delgado. 2013. "Explotación sexual de niños, niñas y adolescentes: Modelo de intervención." *Revista Latinoamericana de Ciencias Sociales, Niñez y Juventud* 11, no. 2: 617–632.

Bernhardt, Paul C., James M. Dabbs Jr., Julie A. Fielden, and Candice D. Lutter. 1998. "Testosterone Changes during Vicarious Experiences of Winning and Losing among Fans at Sporting Events." *Phsyiology & Behavior* 65, no. 1: 59–62.

Bernstein, Basil. 2003. *Class, Codes and Control. Volume II. Applied Studies Towards a Sociology of Language.* London: Routledge.

Bértola, Luis, and José Antonio Ocampo. 2012. *The Economic Development of Latin America since Independence.* Oxford: Oxford University Press.

Betancourt, Íngrid. 2010. *Even Silence Has an End: My Six Years of Captivity in the Colombian Jungle.* New York: Penguin.

Bialowas Pobutsky, Aldona. 2013. "Peddling Pablo: Escobar's Cultural Renaissance." *Hispania* 96, no. 4: 684–699.

Bidwai, Praful. 2005. "Prevent, Prepare & Protect." Rediff, January 4, 2005. http://in.rediff.com/news/2005/jan/04bidwai.htm.

Birenbaum Quintero, Michael. 2018. "Exchange, Materiality and Aesthetics in Colombian *Champeta.*" *Ethnomuiscology Forum* 27, no. 1: 3–24.

Blanquer, Jean-Michel, and Christian Gros. 1996. *La Colombia à l'aube du troisième millénaire.* Paris: Éditions de l'IHEAL.

Boateng, Boatema. 2011. *The Copyright Thing Doesn't Work Here: Adinkra and Kente Cloth and Intellectual Property in Ghana.* Minneapolis: University of Minnesota Press.

Böhm, Robert, Hannes Rusch, and Özgür Gürerk. 2015. "What Makes People Go to War? Defensive Intentions Motivate Retaliatory and Preemptive Intergroup Aggression." *Evolution and Human Behavior* 37, no. 1: 29–34.

Bolívar, Simón. 2003. *El Libertador: Writings of Simón Bolívar.* Translated by Frederick H. Fornoff. Edited by David Bushnell. Oxford: Oxford University Press.

Bolívar-Anillo, Hernando José, Hernando Sánchez Moreno, Ronield Fernandez, and Giorgio Anfuso. 2019. "An Overview on Mangrove Forests Distribution in Colombia: An Ecosystem at Risk." *Journal of Aquatic Science and Marine Biology* 2, no. 1: 16–18.

Bolívar Ramírez, Ingrid Johanna. 2007. "Reinados de belleza y nacionalización de las sociedades latinoamericanas." *Iconos: Revista de Ciencias Sociales* 28: 71–80.

———. 2018. "Antioquia's Regional Narratives and the Challenges of Professional Football in Medellín During the 1950s and 1960s." *Bulletin of Latin American Research* 37, no. 5: 582–597.

Bond, Patrick. 2010. "What South Africa Really Lost at the World Cup." Transnational Institute, June 2010. https://www.tni.org/es/node/12529.

Boot, Max, and Richard Bennet. 2009. "The Colombian Miracle." *Weekly Standard*, December 14, 2009. https://www.weeklystandard.com/max-boot-and-richard-bennet/the-colombian-miracle.

Bourdieu, Pierre. 1978. "Sport and Social Class." *Social Science Information* 17, no. 6: 819–840.

———. 1984. *Distinction: A Social Critique of the Judgement of Taste*. Translated by Richard Nice. Cambridge, MA: Harvard University Press.

Boyer, Marc. 2002. "El turismo en Europa, de la edad moderna al siglo XX." Translated by Carlos Larrinaga Rodríguez. *Historia Contemporánea* 25: 13–31.

Brands, Hal. 2010. *Latin America's Cold War*. Cambridge, MA: Harvard University Press.

Braudel, Fernand. 1984. *Civilization and Capitalism: 15th–18th Century. Volume III: The Perspective of the World*. Translated by Siân Reynolds. London: Collins.

Braun, Herbert. 1994. *Our Guerrillas, Our Sidewalks: A Journey into the Violence of Colombia*. Boulder: University Press of Colorado.

Brecht, Bertolt. 1964. "Emphasis on Sport." In *Brecht on Theatre*, edited by John Willett, 6–9. London: Macmillan.

———. 2000. *Brecht on Film and Radio*. Translated and edited by Marc Silberman. London: Bloomsbury.

Brennan, Denise. 2004. *What's Love Got to Do With it? Transnational Desires and Sex Tourism in the Dominican Republic*. Durham: Duke University Press.

Brida, Juan Gabriel, Isabel Cortes-Jimenez, and Manuela Pulina. 2016. "Has the Tourism-Led Growth Hypothesis Been Validated? A Literature Review." *Current Issues in Tourism* 19, no. 5: 394–430.

Brida, Juan Gabriel, Nicolás Garrido, and María Jesús Such Devesa. 2012. "Cruise Passengers' Satisfaction: Cartagena de Indias." *Benchmarking: An International Journal* 19, no. 1: 52–69.

Brida, Juan Gabriel, Eugenia Riaño, and Sandra Zapata-Aguirre. 2011. "Residents' Attitudes and Perceptions towards Cruise Tourism Development: A Case Study of Cartagena de Indias." *Tourism and Hospitality Research* 11, no. 3: 181–196.

Briggs, Asa, and Peter Burke. 2003. *A Social History of the Media: From Gutenberg to the Internet*. Cambridge: Polity Press.

Britto, Lina. 2016. "Car Bombing Drug War History." *NACLA Report on the Americas* 48, no. 2: 177–180.

Brodzinsky, Sibylla. 2010. "Colombian Football Seeks to Escape Grip of Drug Cartels." *Guardian*, December 28, 2010. https://www.theguardian.com/world/2010/dec/28/colombia-football-drug-cartels.

Brown, Mary Ellen, ed. 1990. *Television and Women's Culture: The Politics of the Popular*. Sydney, NSW: Currency Press.

Browning, Christopher S., and Antonio Ferraz de Oliviera. 2017. "Introduction: Nation Branding and Competitive Identity in World Politics." *Geopolitics* 22, no. 3: 481–501.

Buharin, N. [*sic*] and E. Preobrazhensky. 1922. *The ABC of Communism: A Popular Explanation of the Program of the Communist Party of Russia.* Translated by Eden and Cedar Paul. N. p.: Communist Party of Great Britain.

Buitrago Restrepo, Felipe, and Iván Duque Márquez. 2013. *La economía naranja: Una oportunidad infinita.* Washington, DC: Banco Interamericano de Desarrollo (Inter-American Development Bank).

Bulmer-Thomas, Victor. 2003. *The Economic History of Latin America Since Independence,* 2nd ed. Cambridge: Cambridge University Press.

Burke, Edmund. 1986. *Reflections on the Revolution in France and on the Proceedings in Certain Societies in London Relative to that Event.* Edited by Conor Cruise O'Brien. Harmondsworth: Penguin.

Burke, Peter. 1997. *Varieties of Cultural History*. Ithaca: Cornell University Press.

———. 2004. *Languages and Communities in Early Modern Europe: The 2002 Wiles Lectures Given at Queen's University, Belfast.* Cambridge: Cambridge University Press.

Büscher, Bram, and Robert Fletcher. 2017. "Destructive Creation: Capital Accumulation and the Structural Violence of Tourism." *Journal of Sustainable Tourism* 25, no. 5: 651–667.

Bush, Vannevar. 1945. "As We May Think." *Atlantic Monthly*, July, 101–108.

Butler, Meg. 2018. "The Caribbean Destination That Looks Like a Disney Movie." *Fodor's Travel,* October 5, 2018. https://www.fodors.com/world/south-america/colombia/the-caribbean-coast/experiences/news/the-caribbean-destination-that-looks-like-a-disney-movie.

Butt, Nathalie, Frances Lambrick, Mary Menton, and Anna Renwick. 2019. "The Supply Chain of Violence." *Nature Sustainability* 2: 742–747.

Caballero Fula, Henry. 2016. "Intercultural Indigenous Communication of the Indigenous Communities of Cauca in the Context of the Armed Conflict." In *Journalism in Conflict and Post-Conflict Conditions: Worldwide Perspectives,* edited by Kristin Skare Orgeret and William Tayeebwa, 129–146. Göteborg: NORDICOM.

Cabañas, Miguel. 2012. "*Narcotelenovelas,* Gender, and Globalization in *Sin tetas no hay paraíso.*" *Latin American Perspectives* 39, no. 3: 74–87.

Cabezas, Amalia L. 2009. *Economies of Desire: Sex and Tourism in Cuba and the Dominican Republic.* Philadelphia: Temple University Press.

———. 2019. "Latin American and Caribbean Sex Workers: Gains and Challenges in the Movement." *Anti-Trafficking Review* 12: 37–56.

Cabezas Cortés, Carmen Cecilia. 2016. "Consideraciones alrededor de regímenes de discriminación género/etnia sobre relaciones laborales en Colombia." In *Retos de las relaciones de trabajo y de la seguridad social en el Siglo XXI,* edited by Luis Alberto Montenegro Mora, 71–81. San Juan de Pasto, Nariño, Colombia: Editorial UNIMAR.

Cable, Vincent. 1969. "The 'Football War' and the Central American Common Market." *International Affairs* 45, no. 4: 658–671.

Cabo, Leila. 2018. "From Yatra to Fonseca: The Making of Colombia's Musical 'Land of Sabrisura' Tourism Campaign." *Billboard,* June 8, 2018. https://www.billboard.com/articles/columns/latin/8468809/colombias-musical-tourism-campaign.

Cabral, Amilcar. 1979. *Unity and Struggle: Speeches and Writings: Texts Selected by the PAIGC* [Partido Africano da Independência da Guiné e Cabo Verde]. Translated by Michael Wolfers. New York: Monthly Review Press.

Calderón, María Alejandra. 2015. "El río grande de la Magdalena y el cine." Radio Nacional de Colombia, July 5, 2015. http://www.radionacional.co/noticia/el-rio-grande-de-la-magdalena-y-el-cine.

Calvino Ospina, Hernando. 2008. *Colombia, laboratorio de embrujos: Democracia y terrorismo de estado*. Madrid: Foca.

Camacho Ordoñez, Leidy Bibiana, and María Angélica Trujillo González. 2009. "La explotación sexual comercial infantil: Una ganancia subjetiva." *Revista Latinoamericana de Ciencias Sociales, Niñez y Juventud* 7, no. 2: 1009–1025.

"Cambiar el texto de la placa sería una ofensa a los ingleses." 2014. *El Universal*, November 4, 2014. http://www.eluniversal.com.co/cartagena/cambiar-el-texto-de-la-placa-seria-una-agresion-los-ingleses-sabas-pretelt-175903.

Camus, Albert. 1961. *Resistance, Rebellion, and Death*. Translated by Justin O'Brien. New York: Alfred A. Knopf.

Cañizares, Rubén. 2018. "25 años de la muerte de Pablo Escobar narco fútbol." ABC, February 12, 2018. https://www.abc.es/deportes/futbol/abci-25-anos-muerte-pablo-escobar-patron-narco-futbol-201812020206_noticia.html.

Carbonell, Carlos. 2006. "Narrativa etnográfica y análisis sociocultural de las relaciones entre turismo y sexualidad en Cartagena de Indias." *Turismo y Sociedad* 7: 65–74.

Cardoso, Fernando Henrique. 2009. "New Paths: Globalization in Historical Perspective." *Studies in Comparative International Development* 44, no. 4: 296–317.

Carey, Sabine C., Michael P. Colaresi, and Neil J. Mitchell. 2015. "Governments, Informal Links to Militias, and Accountability." *Journal of Conflict Resolution* 59, no. 5: 850–876.

Carranza-Franco, Francy. 2019. *Demobilisation and Reintegration in Colombia: Building State and Citizenship*. London: Routledge.

Carrillo Romero, Harold, Georgina Cabarcas Cañate, Adineth Vargas Hernández, and Yusleinis Puello Pájaro. 2013. "El desarrollo de la actividad turística en Cartagena de Indias: Implicaciones sociales y urbanas: 1943–1978." *Palobra* 13: 190–210.

Cartagena Cómo Vamos. 2017. *Cartagena Cómo Vamos: Informe Calidad de Vida 2016*. July 2017. http://www.cartagenacomovamos.org/nuevo/wp-content/uploads/2017/07/Presentaci%C3%B3n-para-WEB-ICV-2016.pdf.

"Cartagena de Indias: A Location for Love." 2012. *Hullo!*, February 13, 2012. https://www.hellomagazine.com/travel/201202137184/cartagena-de-indias-colombia/.

"¿Cartagena es Pasión?" 2012. *Revista Semana*, October 13, 2012. http://www.semana.com/nacion/articulo/cartagena-pasion/257186-3.

Carter, Jamie. 2019. "The Best Cities for Instagram Photos, Selfies, Sexy Poses—New York, London, Jakarta Score, Hong Kong Surprises." *South China Morning Post*, May 8, 2019. https://www.scmp.com/lifestyle/travel-leisure/article/3009306/best-cities-instagram-photos-selfies-sexy-poses-new-york.

Cary, Bill. 2019. "Cartagena's 'Old City' Undergoing a Vibrant Rebirth." Mansion Global. https://www.mansionglobal.com/articles/cartagena-s-old-city-undergoing-a-vibrant-rebirth-106173.

Caselli, Irene. 2016. "Soap Operas Get Whitewashed." *Index on Censorship* 45, no. 2: 74–77.

Cassidy, William P. 2005. "Variations on a Theme: Professional Role Conceptions of Print and Online Newspaper Journalists." *Journalism & Mass Communication Quarterly* 82, no. 2: 264–280.

Castells, Manuel. 2010. *The Information Age: Economy, Society, and Culture. Volume III: End of Millennium*, 2nd ed. Malden: Wiley-Blackwell.

———. 2012. *Redes de indignación y esperanza: Los movimientos sociales en la era de internet*. Madrid: Alianza Editorial.

Castillo, Fabio. 1987. *Los jinetes de la cocaina*. Bogotá: Documentos Periodísticos.

Castillo, Juan Sebastián, Alejandra Zuluaga, and Juan José Serrano Rojas. 2016. "Fútbol y racismo: Estudio exploratorio en la hinchada del América de Cali." *Trans-Pasando Fronteras* 10: 57–66.

Castillo Murillejo, Norma Constanza, and Nelson Enrique Rivera Reyes. 2013. "TICS, comunicación humana y violencia de género contra niños y adolescents víctimas de la explotación sexual comercial: Los casos de Bogotá y Cartagena, Colombia." *Actas–V Congreso Internacional Latina de Comunicación Social—V CILCS*. 2013. http://www.revistalatinacs.org/13SLCS/2013_actas/171_Castillo.pdf.

Castoriadis, Cornelius. 2010. *A Society Adrift: Interviews and Debates 1974-1997*. Translated by Helen Arnold, edited by Enrique Escobar, Myrto Gondicas, and Pascal Vernay. New York: Fordham University Press.

Castro, Nazaret. 2013. "Grandeza y miserias del río Magdalena. El desembarco de las multinacionales españolas en Colombia." Observatorio de Multinacionales en América Latina, December 5, 2013. http://omal.info/spip.php?article6118.

Castro-Gómez, Santiago, and Eduardo Restrepo. 2008. "Introducción: Colombianidad, población y diferencia." In *Genealogías de Colombianidad: Formaciones discursivas y tecnologías de gobierno en los siglos XIX y XX*, edited by Santiago Castro-Gómez and Eduardo Restrepo, 10–40. Bogotá: Editorial Pontificia Universidad Javeriana.

Castro Lozano, John Alexander. 2013. "El *carnaval* y el *combate* hacen el *aguante* en una barra brava." *Revista Colombiana de Sociología* 36, no. 1: 77–92.

———. 2019. "De las rivalidades a la violencia del fútbol en Colombia." *Revista Brasileira de Ciências do Esporte* 41, no. 1: 109–115.

Catton, William R., Jr., and Riley E. Dunlap. 1978. "Environmental Sociology: A New Paradigm." *American Sociologist* 13, no. 1: 41–49.

Caycedo, Carolina, and Entre Aguas La Jagua. 2015. "'We Need the River to Be Free'": Activists Fight the Privatization of Colombia's Longest River." Creative Time Reports, March 17, 2015. http://creativetimereports.org/2015/03/17/activists-fight-privatization-colombias-magdalena-river/.

Celis González, Leila Iliana. 2018. *Luchas campesinas Colombia (1970–2016): Resistencias y sueños*. Montréal: RéQUEF; Bogotá: Ediciones desde abajo.

Celis Hernández, Marlon Steve. 2017. "Nación, fútbol e imagen publicitaria: Los significados de la Copa América del 2001 en Colombia." *Revista de Ciencias Sociales* 158: 61–83.

Centro Nacional de Consultoría. 2014. *El poder del fútbol*. Bogotá: Ministerio del Interior.

Centro Nacional de Memoria Histórica. 2018a. *Todo pasó frente a nuestros ojos: El genocidio de la Unión Patriótica 1984–2002*. http://www.centrodememoriahistorica.gov.co/informes/publicaciones-por-ano/2018/todo-paso-frente-a-nuestros-ojos-genocidio-de-la-union-patriotica-1984–2002.

Centro Nacional de Memoria Histórica. 2018b. *Paramilitarismo: Balance de contribución del CNMH al esclarecimiento histórico*. http://www.centrodememoriahistorica.gov.co/informes/publicaciones-por-ano/2018/paramilitarismo-balance-de-la-contribucion-del-cnmh-al-esclarecimiento-historico.

Cepeda, María Elena. 2018. "Putting a "Good Face on the Nation": Beauty, Memes, and the Gendered Rebranding of Global *Colombianidad*." *WSQ: Women's Studies Quarterly* 46, nos. 1–2: 121–138.

Cepeda Jiménez, José Alejandro, Camilo Andrés Montoya Pardo, and Magda Catalina Jiménez Jiménez. 2011. "Entre la formación de la opinión pública y la movilización: El proceso independentista de Cartagena de Indias." *Panorama*: 11–19.

Chakrabarty, Dipesh. 2014. "Climate and Capital: On Conjoined Histories." *Critical Inquiry* 41, no. 1: 1–23.

Chandler, Raymond. 1949. *The Little Sister*. New York: Houghton Mifflin.

Chaparro, María Paula, and Mimi Yagoub. 2018. "Attacks on Multinationals in Colombia: Signs of New Criminal Era." InSight Crime, October 3, 2018. https://www.insightcrime

.org/news/analysis/attacks-multinational-companies-colombia-signs-new-criminal-era/.

Chaparro Valderrama, Hugo. 2007. "Once Upon a Time: A Short Story on Violence." In *The Flight of the Condor: Stories of Violence and War from Colombia*, translated and compiled by Jennifer Gabrielle Edwards, xiii–xxiii. Madison: University of Wisconsin Press.

Charles, Mathew. 2018. "Child Sex Trafficking Rife in Colombia's Picturesque Cartagena." *Guardian*, December 23, 2018. https://www.theguardian.com/global-development/2018/dec/23/child-sex-trafficking-rife-colombia-cartagena.

Children's Climate Rallies Gain Momentum in Europe." 2019. *BBC News*, January 25, 2019. https://www.bbc.co.uk/news/world-europe-46999381.

Chin, Christine B. N. 2013. *Cosmopolitan Sex Workers: Women and Migration in a Global City*. New York: Oxford University Press.

Chua-Eoan, Howard. 1994. "The Case of the Fatal Goal." *Time*, July 11, 1994. http://content.time.com/time/magazine/article/0,9171,981082,00.html.

"Citan a Alcaldía de Cartagena para responder por polémica placa." 2014. *El Tiempo*, November 4, 2014. http://www.eltiempo.com/archivo/documento/CMS-14787676.

Clarke, Natalie. 2007. "The Night Camilla Lost Her Virginity—and Changed the History of the Royals." *Daily Mail*, June 3, 2007. http://www.dailymail.co.uk/femail/article-459315/The-night-Camilla-lost-virginity—changed-history-royals.html.

Clarkson, Jeremy. 2019. "Cheat, Love Bray—Let Me Put My Ass on the Line and Tell You That the Donkey Sex Scene Was Real." *Sunday Times*, February 3, 2019. https://www.thetimes.co.uk/edition/news-review/jeremy-clarkson-cheat-love-bray-let-me-put-my-ass-on-the-line-and-tell-you-that-the-donkey-sex-scene-was-real-2zrpzczzo.

Clausen, Helene Balslev, and Mario Alberto Velázquez García. 2017. "Collaborative Economy in Tourism in Latin America: The Case of Argentina, Colombia, Chile and Mexico." In *Collaborative Economy and Tourism: Perspectives, Politics, Policies and Prospects*, edited by Dianne Dredge and Szilvia S. Gyimóthy, 271–284. New York: Springer.

Clavijo Poveda, Jairo. 2004. "Estudio de barras de fútbol de Bogotá: Los Comandos azules." *Universidad Humanística* 31, no. 58: 43–59.

CO. 2017. *ColombiaTravel*. http://www.colombia.travel/es/ferias-y-fiestas/independencia-de-cartagena-y-reinado-nacional-de-belleza (site discontinued).

Colla, Elliott. 2012. "Roundtable on Language of Revolution: The Revolution Continues (Present Continuous) (Colla)." *Jadaliyya*, August 12, 2012. http://arabic.jadaliyya.com/pages/index/6829/roundtable-on-language-of-revolution_the-revolutio.

Colmenares, Germán. 1996. "La formación de la economía colonial (1500–1740)." In *Historia económica de Colombia*, edited by José Antonio Campo, 2–22. Bogotá: Tercer Mundo Editores.

"Colocados $400 mil millones en primera subasta de bonos naranja." 2018. *El Tiempo*, November 29, 2018. https://www.eltiempo.com/politica/gobierno/primera-subasta-de-bonos-naranja-299580.

"Colombia Anti-Government Protestors Clash with Police." 2019. *Deutsche Welle*, November 22, 2019. https://www.dw.com/en/colombia-anti-government-protesters-clash-with-police/a-51360862.

"Colombia cierra 2019 con más de 10 mil homicidios y 230 líderes de DDHH asesinados." 2019. *Nodal*, December 30, 2019. https://www.nodal.am/2019/12/colombia-cierra-2019-con-mas-de-10-mil-homicidios-y-230-lideres-de-ddhh-asesinados/?fbclid=IwAR2l3shgcFuGCRFw8n9nAU4v60W_RBy277a7Bw6JNY0_K8fB95AefBLrNNM.

"Colombian Player Survives Shooting Attack after Match." 2018. Reuters, November 12, 2018. https://uk.reuters.com/article/uk-soccer-colombia/colombian-player-survives-shooting-attack-after-match-idUKKCN1NH2KY.

"Colombia pide explicaciones a Holanda y a Unicef por meme ofensivo." 2014. *El Espectador,* June 19, 2014. http://www.elespectador.com/noticias/nacional/colombia-pide-explicaciones-holanda-y-unicef-meme-ofens-articulo-499327.

"Colombia's Santos 'in Serious Difficulty' if FARC Deal Fails." 2015. *BBC News,* November 18, 2015. http://www.bbc.com/news/world-latin-america-34864194.

"Colombia—Travel and Tourism." 2019. *export.gov,* October 16. https://www.export.gov/article?id=Colombia-Travel-and-Tourism.

Comisión Histórica del Conflicto y sus Víctimas. 2015. *Contribución el entendimiento del conflicto armado en Colombia.* https://web.archive.org/web/20160121194351/https://www.mesadeconversaciones.com.co/sites/default/files/Informe%20Comisi_n%20Hist_rica%20del%20Conflicto%20y%20sus%20V_ctimas.%20La%20Habana%2C%20Febrero%20de%202015.pdf.

Comisión Nacional de Seguridad, Comodidad y Convivencia en el Fútbol. 2014. *Plan Decenal de Seguridad, Comodidad y Convivencia en el Fútbol 2014–2024.* https://www.mininterior.gov.co/el-poder-del-futbol-la-gran-encuesta.

Committee on the Elimination of All Forms of Discrimination against Women. 2017. *Ninth Periodic Report of Colombia Under Article 18 of the Convention, Due in 2017.* CEDAW/C/COL/9.

Comunidades con Paz. 2014. "Carta abierta a James Rodríguez: Construyamos más esperanza, sumemos voluntades." Comunidades con Paz, July 1, 2014. https://comunidadesconpaz.wordpress.com/2014/07/01/carta-abierta-a-james-rodriguez-construyamos-mas-esperanza-sumemos-voluntades/.

Conan Doyle, Arthur. 1960. *The Complete Sherlock Holmes.* Harmondsworth: Penguin Books.

Concept Media S. A., n.d. *Las Mil y Una Noches: Cuales son las claves de este éxito y cómo son sus televidentes.* http://www.conceptmedia.com.ar/notas mail/las mil y una noches.html.

"Con fútbol se preparan las FARC para la paz." 2016. *Fútbol Rebelde,* (blog) June 27, 2016. http://futbolrebelde.blogspot.com.co/2016/06/con-futbol-se-preparan-las-farc-para-la.html.

Conley, Verena Andermatt. 1997. *Ecopolitics: The Environment in Poststructuralist Thought.* London: Routledge.

Connell, R. W. 2003. *Masculinidades.* Mexico City: Programa Universitario de Estudios in Género, Universidad Nacional Autónoma de México.

———. 2005. *Masculinities,* 2nd ed. Berkeley: University of California Press.

Conor, Bridget. 2014. *Screenwriting: Creative Labour and Professional Practice.* London: Routledge.

"Consejo Nacional de Economía Naranja anuncia inversiones para el emprendimiento nacional." 2019. *Ministerio de Tecnologías de la Información y las Comunicaciones de Colombia,* March 8, 2019. https://www.mintic.gov.co/portal/604/w3-article-82648.html?_noredirect=1.

Cook, Philip, and Conrad Heilmann. 2013. "Two Types of Self-Censorship: Public and Private." *Political Studies* 61, no. 1: 178–196.

Cooley, Laurence, and Jasmin Mujanović. 2015. "Changing the Rules of the Game: Comparing FIFA/UEFA and EU Attempts to Promote Reform of Power-Sharing Institutions in Bosnia-Herzegovina." *Global Society* 29, no. 1: 42–63.

"Copa América: ¿Por qué Caracol TV le gana la batalla a RCN?" 2016. *Semana,* June 10, 2016. http://www.semana.com/tecnologia/articulo/copa-america-caracol-television-gana-a-rcn-por-raiting/477164. "Dos primeras jornadas de Copa América transcurren sin incidentes pese a temor a violencia." 2001. *La Nación,* July 13, 2001. http://www.nacion.com/deportes/Copa-America-transcurren-incidentes-violencia_0_476952357.html.

Coronell, Daniel. 2014. "Placa que debe avergonzar a Cartagena. Por la lagartería de unos cuantos terminamos homenajeando a un verdugo." Twitter, November 2, 2014. https://

twitter.com/search?q=Placa%20que%20debe%20avergonzar%20a%20Cartagena.%20Por%20la%20lagarteri%CC%81a%20de%20unos%20cuantos%20terminamos%20homenajeando%20a%20un%20verdugo&src=typd.

Cote, Jorge. 2019. "Las promesas incumplidas a los indígenas y afrocolombianos." *Semana*, August 4, 2019. https-//www.semana.com/nacion/articulo/promesas-incumplidas-a-los-indigenas-y-afrocolombianos-tras-la-independencia/626266.pdf.

Cotte Poveda, Alexander. 2011. "Economic Development, Inequality and Poverty: An Analysis of Urban Violence in Colombia." *Oxford Development Studies* 39, no. 4: 453–468.

———. 2012. "Empirical Research on the Relationship between Violence and Social Development in Colombia." *Ensayos Revista de Economía* 31, no. 2: 37–56.

Cottle, Robin. 2018. "Cocaine Tourism Boom: Brits Flocking to South America to Get Drug 20 TIMES Cheaper." *Daily Star*, September 9, 2018. https://www.dailystar.co.uk/news/world-news/728446/cocaine-south-america-holidays-tourism-brits-peru-bolivia-colombia.

Cottle, Simon, Richard Sambrook, and Nick Mosdell. 2016. *Reporting Dangerously: Journalist Killings, Intimidation and Security*. London: Palgrave Macmillan.

Council of Europe. 2019. *Democracy at Risk: Threats and Attacks against Media Freedom in Europe*. https://rm.coe.int/annual-report-2018-democracy-in-danger-threats-and-attacks-media-freed/1680926453.

Craft, Stephanie, Tim P. Vos, and J. David Wolfgang. 2016. "Reader Comments as Press Criticism: Implications for the Journalistic Field." *Journalism* 17, no. 6: 677–693.

Criscione, Giacomo, and Paolo Vignolo. 2014. "¿Del terrorismo al turismo? 'Vive Colombia viaja por ella' como dispositivo de movilidad, entre conflicto armado y patrimonio cultural." In *El valor del patrimonio: Mercado, políticas culturales y agenciamientos sociales*, edited by Margarita Chaves, Mauricio Montenegro, and Marta Zambrano, 473–517. Bogotá: Instituto Colombiano de Antropología e Historia.

Critchley, Simon. 2014. "Why There Is No Such Thing as a Bad World Cup." *New Republic*, June 11, 2014. https://newrepublic.com/article/117879/world-cup-2014-philosophy-soccer-fandom.

Cronin, Brian. 2010. "Sports Legend Revealed: Did Johan Cruyff Sit Out the 1978 World Cup as a Political Protest?" *Los Angeles Times*, June 22, 2010. http://latimesblogs.latimes.com/sports_blog/2010/06/sports-legend-revealed-did-johan-cruyff-sit-out-the-1978-world-cup-as-a-political-protest.html.

Cross, Kathleen, Shane Gunster, Marcelina Piotrowski, and Shannon Daub. 2015. *News Media and Climate Politics: Civic Engagement and Political Efficacy in a Climate of Reluctant Cynicism*. Canadian Centre for Policy Alternatives/Centre Canadien de Politiques Alternatives, September 2015. https://www.policyalternatives.ca/sites/default/files/uploads/publications/BC%20Office/2015/09/CCPA-BC-News_Media_Climate_Politics.pdf.

Cuartas, Jorge. 2018. "Physical Punishment against the Early Childhood in Colombia: National and Regional Prevalence, Sociodemographic Gaps, and Ten-Year Trends." *Children and Youth Services Review* 93: 428–440.

Cumbre Agraria: Campesina, Étnica y Popular, Equipo Operativo Nacional Garantías y Derechos Humanos, Coordinación Social y Política "Marcha Patriótica," and Instituto de Estudios para el Desarrollo y la Paz—Indepaz. 2018. *Todos los nombres, todos los rostros: Informe de derechos humanos sobre la situación de líderes/as y defensores de derechos humanos en los territorios*. Marcha Patriotica, June 2018. https://www.marchapatriotica.org/wp-content/uploads/2018/06/Informe-l%C3%ADderes-y-defensores-2018-1.pdf.

Cunin, Elisabeth, and Christian Rinaudo. 2008. "Consuming the City in Passing: Guided Visits and the Marketing of Difference in Cartagena de Indias (Colombia)." *Turist Studies* 9, no. 2.

Cunningham, Stuart. 1981. "The "Force-Field" of Melodrama." *Quarterly Review of Film Studies* 6, no. 4: 347–364.

Curtis, Debra. 2009. *Pleasures and Perils: Girls' Sexuality in a Caribbean Consumer Culture.* New Brunswick, NJ: Rutgers University Press.

da Silva, Marisa Torres. 2013. "Professional Views on Letters-to-the-Editor as a Means of Audience Participation." *Participations: Journal of Audience & Reception Studies* 10, no. 1. http://www.participations.org/Volume%2010/Issue%201/36%20Silva%2010.1.pdf.

Dabashi, Hamid. 2013. "Can Non-Europeans Think?" Al Jazeera, January 15, 2013. http://www.aljazeera.com/indepth/opinion/2013/01/2013114142638797542.html

Daniels, Joe Parkin. 2019. "Journalist Finally Brings Attackers to Justice but Warns: 'Colombia's Sliding Backwards.'" *Guardian*, June 16, 2019. https://www.theguardian.com/world/2019/jun/16/colombia-journalist-threats-violence.

Darwin, Charles. 2008. *Evolutionary Writings*. Edited by James A. Secord. New York: Oxford University Press.

Dávila, Andrés, and Catalina Londoño. 2005. "La nación bajo un uniforme: Fútbol e identidad nacional en Colombia, 1985–2000." In *Futbologías: Fútbol, identidad y violencia en América Latina*, edited by Pablo Alabarces, 135–158. Buenos Aires: Consejo Latinoamericano de Ciencias Sociales.

de Beauvoir, Simone. 1999. *America Day by Day.* Translated by Carol Cosman. Berkeley: University of California Press.

De la Hoz Bohórquez, German Alberto, and Jhon Henry Romero Quevedo. 2016. *Enterremos las armas para que florezca la Vida!!! Comportamiento del homicidio. Colombia, 2015.* Instituto Nacional de Medicina Legal y Ciencias Forenses. http://www.medicinalegal.gov.co/documents/88730/3418907/2.+HOMICIDIOS.pdf/70a4c34b-920c-465b-9902-936ffeab4afd.

de la Torre, Renée, and Eloisa Martín. 2016. "Religious Studies in Latin America." *Annual Review of Sociology*, no. 42: 473–492.

de Nebrija, Antonio. 2016. "On Language and Empire: The Prologue to *Grammar of the Castilian Language* (1492)." Translated by Magalí Armillas-Tiseyra. *PMLA* 131, no. 1: 197–208.

de Pablos, Emiliano. 2019. "LatAm Scripted: The End of Telenovelas?" *Television Business International*, January 21, 2019. https://tbivision.com/2019/01/21/latin-american-scripted-raising-the-bar/.

De Sanctis, Fausto Martin. 2014. *Football, Gambling, and Money Laundering: A Global Criminal Justice Perspective.* New York: Springer.

de Sousa Santos, Boaventura. 2007. *Democratizing Democracy: Beyond the Liberal Democratic Canon.* London: Verso.

de Spinoza, Benedictus. 2016. *The Collected Works of Spinoza Volume II.* Edited and Translated by Edwin Curley. Princeton: Princeton University Press.

Deas, Malcolm. 2015. "The Colombian Conflict: A Historical Perspective." In *Colombia's Political Economy at the Outset of the Twenty-First Century: From Uribe to Santos and Beyond*, edited by Bruce M. Bagley and Jonathan D. Rosen, 91–109. Lanham: Lexington Books.

Debnath, Neela. 2018. "The Last Ship Season 5 Location: Where is The Last Ship Filmed? Where's It Set?" *Daily Express*, September 21, 2018. https://www.express.co.uk/showbiz/tv-radio/1021001/The-Last-Ship-season-5-location-Where-is-The-Last-Ship-filmed-series-TNT-Sky.

Della Giusta, Marina, Maria Laura Di Tommaso, and Steinar Strøm. 2008. *Sex Markets: A Denied Industry.* London: Routledge.

Dennis, Marisol. 2006. "National Identity and Violence: The Case of Colombia." In *Political Violence and the Construction of National Identity in Latin America*, edited by Will Fowler and Peter Lambert, 91–109. New York: Palgrave Macmillan.

Departamento Administrativo Nacional de Estadística. 2007. *Colombia una nación multicultural: Su diversidad étnica*. https://www.dane.gov.co/files/censo2005/etnia/sys/colombia_nacion.pdf.

Descartes, René. 2007. *Discourse on the Method of Rightly Conducting One's Reason and Seeking Truth in the Sciences*. http://www.earlymoderntexts.com/assets/pdfs/descartes1637.pdf.

de-Shalit, Avner. 2006. "Nationalism." In *Political Theory and the Ecological Challenge*, edited by Andrew Dobson and Robyn Eckersley, 75–90. Cambridge: Cambridge University Press.

Díaz Granados, Orlando Scoppetta D., and Rolando Rodríguez Cruz. 2006. "La explotación sexual de los niños en Cartagena de Indias y Bogotá, Colombia." *Revista Infancia Adolescencia y Familia* 1, no. 2: 247–258.

Díaz Nosty, Bernardo, and Ruth A. de Frutos García. 2017. "Murders, Harassment and Disappearances: The Reality of Latin American Journalists in the XXI Century." *Revista Latina de Comunicación Social*, no. 72: 1418–1434.

Dinnie, Keith. 2016. *Nation Branding: Concepts, Issues, Practice*, 2nd ed. London: Routledge.

Diz Caraballo, Alexander. 2014. "Turismo, modernidad y exclusión social en Cartagena de Indias, 1913–1946." *Alaüla—Revista Estudiantil* 2: 24–38.

Djellouli, Nehla, and María Cristina Quevedo-Gómez. 2015. "Challenges to Successful Implementation of HIV and AIDS-Related Health Policies in Cartagena, Colombia." *Social Science & Medicine* 133: 36–44.

Dmowski, Seweryn. 2015. "Football Sites of Memory in the Eastern Bloc 1945–1991." In *European Football and Collective Memory*, edited by Wolfram Pyta and Nils Havermann, 171–184. London: Palgrave Macmillan.

Doherty, Simon. 2019. "The Activists Going on 'Birth Strike' to Protest Climate Change." *Vice*, March 13, 2019. https://www.vice.com/en_ca/article/wjmkmz/the-activists-going-on-birth-strike-to-protest-climate-change.

Donzelot, Jacques. 2006. "Refonder la cohésion sociale." *Esprit*, December 2006. https://esprit.presse.fr/article/jacques-donzelot/refonder-la-cohesion-sociale-13800.

Dorfman, Ariel, and Armand Mattelart. 1971. *Para leer al pato Donald*. Santiago de Chile: Ediciones Universitarias de Valparaíso.

Dragomir, Marius. 2018. "Control the Money, Control the Media: How Government Uses Funding to Keep Media in Line." *Journalism* 19, no. 8: 1131–1148.

Dube, Oeindrila, and Suresh Naidu. 2014. "Bases, Bullets and Ballots: The Effect of U.S. Military Aid on Political Conflict in Colombia." National Bureau of Economic Research Working Paper 20213. http://www.nber.org/papers/w20213.

Dubois, Laurent. 2013. "The Blood of the Impure." Africa Is a Country, March 2013. https://africasacountry.com/2013/03/the-blood-of-the-impure.

Dudley, Steven. 2004. *Walking Ghosts: Murder and Guerrilla Politics in Colombia*. London: Routledge.

Dugas, John C. 2005. "The Colombian Nightmare: Human Rights Abuses and the Contradictory Effects of U.S. Foreign Policy." In *When States Kill: Latin America, the U.S., and Technologies of Terror*, edited by Cecilia Menjívar and Néstor Rodríguez, 227–251. Austin: University of Texas Press.

Duncan, Gustavo. 2015. "El narco y los economistas." *El Tiempo*, August 12, 2015. http://www.eltiempo.com/opinion/columnistas/el-narco-y-los-economistas-gustavo-duncan-columna-el-tiempo/16226336.

Durán-Martínez, Angélica. 2018. *The Politics of Drug Violence: Criminals, Cops, and Politicians in Colombia and Mexico*. New York: Oxford University Press.

Durkheim, Émile. 1961. "The Solidarity of Occupational Groups." In *Theories of Society: Foundations of Modern Sociological Theory. Volume I*, edited by Talcott Parsons, Edward Shils, Kaspar D. Naegle, and Jesse R. Pitts, 356–363. New York: Free Press of Glencoe.

Duzán, Maria Jimena. 1994. *Death Beat: A Colombian Journalist's Life Inside the Cocaine Trade.* Translated by Peter Eisner. New York: Harper Collins.

Eagleton, Terry. 2010. "Football: A Dear Friend to Capitalism." *Guardian*, June 15, 2010. http://www.theguardian.com/commentisfree/2010/jun/15/football-socialism-crack-cocaine-people.

Earle, Rebecca. 1996. "'A Grave for Europeans'? Disease, Death, and the Spanish-American Revolutions." *War in History* 3, no. 4: 371–383.

Echeverri, Lina María, Eduardo Rosker, and Martha Lucía Restrepo. 2010. "Los orígenes de la marca país Colombia es pasión." *Estudios y Perspectivas en Turismo* 19, no. 3: 409–421.

Echeverri, Lina María, Enrique ter Horst, German Molina, and Zarifa Mohamad. 2019. "Nation Branding: Unveiling Factors That Affect the Image of Colombia from a Foreign Perspective." *Tourism Planning & Development* 16, no. 1: 1–21.

Eco, Umberto. 1987. *Travels in Hyperreality*. Translated by William Weaver. London: Picador.

Economic Commission for Latin America and the Caribbean. 2018. *Economic Survey of Latin America and the Caribbean, 2018* (LC/PUB.2018/17-P).

———. 2019a. *Statistical Yearbook for Latin America and the Caribbean, 2018* (LC/PUB.2019/2-P).

———. 2019b. *Social Panorama of Latin America, 2018* (LC/PUB.2019/3-P).

Economist Intelligence Unit. 2019. *Colombia: Fact Sheet.* EIU, May 1, 2019. http://country.eiu.com/article.aspx?articleid=1048240888&Country=Colombia&topic=Summary&subtopic=Fact+sheet.

EFE. 2007. "El capitán de Perú en el 78: 'Pongo la mano en el fuego por mis compañeros.'" *El Mundo*, May 12, 2007. http://www.elmundo.es/elmundodeporte/2007/12/05/futbol/1196888260.html.

Eisenstein, Sergei. 1987. *Nonindifferent Nature*. Translated by Herbert Marshall and Roberta Reader. New York: Cambridge University Press.

"El Batallón Guardia Presidencia cree en la Selección Colombia." 2016. *Noticias RCN*, June 3, 2016. http://www.noticiasrcn.com/videos/. Elias, Norbert. 1978. "On Transformations of Aggressiveness." *Theory and Society* 5, no. 2: 229–242.

"El desafortunado trino de barra brava del América." 2019. *Kien y Ke*, August 15, 2019. https://www.kienyke.com/radark/baron-rojo-sur-mensaje-twitter-miguel-angel-rodriguez-orejuela.

"El futuro del Magdalena, según Hydrochina." 2014. *La Nación*, August 10, 2014. http://www.lanacion.com.co/2014/08/10/el-futuro-del-magdalena-segun-hydrochina/.

Elias, Norbert, and Eric Dunning. 1986. *Quest for Excitement: Sport and Leisure in the Civilizing Process*. Oxford: Basil Blackwell.

"El maratón de partidos de Junior en el 2018." 2018. *Marca Claro*, December 2, 2018. http://co.marca.com/claro/futbol/junio-barranquilla/2018/12/02/5c030c7be2704e68648b45b2.html.

Eloranta, Jan. 2016. "Cliometric Approaches to War." In *Handbook of Cliometrics*, edited by Claude Diebolt and Michael Haupert, 563–586. Berlin: Springer-Verlag.

"El último antecedente de un intento de paro en el fútbol colombiano." 2019. *El Tiempo*, October 16, 2016. https://www.eltiempo.com/deportes/futbol-colombiano/cuando-fue-el-ultimo-intento-de-paro-en-el-futbol-colombiano-423844.

Engels, Federico. 1968. *Anti-Dühring: La subversión de la ciencia por el señor Eugen Dühring.* Translated by Manuel Sacristan Luzon. México: Editorial Grijalbo, S. A.

Engels, Frederick. 1946. *The Dialectics of Nature.* Translated and edited by Clemens Dutt. London: Lawrence and Wishart.

Enloe, Cynthia. 1983. *Does Khaki Become You? The Militarisation of Women's Lives.* Boston: South End Press.

Escobar, Arturo. 1995. *Encountering Development: The Making and Unmaking of the Third World.* Princeton, NJ: Princeton University Press.

———. 1998. "Whose Knowledge, Whose Nature? Biodiversity, Conservation, and the Political Ecology of Social Movements." *Journal of Political Ecology* 5, no. 1: 53–82.

———. (2012). "Más allá del desarrollo: Postdesarrollo y transiciones hacia el pluriverso." *Revista de Antropología Social* 21 https://revistas.ucm.es/index.php/RASO/article/view/40049.

Escobar Ramírez, Jairo J., and Uwe Barg. 1990. *La contaminación de las aguas continentales de Bolivia, Colombia, Costa Rica, Ecuador, Panama, Perá y Venezuela, 8.* Food and Agriculture Organization. ftp://ftp.fao.org/fi/Cdrom/aquaculture/a0844t/docrep/008/T0311S/T0311S00.htm.

Escovar, Alberto. 2012. "Turismo religioso en Colombia." In *Difusión y protección del patrimonio religioso en América Latina,* edited by Carmen María Ramos de Balcarce and Susana Malnis de Bestani, 343–360. Sáenz Peña: Editorial de la Universidad Nacional de Tres de Febrero.

España Eljaiek, Irina Rosa. 2017. *Actors, Institutional Change and Reproduction: The Colombian Case of Racial Exclusion and Local Socio-Economic Performance 1886–1950.* Cologne, Germany: International Max Planck Research School on the Social and Political Constitution of the Economy.

Espinosa Pezzia, Agustín, Alessandro Soares Da Silva, Carlos Contreras Ibáñez, Rosa María Cueto, Aldo García Rengifo, Fabio Ortolano, Juan Valencia, and Angela Vera Ruíz. 2017. "Identidad nacional y sus relaciones con la ideología y el bienestar en cinco países de América Latina." *Avances en Psicología Latinoamericana* 35, no. 2: 351–374.

Estella Nagle, Luz. 2013. "How Conflict and Displacement Fuel Human Trafficking and Abuse of Vulnerable Groups: The Case of Colombia and Opportunities for Real Action and Innovative Solutions." *Groningen Journal of International Law* 1, no. 2: 1–53.

Estrada Alvarez, Jairo. 2015. *Acumulación capitalista, dominación de clase y rebelión armada: Elementos para una interpretación histórica del conflicto social y armado.* Comisión Histórica del Conflicto y sus Víctimas. http://www.corteidh.or.cr/tablas/r33453.pdf.

Eu, Geoffrey. 2018. "Captivating Colombia." *Business Times,* July 27, 2018. https://www.businesstimes.com.sg/lifestyle/feature/captivating-colombia.

Evans, Claire Q., and Elizabeth J. Zechmeister. 2018. *Education and Risk Assessments Predict Climate Change Concerns in Latin America and the Caribbean.* USAID, Vanderbilt University, LAPOP and AmericasBarometer. https://www.vanderbilt.edu/lapop/insights/IO929en.pdf.

Fals Borda, Orlando. 1986. *Historia doble de la costa, vol. 1.* Bogotá: Universidad Nacional de Colombia/Banco de la República/El Ancora.

Fals Borda, Orlando, Germán Guzmán Campos, Camilo Restrepo, and Eduardo Umaña Luna. 1962. *La violencia en Colombia.* Bogotá: Universidad Nacional.

Fanon, Frantz. 1965. *A Dying Colonialism.* Translated by Haakon Chevalier. New York: Grove Press.

———. 2004. *The Wretched of the Earth.* Translated by Richard Philcox. New York: Grove Press.

"FARC enviaron mensaje de apoyo a los jugadores de la Selección Colombia." 2014. *El País,* June 11, 2014. https://www.elpais.com.co/elpais/judicial/noticias/farc-enviaron-mensaje-apoyo-jugadores-seleccion-colombia.

Farnsworth-Alvear, Ann, Marco Palacios, and Ana María Gómez López, eds. 2017. *The Colombia Reader: History, Culture, Politics*. Durham, NC: Duke University Press.

Fedesarrollo. 1972. "Turismo." *Coyuntura Económica* (December). https://www.repository.fedesarrollo.org.co/handle/11445/2846.

Feinberg, Matthew, and Robb Willer. 2013. "The Moral Roots of Environmental Attitudes." *Psychological Science* 24, no. 1: 56–62.

Feinman, Ilene Rose. 2000. *Citizenship Rites: Feminist Soldiers and Feminist Antimilitarists*. New York: New York University Press.

Fernández L'Hoeste, Héctor. 2015. "Race, Sports, and Regionalism in the Construction of Colombian Nationalism." In *Sports and Nationalism in Latin/o America*, edited by Héctor Fernández L'Hoeste, Robert McKee Irwin, and Juan Poblete, 85–104. New York: Palgrave Macmillan.

Fernández Moores, Ezequiel. 2014. "El cártel." *La Nación*, December 2, 2014. http://canchallena.lanacion.com.ar/1748972-el-cartel.

Ferrier, Michelle. 2019. *Attacks and Harassment: The Impact on Female Journalists and Their Reporting*. Troll-Busters and International Women's Media Foundation, March 2019. https://16dayscampaign.org/wp-content/uploads/2019/03/Attacks-and-Harassment-PDF.pdf.

Fielder, Anke, and Michael Meyen. 2015. "A Quasi-Public Sphere: Letters to the Editor in the German Democratic Republic." *Javnost—The Public: Journal of the European Institute for Communication and Culture* 22, no. 2: 181–195.

Financial Action Task Force. 2009. *Money Laundering through the Football Sector*. Paris: Financial Action Task Force.

Fine, Ben, and Juan Pablo Durán Ortiz. 2016. "Social Capital: From the Gringo's Tale to the Colombian Reality." SOAS (University of London) Department of Economics Working Paper Series, 195.

Finlay, Christopher. 2019. *Is Just War Possible?* Cambridge: Polity Press.

Fisher, Dana R. 2019. "The Broader Importance of #FridaysForFuture." *Nature Climate Change*, no. 9: 430–431.

Fleetwood, Jennifer. 2014. *Drug Mules: Women in the International Cocaine Trade*. London: Palgrave Macmillan.

Fletcher, Alex. 2019. "The Grand Tour Colombia Special: Everything You Need to Know." *BT TV*, January 25, 2019. https://tv.bt.com/tv/amazon-prime-video-on-bt-tv/grand-tour-colombia-special-release-date-spoilers-pictures-11364325638594.

FLIP. 2017. *Estado depredador: Informe sobre el estado de la libertad de prensa en Colombia 2017*. https://flip.org.co/index.php/es/publicaciones/informes-anuales/item/2188-informe-anual-2017-un-estado-depredador-de-la-libertad-de-prensa.

———. 2018a. *Alerta por incremento en el número amenazas de muerte a periodistas en Colombia*. https://flip.org.co/index.php/es/informacion/pronunciamientos/item/2252-alerta-por-incremento-en-el-numero-amenazas-de-muerte-a-periodistas-en-colombia.

———. 2018b. *Cartografías de la información*. https://flip.org.co/cartografias-informacion/.

———. 2018c. *War in Colombia Is Silencing Local Journalism*. https://flip.org.co/index.php/en/publications/item/2268-about-cartographies-of-information.

———. 2018d. *Prensa acorralada: Un juego de violentos y poderosos: Informe sobre el estado de la libertad de prensa en Colombia 2018*. https://flip.org.co/index.php/es/publicaciones/informes-anuales/item/2315-informe-anual-prensa-acorralada-un-juego-de-violentos-y-poderosos.

"FLIP alerta por aumento de amenazas a periodistas en varias regiones del país." 2018. *El Espectador*, July 12, 2018. https://www.elespectador.com/noticias/nacional/flip-alerta-por-aumento-de-amenazas-periodistas-en-varias-regiones-del-pais-articulo-799693.

Florida, Richard. 2009. *Who's Your City? How the Creative Economy Is Making Where to Live the Most Important Decision of Your Life*. New York: Basic Books.

———. 2012. *The Rise of the Creative Class, Revisited*. New York: Basic Books.

Ford, Henry. 1929. *My Philosophy of Industry: An Authorized Interview by Ray Leone Faurote*. New York: Coward-McCann.

Forero, Germán Arango. 2005. "Siglo XXI: Hacia una nueva deontología del periodismo deportivo." *Palabra Clave* 13: 139–151.

Foucault, Michel. 1984. *The History of Sexuality: An Introduction*. Translated by Robert Hurley. Harmondsworth: Penguin.

———. 1991. "Governmentality." Translated by Pasquale Pasquino. In *The Foucault Effect: Studies in Governmentality*, edited by Graham Burchell, Colin Gordon, and Peter Miller, 87–104. London: Harvester Wheatsheaf.

———. 2007. *The Politics of Truth*. Edited by Sylvère Lotringer. Translated by Lysa Hochroth and Catherine Porter. Los Angeles: Semiotext(e).

Franco, Jean. 2001. "Bodies in Contention." *NACLA Report on the Americas* 34, no. 5: 41–45.

Freedom House. 2017. *Freedom of the Press 2017*. https://freedomhouse.org/sites/default/files/FOTP_2017_booklet_FINAL_April28.pdf.

Freston, Paul. 2004. *Evangelicals and Politics in Africa, Asia and Latin America*. Cambridge: Cambridge University Press.

Fridman Stalnicovitz, Dan. 2016. "La Copa América incompleta." Univision, June 5, 2016. http://www.univision.com/deportes/futbol/copa-america-centenario-2016/la-copa-america-incompleta-colombia-2001-sufrimiento-dudas-y-jubilo-al-final.

Frith, Simon. 1991. "The Good, the Bad, and the Indifferent: Defending Popular Culture from the Populists." *diacritics* 21, no. 4: 102–115.

Funari, Pedro Paulo A. 2019. "The British in Latin America: Material Evidence of Empire and Beyond." In *Archaeologies of the British in Latin America*, edited by Charles E. Orser Jr., 255–260. New York: Springer.

Fundación Renacer. 2016. *Global Study on Sexual Exploitation of Children in Travel and Tourism Country-Specific Report: Colombia*. http://www.ecpat.org/wp-content/uploads/2016/10/3.-SECTT-COLOMBIA.pdf.

Fundar Centro de Análisis e Investigación. 2015. *Libertad de expresión en venta: Acceso a información y censura indirecta en publicidad oficial*. http://www.fundar.org.mx/mexico/pdf/LibertadDigitalOk.pdf.

"Fútbol colombiano vendió sus derechos de televisión internacional por los próximos 10 años." 2019. *La República*, July 19, 2019. https://www.larepublica.co/empresas/futbol-colombiano-vendio-sus-derechos-de-television-internacional-por-los-proximos-10-anos-2886697.

Gagliano, Monica. 2013. "Green Symphonies: A Call for Studies on Acoustic Communication in Plants." *Behavioral Ecology* 24, no. 4: 789–796.

Galeano, Edgar Antonio, Bettsy T. Cruz Ortiz, Jeffrey S. Cruz Jiménez, Edward F. Escovar Álvarez, Andrés S. Gómez Gómez, Juan D. Nieto Manrique, and Luisa F. Rodríguez Lesmes. 2015. "Barras bravas: ¿Realización desde la marginalidad y las falencias académicas?" *Revista Papeles* 7, no. 14: 31–41.

Galeano, Eduardo. 1997. *Open Veins of Latin America: Five Centuries of the Pillage of a Continent*. Translated by Cedric Belfrage. London: Latin America Bureau.

———. 2013. *Soccer in Sun and Shadow*, rev. ed. Translated by Mark Field. New York: Nation Books.

———. 2016, "Fútbol a sol y a sombra." *Don Patadon*, September 16, 2016. http://www.don-patadon.com/2018/10/futbol-sol-y-sombra-de-eduardo-galeano.html.

Garcés-Prettel, Miguel E., and Jesús Arroyave Cabrera. 2017. "Autonomía profesional y riesgos de seguridad de los periodistas en Colombia." *Perfiles Latinoamericanos* 49: 1–19.

Garcés-Prettel, Miguel, Luis Guillermo Jaramillo, Jesús Arroyave-Cabrera, and Alí De Ávila-Majul. 2019. "Libertad de prensa y conflicto armado en Colombia: Un análisis desde la autonomía profesional percibida por los periodistas colombianos." *Saber, Cinencia y Libertad* 14, no. 1: 21–34.

Garcia, Patricia. 2017. "A Stylish, James Bond-Esque Wedding in Cartagena." *Vogue*, February 17, 2017. https://www.vogue.com/article/pili-restrepo-josh-hackler-wedding-cartagena-colombia.

Garcia Canclini, Néstor. 2008. "Interview for the 9th Spanish Sociology Conference, 2007." Translated by Toby Miller. *Social Identities* 14, no. 3: 389–394.

García Márquez, Gabriel. 1981. "El río de la vida." *El País*, March 25, 1981. https://elpais.com/diario/1981/03/25/opinion/354322807_850215.html.

———. 1987. *La mala hora*. https://www.cobachsonora.edu.mx/bibliotecacobach/files/libros/Gabriel_Garcia_Marquez_La_mala_hora.pdf.

———. 1988. *Love in the Time of Cholera*. Translated by Edith Grossman. New York: Alfred A. Knopf.

———. 1994. "Por un país al alcance de los niños." *El Espectador*, July 23, 1994, 12A.

———. 1996. *Noticia de un secuestro*. Mexico City: Editorial Diana.

———. 1997. *News of a Kidnapping*. Translated by Edith Grossman. New York: Alfred A. Knopf.

———. 1998. *Por un país al alcance de los niños*, 2nd ed. Bogotá: Villegas Editores.

———. 2015. *El general en su laberinto*. Literatura Random House. http://www.educando.edu.do/files/8914/0932/5229/Garcia_Marquez_Gabriel_-_El_general_en_su_laberinto.pdf.

García Marrugo, Alexandra. 2017. "'On the Grammar of Death': The Construal of Death and Killing in Colombian Newspapers." *Functional Linguistics* 4: 1–17.

García Villegas, Mauricio. 2015. "Violentólogos." *El Espectador*, November 6, 2015. https://www.elespectador.com/opinion/opinion/violentologos-columna-597630.

Garnica, Alejandro. 2011. "Las televisiones de un visionario: Cómo Miguel Sabido contribuyó a la telenovela mexicana y al entretenimiento educativo." In *Telenovelas en México: Nuestras íntimas extrañas*, edited by Álvaro Cueva, Carla Estrada, Alejandro Garnica, Rubén Lara, Heriberto López Romo, Guillermo Orozco, and Silvano Soto Hernández, 94–120. México City: Delphi.

Gaviria Castellanos, Jorge Luis, V. Gómez-Ortega, and P. Gutiérrez. 2015. "Quemaduras químicas por agresión: Caracteristicas e incidencia recogidas en el Hospital Simón Bolívar, Bogotá, Colombia." *Cirugía Plástica Ibero-Latinoamericana* 41, no. 1: 73–82.

Gellner, Ernest. 1988. *Plough, Sword and Book: The Structure of Human History*. Chicago: University of Chicago Press.

George, Babu P., and Thomas R. Panko. 2011. "Child Sex Tourism: Facilitating Conditions, Legal Remedies, and Other Interventions." *Vulnerable Children and Youth Studies* 6, no. 2: 134–143.

Gill, Lesley. 2016. *A Century of Violence in a Red City: Popular Struggle, Counterinsurgency, and Human Rights in Colombia*. Durham, NC: Duke University Press.

Gill, Nicholas. 2018. "Colombia: With the War Finally Over, the Entire Country Is Opening" in "52 Places to Go in 2018." *New York Times*. https://www.nytimes.com/interactive/2018/travel/places-to-visit.html.

Giraldo, Isis. 2015. "Machos y mujeres de armas tomar: Patriarcado y subjetividad femenina en la narco-telenovela colombiana contemporánea." *La Manzana de la Discordia* 10, no. 1: 67–81.

Giraldo Durán, Angélica, and Adrián Gutiérrez Álvarez de Castillo. 2018. "Violencia y paz en Colombia: Una mirada desde la reproducción del capital en América Latina." *Interdisciplina* 6, no. 15: 61–81.

Giraudat, Jules. 2018. "'This Border Is Out of Control': Journalists' Murders Shock Ecuador." *Guardian*, October 24, 2018. https://www.theguardian.com/world/2018/oct/24/ecuador-journalist-safety-colombia-mataje-murders.

Giulianotti, Richard. 1999. *Football: A Sociology of the Global Game*. Cambridge: Polity.

Glade, Jim. 2017. "From Escobar Hitman to YouTube Star: Meet Jhon Jairo 'Popeye' Velasquez." *Rolling Stone*, June 14, 2017. https://www.rollingstone.com/culture/culture-features/from-escobar-hitman-to-youtube-star-meet-jhon-jairo-popeye-velasquez-196369/#!

Gladwell, Valerie F., Daniel K. Brown, Carly Wood, Gavin R. Sandercock, and Jo L. Barton. 2013. "The Great Outdoors: How a Green Exercise Environment Can Benefit All." *Extreme Physiology & Medicine*, no. 2: 3.

Global Burden of Disease 2016 Injury Collaborators. 2018. "Global Mortality from Firearms, 1990–2016." *Journal of the American Medical Association* 320, no. 8: 792–814.

Global Initiative to End All Corporal Punishment of Children. 2018, June. *Ending Family Violence in Colombia—Challenging Physical Punishment of Girls and Boys*. https://endcorporalpunishment.org/reports-on-every-state-and-territory/colombia/.

Global Witness. 2019. *Enemies of the State? How Government and Business Silence Land and Environmental Defenders*. https://www.globalwitness.org/en/campaigns/environmental-activists/enemies-state/.

Gmelch, George. 2003. *Behind the Smile: The Working Lives of Caribbean Tourism*. Bloomington: Indiana University Press.

"Gobernador de Bolívar critica placa que descubrió príncipe Carlos." 2014. *El Tiempo*, November 4, 2014. http://www.eltiempo.com/colombia/otras-ciudades/gobernador-de-bolivar-critica-placa-que-descubrio-principe-carlos/14786136.

Goel, Rashmi and Leigh Goodmark, eds. 2015. *Comparative Perspectives on Gender Violence: Lessons from Efforts Worldwide*. Oxford: Oxford University Press.

Gohdes, Anita R., and Sabine C. Carey. 2017. "Canaries in a Gold Mine? What the Killings of Journalists Tell Us About Future Repression." *Journal of Peace Research* 54, no. 2: 157–174.

Goldberg, Beverly. 2018. "Being a Female Social Leader in Colombia: A Black Hole." Democracia Abierta, September 14, 2018. https://www.opendemocracy.net/democraciaabierta/beverly-goldberg/being-female-social-leader-in-colombia-black-hole.

Goldman, Emma. 1917. *Anarchism and Other Essays*, 3rd ed. New York: Mother Earth Publishing Association.

Goldman, Michael, and Rachel A. Schurman. 2000. "Closing the "Great Divide": New Social Theory on Society and Nature." *Annual Review of Sociology* 26: 563–584.

Gómez, J.A.M., n.d. "Presencia del río Magdalena en el audiovisual." *Patrimonio Fílmico*. January 27, 2020. http://www.patrimoniofilmico.org.co/anterior/noticias/163.htm.

Gómez-Barris, Macarena. 2017. *The Extractive Zone: Social Ecologies and Decolonial Perspectives*. Durham, NC: Duke University Press.

Gómez Cano, Carlos Alberto, Verenice Sánchez Castillo, and Karen Viviana Díaz. 2015. "Analysis of Public Gender Policy in Colombia 1990–2014)." *Revista Facultad de Ciencias Contables, Económicas y Administrativas* 5, no. 2: 175–181.

González Castaño, Theo. 2014. "El día que mataron el fútbol." *El Espectador*, November 15, 2014. https://www.elespectador.com/deportes/futbolcolombiano/el-dia-mataron-el-futbol-articulo-527767.

González de Bustamante, Celeste, and Jeannine E. Relly. 2016. "Professionalism under Threat of Violence: Journalism, Reflexivity, and the Potential for Collective Professional Autonomy in Northern Mexico." *Journalism Studies* 17, no. 6: 684–702.

Goodwin, Christopher. 2009. "Latino TV Station Tops US Ratings." *Observer*, January 18, 2009. http://www.theguardian.com/world/2009/jan/18/usa-television.

Gootenberg, Paul. 2006. "Cocaine in Chains: The Rise and Demise of a Global Commodity, 1860–1950." In *From Silver to Cocaine: Latin American Commodity Chains and the Building of the World Economy, 1500–2000*, edited by Steven Topik, Carlos Marichal, and Zephyr Frank, 321–351. Durham, NC: Duke University Press.

Graham, David. 2000. "A Declaration of Independence." *Economic Affairs* (December): 7–12.

Gramsci, Antonio. 1978. *Selections from the Prison Notebooks of Antonio Gramsci*. Translated and edited by Quentin Hoare and Geoffrey Nowell-Smith. New York: International Publishers.

———. 2000. *The Antonio Gramsci Reader: Selected Writings 1916-1935*. Edited by David Forgacs. New York: New York University Press.

Green, W. John. 2000. "Left Liberalism in the Evolution of Colombian Popular National Identity." *The Americas* 57, no. 1: 95–124.

Gregory, Kenneth, ed. 1976. *The First Cuckoo: Letters to the Times, 1900–75*. London: Times Books/George Allen & Unwin.

Griffiths, George. 2019. "Jack Ryan Stars John Krasinski and Wendall Pierce Followed by Russian Spies and Entered Warzones for Season 2." *Metro*, November 1, 2019. https://metro.co.uk/2019/11/01/jack-ryan-stars-john-krasinski-and-wendall-pierce-followed-by-russian-spies-and-entered-warzones-for-season-2-11020440/.

Gruffydd Jones, Branwen, ed. 2006. *Decolonizing International Relations*. Plymouth: Rowman & Littlefield.

Grupo de Memoria Histórica. 2013. *¡Basta ya! Colombia: Memorias de guerra y dignidad*. http://www.centrodememoriahistorica.gov.co/descargas/informes2013/bastaYa/basta-ya-memorias-guerra-dignidad-new-9-agosto.pdf.

Guattari, Pierre-Félix. 1996. *The Guattari Reader*. Edited by Gary Genosko. Oxford: Blackwell.

Guerrero, Linda. 2013. "Burns Due to Acid Assaults in Bogotá, Colombia." *Burns* 39, no. 5: 1018–1023.

Guerrero, Rodrigo, and Andrés Fandiño-Losada. 2017. "Is Colombia a Violent Country?" *Colombia Médica* 48, no. 1: 9–11.

Guerrero-Figueroa Guerrero, Guillermo. 2016. "Incidencias del ESCNNA (explotación sexual comercial de niños, niñas, y adolescentes) en el turismo." *Revista Adelante Ahead* 7, no. 1: 88–96.

Guest, Greg, Kathleen M. MacQueen, and Emily E. Namey. 2012. *Applied Thematic Analysis*. Thousand Oaks, CA: Sage.

"Hablan de veto o censura para transmitir protestas de jugadores del fpc." 2019. *Comutricolor*, October 7, 2019. https://comutricolor.com/futbol-colombiano/hablan-de-veto-o-censura-para-transmitir-protestas-de-jugadores-del-fpc/.

Hall, Stuart. 1998. "The Windrush Issue: *Postscript*." *Soundings* 10: 188–192.

———. 2016. *Cultural Studies 1983: A Theoretical History*. Edited by Jennifer Daryl Slack and Lawrence Grossberg. Durham, NC: Duke University Press.

Hall, Stuart, and Tony Jefferson, eds. 1976. *Resistance through Rituals: Youth Subcultures in Post-War Britain*. London: Hutchinson.

Halliday, Fred. 1990. "'The Sixth Great Power': On the Study of Revolution and International Relations." *Review of International Studies* 16, no. 3: 207–221.

———. 2009. “International Relations in a Post-Hegemonic Age.” *International Affairs* 85, no. 1: 50.

Hammond, David S., Judith Rosales, and Paul E. Ouboter. 2013. *Managing the Freshwater Impacts of Surface Mining in Latin America.* Inter-American Development Bank Environmental Safeguards Unit Technical Note IDB-TN-519. http://hispagua.cedex.es/sites/default/files/hispagua_documento/Managing_the_Freshwater_Impacts_of_Surface_Mining_in_Latin_America.pdf/.

Hanitzsch, Thomas, Maria Anikina, Rosa Berganza, Incilay Cangoz, Mihai Coman, Basyouni Hamada, Folker Hanusch, Christopher D. Karadjov, Claudia Mellado, Sonia Virginia Moreira, Peter G. Mwesige, Patrick Lee Plaisance, Zvi Reich, Josef Seethaller, Elizabeth A. Skewes, Dani Vardiansyah Noor, and Kee Wang Yuen. 2010. “Modeling Perceived Influences on Journalism: Evidence from a Cross-National Survey of Journalists.” *Journalism and Mass Communication Quarterly* 87, no. 1: 5–22.

Hardin, Garrett. 1968. “The Tragedy of the Commons.” *Science* 162, no. 3859: 1243–1248.

Harrison, Jackie, and Stefanie Pukallus. 2018. “The Politics of Impunity: A Study of Journalists’ Experiential Accounts of Impunity in Bulgaria, Democratic Republic of Congo, India, Mexico and Pakistan.” *Journalism*, June 5, 2018. http://journals.sagepub.com/doi/10.1177/1464884918778248.

Hartley, John. 1992. *The Politics of Pictures: The Creation of the Public in the Age of Popular Media.* London: Routledge.

Hearn, Jeff. 2012. “The ‘Missing’ Men of International Relations.” *E-International Relations*, May 23, 2012. http://www.e-ir.info/2012/05/23/the-missing-men-of-international-relations/.

Hegel, Georg Wilhelm Friedrich. 1954. *The Philosophy of Hegel.* Edited by Carl J. Friedrich. Translated by Carl J. Friedrich, Paul W. Friedrich, W. H. Johnston, L. G. Struthers, B. Bosanquet, W. M. Bryant, and J. B. Baillie. New York: Modern Library.

———. 1988. *Lectures on the Philosophy of World History. Introduction: Reason in History.* Translated by H. B. Nisbet. Cambridge: Cambridge University Press.

Heidegger, Martin. 1977. *Basic Writings from Being and Time (1927) to The Task of Thinking (1964).* Edited by David Farrell Krell. Translated by Joan Stambaugh, J. Glenn Gray, David Farrell Krell, John Sallis, Frank A. Capuzzi, Albert Hofstadter, W. B. Barton Jr., Vera Deutsch, William Lovitt, and Fred D. Wieck. New York: Harper & Row.

Helg, Aline. 2012. “Simón Bolívar’s Republic: A Bulwark Against the “Tyranny” of the Majority.” *Revista de Sociologia e Política*, no. 20: 21–37.

Heller, Agnes. 1984. *Everyday Life.* Translated by G. L. Campbell. London: Routledge & Kegan Paul.

Hellinger, Daniel C. 2015. *Comparative Politics of Latin America: Democracy at Last?* 2nd ed. New York: Routledge.

Helman, Gerald B. and Steven R. Ratner. 1992–1993. “Saving Failed States.” *Foreign Policy* 89: 3–20.

Herder, Johann Gottfried von. 2002. *Philosophical Writings.* Translated and edited by Michael N. Forster. Cambridge: Cambridge University Press.

Hernández-Mora, Salud. 2014. “Colombia: El ridículo histórico del Príncipe Carlos de Inglaterra y del alcalde de Cartagena a cuenta de una placa homenaje al almirante que intentó conquistar la ciudad.” *Radio Tierra Viva* (blog), November 6, 2014. http://radiotierraviva.blogspot.com.co/2014/11/colombia-el-ridiculo-historico-del.html.

Hersh, Phil. 1990. “Group Demands Colombia Drop Alleged Drug Ties.” *Chicago Tribune*, February 5, 1990. http://articles.chicagotribune.com/1990-02-05/sports/9001110186_1_colombian-soccer-colombian-people-narcotics-industry.

Higuera, Silvia. 2019. "Colombia's Attorney General Orders Detention of Former Hitman, Links Him to Murder of Journalist Guillermo Cano Isaza." *Journalism in the Americas*, May 29, 2019. https://www.knightcenter.utexas.edu/blog/00-20921-colombia%E2%80%99s-attorney-general-orders-detention-former-hitman-links-him-murder-journalist.

Hill, Christopher. 1991. *The World Turned Upside Down: Radical Ideas During the English Revolution*. Harmondsworth: Penguin.

Hill, Kendall. 2015. "Cartagena de Indias, Colombia Travel Guide." *Gourmet Traveller*, August 4, 2015. https://www.gourmettraveller.com.au/travel/destinations/cartagena-de-indias-colombia-travel-guide-5634.

Hiller, Herbert L. 1976. "Escapism, Penetration, and Response: Industrial Tourism and the Caribbean." *Caribbean Studies* 16, no. 2: 92–116.

Hobbes, Thomas. 1998. *On the Citizen*. Translated and edited by Richard Tuck and Michael Silverthorne. Cambridge: Cambridge University Press.

Hobsbawm, Eric. 1994. "Barbarism: A User's Guide." *New Left Review*, no. 206: 44–54.

———. 1995. *The Age of Extremes: The Short Twentieth Century, 1914–1991*. London: Abacus.

———. 1998. *Uncommon People: Resistance, Rebellion and Jazz*. New York: The New Press.

Hobsbawm, Eric, and Terence Ranger, eds. 2002. *La invención de la tradición*. Translated by Omar Rodríguez. Barcelona: Editorial Crítica.

Hobson, J. A. 1902. *Imperialism: A Study*. London: James Nisbet & Co.

Høiby, Marte, and Rune Ottosen, eds. 2015. *Journalism under Pressure: A Mapping of Editorial Policies for Journalists Covering Conflict*. Oslo: Høgskolen i Oslo og Akershus.

Holland, Kaye. 2019. "Cartagena Cool—an Expert Guide to Colombia's Most Alluring City." *Telegraph*, February 22, 2019. https://www.telegraph.co.uk/travel/cruises/port-guides/cartagena-cruise-port-guide/.

Holland, Mary. 2017. "A Travel Guide to Cartagena, the Romantic Caribbean Capital You Need to Visit." *GQ*, May 5, 2017. https://www.gq.com/story/cartagena-travel-guide.

Homewood, Brian. 2016. "Life Bans for ex-South America FA Duo Jadue, Bedoya." Reuters, May 6, 2016. http://www.reuters.com/article/us-fifa-chile-ban-idUSKCN0XX0ZF.

Horkheimer, Max. 1996. *Critique of Instrumental Reason: Lectures and Essays Since the End of World War II*. Translated by Matthew J. O'Connell et al. [unnamed]. New York: Continuum.

———. 2002. *Critical Theory: Selected Essays*. Translated by Matthew J. O'Connell et al. [unnamed]. New York: Continuum.

Howard, Michael. 1984. "The Causes Of Wars." *Wilson Quarterly* 8, no. 3: 90–103.

Hoyos, Catalina. 2015. "'Tenemos los jugadores para ganar la Copa': 'Totono' Grisales." *FutbolRed*, June 11, 2015. https://www.futbolred.com/copa-america-2015/totono-grisales-habla-antes-de-la-copa-america+15936696.

Hristov, Jasmin. 2014. *Paramilitarism and Neoliberalism: Violent Systems of Capital Accumulation in Colombia and Beyond*. London: Pluto.

Hudson, Rex A., ed. 2010. *Colombia: A Country Study*, 5th ed. Library of Congress. https://cdn.loc.gov/master/frd/frdcstdy/co/colombiacountrys00huds/colombiacountrys00huds.pdf.

Huertas, Omar Díaz, and Nayibe Jiménez Rodríguez. 2016. "Feminicidio en Colombia: Reconocimiento de fenómeno social a delito." *Pensamiento Americano* 9, no. 16: 110–120.

Hughes, Sallie, Claudia Mellado, Jesús Arroyave, José Luiz Benitez, Aarnold de Beer, Miguel Garcés, and Mireya Márquez-Ramírez. 2017. "Expanding Influences Research to Insecure Democracies: How Violence, Public Insecurity, Economic Inequality, and Uneven Democratic Performance Shape Journalists' Perceived Work Environments." *Journalism Studies* 18, no. 5: 645–665.

Human Rights Watch. 2015. *World Report 2015: Events of 2014*. https://www.hrw.org/sites/default/files/wr2015_web.pdf.

———. 2017. *World Report 2018: Events of 2017*. https://www.hrw.org/world-report/2018.

———. 2019. *Submission by Human Rights Watch to the Committee on the Elimination of All Forms of Discrimination against Women on Colombia*. February 1, 2019. https://www.hrw.org/news/2019/02/01/submission-human-rights-watch-committee-elimination-all-forms-discrimination-against.

Hume, David. 1739. *A Treatise of Human Nature*. http://michaeljohnsonphilosophy.com/wp-content/uploads/2012/01/5010_Hume_Treatise_Human_Nature.pdf.

———. 1955. *An Inquiry Concerning Human Understanding with a Supplement: An Abstract of a Treatise of Human Nature*. Edited by Charles W. Hendel. Indianapolis: Bobbs-Merrill.

Hunt, Stacey L. 2009. "Rethinking State, Civil Society and Citizen Participation: The Case of the Colombian Paramilitaries." *Behemoth: A Journal on Civilisation* 1: 64–87.

Hurtado, Aída, and Mrinal Sinha. 2016. *Beyond Machismo: Intersectional Latino Masculinities*. Austin: University of Texas Press.

Hyde, Marina. 2010. "Fans, Robbers and a Marketing Stunt Face Justice, FIFA Style." *Guardian*, June 20, 2010. http://www.guardian.co.uk/football/2010/jun/20/world-cup-2010-fans-marketing-justice-fifa.

Hylton, Forrest. 2006. *Evil Hour in Colombia*. London: Verso.

Iglesias, Waldemar. 2014. "El fútbol en los tiempos de Pablo Escobar." *Clarín*, February 26, 2014. http://www.clarin.com/deportes/futbol-tiempos-Pablo-Escobar_0_1091291136.html.

"'I Have Been Honorable.'" 2002. *Newsweek*, March 24, 2002. http://www.newsweek.com/i-have-been-honorable-141719.

Ihlebæk, Karoline Andrea, and Arne H. Krumsvik. 2015. "Editorial Power and Public Participation in Online Newspapers." *Journalism* 16, no. 4: 470–487.

"Imputarán cargos por amenazas contra María Jimena Duzán y otros dos periodistas." 2018. *Revista Semana*, August 8, 2018. https://www.semana.com/nacion/articulo/imputaran-cargos-por-amenazas-contra-maria-jimena-duzan-y-otros-dos-periodistas/578774.

Institute for Economics & Peace. 2018. *Global Terrorism Index 2018: Measuring the Impact of Terrorism*. IEP, December 2018. http://visionofhumanity.org/app/uploads/2018/12/Global-Terrorism-Index-2018-1.pdf.

Instituto Colombiano de Medicina Legal. 2015. *Forensis, datos para la vida*. http://www.medicinalegal.gov.co/documents/88730/1656998/Forensis+Interactivo+ 2014.24-JULpdf.pdf/9085ad79-d2a9-4c0d-a17b-f845ab96534b.

Inter-American Development Bank, Oxford Economics, British Council, and Organization of American States. 2014. *The Economic Impact of the Creative Industries in the Americas*. Inter-American Development Bank/British Council/Organization of American States, July 2014. https://publications.iadb.org/en/publication/12503/economic-impact-creative-industries-americas.

International Commission for the Study of Communication Problems. 1980. *Many Voices One World: Towards a New More Just and More Efficient World Information and Communication Order*. Paris: UNESCO; London: Kogan Page; New York: Unipub.

International Congress and Convention Association. 2018. *ICCA Statistics Report: Country and City Rankings: Public Abstract*. https://www.iccaworld.org/knowledge/benefit.cfm?benefitid=4036.

International Federation of Journalists. 2019. *In the Shadow of Violence: Journalists and Media Staff Killed in 2018*. https://www.ifj.org/fileadmin/user_upload/IFJ_2018_Killed_Report_FINAL_pages.pdf.

International Monetary Fund. 2019. *Colombia: Selected Issues.* IMF Country Report 19/107, April 29, 2019. https://www.imf.org/en/Publications/CR/Issues/2019/04/29/Colombia-Selected-Issues-46829.

Irigaray, Luce, ed. 2004. *Luce Irigaray: Key Writings.* New York: Continuum.

Jackson, Matthew O., and Massimo Morelli. 2011. "The Reasons for Wars: An Updated Survey." In *The Handbook on the Political Economy of War,* edited by Christopher J. Coyne and Rachel L. Mathers, 34–57. Cheltenham: Edward Elgar Publishing.

Jacobs, Daniel, and Stephen Keeling. 2015. *The Rough Guide to Colombia.* London: Rough Guide.

James, Meg. 2009. "Univision, Televisa Settle High-Stakes Lawsuit." *Los Angeles Times,* January 23, 2009. http://articles.latimes.com/2009/jan/23/business/fi-televisa23.

James, William. 1909. *A Pluralistic Universe: Hibbert Lectures at Manchester College on the Present Situation in Philosophy.* http://hudsoncress.net/hudsoncress.org/html/library/western-philosophy/James,%20William%20-%20A%20Pluralistic%20Universe.pdf.

Jaramillo Marín, Jefferson. 2015. "The Commissions for the Study of Violence in Colombia: An Analysis of the Official Devices and Narratives of the Past and Present of Violence." In *The Struggle for Memory in Latin America: Recent History and Political Violence,* edited by Eugenio Allier-Montaño and Emilio Crenzel, 147–163. New York: Palgrave Macmillan.

Jaramillo Racines, Rafael. 2011. "El fútbol de el Dorado 'El punto de inflexión que marcó la rápida evolución del 'amateurismo' al 'profesionalismo.'" *Curitiba: Revista de Asociación Latinoamericana de Estudios Socioculturales del Deporte* 1, no. 1: 111–128.

Jenke, Libby, and Christopher Gelpi 2017. "Theme and Variations: Historical Contingencies in the Causal Model of Interstate Conflict." *Journal of Conflict Resolution* 61, no. 10: 2262–2284.

Jenkins, Simon. 2007. "Passion Alone Won't Rescue Colombia from Its Narco-Economy Stigma." *Guardian,* February 2, 2007. https://www.theguardian.com/commentisfree/2007/feb/02/comment.colombia.

Jerryson, Michael, Mark Juergensmeyer, and Margo Kitts, eds. 2013. *The Oxford Handbook of Religion and Violence.* New York: Oxford University Press.

Jiménez Botta, Felix A. 2017. "'Yes to Football, No to Torture!': The Politics of the 1978 Football World Cup in West Germany." *Sport in Society* 20, no. 10: 1440–1456.

Jimeno, Myriam, Daniel Varela, and Angela Castillo. 2018. "Violence, Emotional Communities, and Political Action in Colombia." In *Resisting Violence: Emotional Communities in Latin America,* edited by Morna Macleod and Natalia De Marinis, 23–52. New York: Palgrave Macmillan.

Jones, Finn-Olaf. 2018. "Why Bogotá Is Now on Ambitious Travelers' Agendas." *Wall Street Journal,* March 22, 2018. https://www.wsj.com/articles/why-bogota-is-back-on-ambitious-travelers-agendas-1521744253.

Jungblut, Marc, and Abit Hoxha. 2016. "Conceptualizing Journalistic Self-Censorship in Post-Conflict Societies: A Qualitative Perspective on the Journalistic Perception of News Production in Serbia, Kosovo, and Macedonia." *Media, War and Conflict* 10, no. 2: 222–238.

Kacowicz, Arie M., and David R. Mares. 2016. "Security Studies and Security in Latin America: The First 200 Years." In *Routledge Handbook of Latin American Security,* edited by Arie M. Kacowicz and David R. Mares, 11–29. Abingdon: Routledge.

Kaldor, Mary. 2012. *New and Old Wars: Organised Violence in a Global Era,* 3rd ed. Cambridge: Polity.

Kant, Immanuel. 1996. "An Answer to the Question: What Is Enlightenment?" Translated by James Schmidt. In *What Is Enlightenment? Eighteenth-Century Answers and Twentieth-*

Century Questions, edited by James Schmidt, 58–64. Berkeley: University of California Press.

———. 2000. *Critique of the Power of Judgement*. Edited by Paul Guyer. Translated by Paul Guyer and Eric Matthews. Cambridge: Cambridge University Press.

———. 2006. *Anthropology from a Pragmatic Point of View*. Translated and edited by Robert B. Louden. Cambridge: Cambridge University Press.

———. 2007. *Critique of Judgment*. Translated by James Creed Meredith and edited by Nicholas Walker. Oxford: Oxford University Press.

———. 2011. *Observations on the Feeling of the Beautiful and Sublime and Other Writings*. Edited by Patrick Frierson and Paul Guyer. Cambridge: Cambridge University Press.

Karl, Robert A. 2017. *Forgotten Peace: Reform, Violence, and the Making of Contemporary Colombia*. Berkeley: University of California Press.

Karlsson, Michael, Annika Bergström, Christer Clerwall, and Karin Fast. 2015. "Participatory Journalism—the Revolution That Wasn't. Content and User Behavior in Sweden 2007–2013." *Journal of Computer-Mediated Communication* 20, no. 3: 295–311.

Kasper, Joe. 2019. "Wheel Be Off." *Sun*, January 7, 2019. https://www.thescottishsun.co.uk/tvandshowbiz/3713211/jeremy-clarkson-richard-hammon-james-may-bbc-return-old-white-middle-class/.

Keane, John. 2004. *Violence and Democracy*. Cambridge: Cambridge University Press.

Kempadoo, Kamala. 2004. *Sexing the Caribbean: Gender, Race, and Sexual Labor*. New York: Routledge.

Keynes, John Maynard. 1936. *The General Theory of Employment, Interest and Money*. London: Palgrave Macmillan.

Kidd, Benjamin. 2009. *Social Evolution*. Cambridge: Cambridge University Press.

Kim, Hun Shik. 2010. "Forces of Gatekeeping and Journalists' Perceptions of Physical Danger in Post-Saddam Hussein's Iraq." *Journalism and Mass Communication Quarterly* 87, nos. 3–4: 484–500.

Kitzinger, Jenny, and Jacquie Reilly. 1997. "The Rise and Fall of Risk Reporting: Media Coverage of Human Genetics Research, 'False Memory Syndrome' and 'Mad Cow Disease.'" *European Journal of Communication* 12, no. 3: 319–350.

Kollontai, Alexandra. 1978. *Selected Writings of Alexandra Kollontai*. Translated by Alix Holt. Wesport, CT: Lawrence Hill and Company.

Krauze, Enrique. 1994. "México en un balón." *El País*, June 28, 1994. http://elpais.com/diario/1994/06/28/opinion/772754409_850215.html.

Kristeva, Julia and Philippe Sollers. 2016. *Marriage as a Fine Art*. Translated by Lorna Scott Fox. New York: Columbia University Press.

Krøvel, Roy. 2017. "Violence against Indigenous Journalists in Colombia and Latin America." In *The Assault on Journalism: Building Knowledge to Protect Freedom of Expression*, edited by Ulla Carlsson and Reeta Pöyhtäri, 191–203. Göteborg: NORDICOM.

Kuper, Simon. 2008. "Political Football: René Higuita." *Channel 4 News*, May 8, 2008. http://www.channel4.com/news/articles/world/americas/political+football+rene+higuita/2154447.html.

Laclau, Ernesto and Chantal Mouffe. 1987. "Post-Marxism Without Apologies." *New Left Review* 166: 79–106.

"La Copa Rosa." 2001. *El Tiempo*, July 13, 2001. http://www.eltiempo.com/archivo/documento/MAM-436708.

"La disputa en la dimayor por los derechos de television." 2016. *Semana*, September 30, 2016. https://www.semana.com/deportes/articulo/la-disputa-en-la-dimayor-por-los-derechos-de-television/496037.

Ladrón de Guevara, Andrés Dávila. 2014. "Fútbol y política en Colombia: Reflexiones politológicas en un año mundialista." *Desbordes: Revista de Investigaciones de la Escuela de Ciencias Sociales, Artes y Humanidades* 5: 11–22.

Lago Martínez, Silvia, ed. 2012. *Ciberespacio y resistencias: Exploración en la cultura digital*. Buenos Aires: Hekht Libros.

Lakoff, George. 2010. "Why It Matters How We Frame the Environment." *Environmental Communication* 4, no. 1: 70–81.

La Liga Contra Silencio. 2018. "Postobón hace pruebas de laboratorio con niños en La Guajira." *Vice*, February 13, 2018. https://www.vice.com/es_co/article/vbpb8m/postobon-pruebas-laboratorio-ninos-guajira-nutricion-bebidas-liga-contra-silencio.

"'La Madame' finalmente fue recluida en la ciudad de Ibagué." 2019. *El Universal*, December 22, 2019. https://www.eluniversal.com.co/cartagena/la-madame-finalmente-fue-recluida-en-la-ciudad-de-ibague-FN2168447.

Lamus, Doris. 2008. "Resistencia contra-hegemónica y polisemia: Conformación actual del movimiento de mujeres/feministas en Colombia." *Manzana de la Discordia* 3, no. 1: 25–37.

La Pastina, Antonio C. 2004. "*Telenovela* Reception in Rural Brazil: Gendered Readings and Sexual Mores." *Critical Studies in Media Communication* 21, no. 2: 162–181.

Laroussi, Sabrina S. 2014–2015. "Dicotomía grotesca de la mujer en la narconovela colombiana: ¿virgen o puta?" *Forum*, no. 22: 65–84.

Larraín, América. 2015. "Bailar fútbol: Reflexiones sobre el cuerpo y la nación en Colombia." *Boletín de Antropología* 30, no. 50: 191–207.

"Las FARC querían ver la Copa América del 2001: Nicolás Leoz." 2013. *El Espectador*, June 14, 2013. http://www.elespectador.com/deportes/futbolcolombiano/farc-querian-ver-copa-america-2001-nicolas-leoz-articulo-427844.

Latour, Bruno. 2004. *Politics of Nature: How to Bring the Sciences into Democracy*. Translated by Catherine Porter. Cambridge, MA: Harvard University Press.

———. 2009. "Will Non-Humans Be Saved? An Argument in Ecotheology." *Journal of the Royal Anthropological Institute* 15, no. 3: 459–475.

———. 2015. "Fifty Shades of Green." *Environmental Humanities* 7: 219–225.

———. 2018. *Down to Earth: Politics in the New Climatic Regime*. Translated by Catherine Porter. Cambridge: Polity.

Latour, Bruno, Pablo Jensen, Tommaso Venturini, Sébastian Grauwin, and Dominique Boullier. 2012. "The Whole Is Always Smaller Than Its Parts: A Digital Test of Gabriel Tarde's Monads." *British Journal of Sociology* 63, no. 4: 590–615.

Laurienti, Jerry M. 2007. *The U.S. Military and Human Rights Promotion: Lessons from Latin America*. Westport: Praeger Security International.

Lazarsfeld, Paul Felix. 1941. "Remarks on Administrative and Critical Communications Research." *Studies in Philosophy and Social Science*, no. 9: 2–16.

Leadbeater, Chris. 2018. "11 Reasons Why Colombia Should Be Your Next Holiday, Whatever Tonight's Result." *Telegraph*, July 3, 2018. https://www.luxurytraveladvisor.com/destinations/11-reasons-why-colombia-should-be-your-next-holiday-whatever-tonight-s-result.

Leavis, Q. D. 1939. *Fiction and the Reading Public*. London: Chatto & Windus.

Lee, Bandy X. 2019. *Violence: An Interdisciplinary Approach to Causes, Consequences, and Cures*. Oxford: Wiley Blackwell.

Lemaitre, Eduardo. 1998. *Breve historia de Cartagena*. Medellín: Editorial Colina.

Lenin, V. I. 1964. *Collected Works. Volume 22. December 1915–July 1916*. Translated by Yuri Sdobnikov. Edited by George Hanna. Moscow: Progress Publishers.

Lennon, John. 1971. "Interview with Tariq Ali and Robin Blackburn." *Red Mole*, January 21, 1971. http://www.beatlesinterviews.org/db1971.0121.beatles.html.

León Soler, Natalia. 2019. "Emancipación feminina." *Semana*, August 4, 2019. https-//www.semana.com/nacion/articulo/emancipacion-femenina-en-la-independencia/626260.

Leong, Laurence Wei-Teng. 1992. "Cultural Resistance: The Cultural Terrorism of British Male Working-Class Youth." *Current Perspectives in Social Theory* 12: 29–58.

Levy, Jack S. 1998. "The Causes of War and the Conditions of Peace." *Annual Review of Political Science* 1: 139–65.

Lewandowsky, Stephan, Naomi Oreskes, James S. Risbey, Ben R. Newell, and Michael Smithson. 2015. "Seepage: Climate Change Denial and Its Effect on the Scientific Community." *Global Environmental Change* 33: 1–13.

Lezcano, Arturo. 2018. "Historias del narcofútbol." *Jot Down*, January 2018. https://www.jotdown.es/2018/01/historias-del-narcofutbol/.

"Liga aguila hoy decisiones para el campeonato 2020." 2019. *Futbolred*, October 31, 2019. https://www.futbolred.com/futbol-colombiano/liga-aguila/liga-aguila-hoy-decisiones-para-el-campeonato-2020-108860.

Lightle, David. 2017. *David Lightle Nation Branding & Promotion Specialist. David Lightle* (blog). https://davidlightleblog.wordpress.com/my-practice/.

Lindsay-Poland, John. 2018. *Plan Colombia: U.S. Ally Atrocities and Community Activism*. Durham, NC: Duke University Press.

Lindsay-Poland, John, and Arlene B. Tickner. 2016. "De- or Re-militarization in Post Peace-Accord Colombia?" *NACLA News*, May 11, 2016. http://nacla.org/news/2016/05/11/de-or-re-militarization-post-peace-accord-colombia.

Lisle, Debbie. 2016. *Holidays in the Danger Zone: Entanglements of War and Tourism*. Minneapolis: University of Minnesota Press.

Löfgren Nilsson, Monica, and Henrik Örnebring. 2016. "Journalism under Threat." *Journalism Practice* 10, no. 7: 880–890.

Londoño, Nora H., Diana Valencia, Mario García, and Catalina Restrepo. 2014. "Factores causales de la explotación sexual infantil en niños, niñas y adolescentes en Colombia." *El Ágora USB Medellín-Colombia* 15, no. 1: 241–254.

López, Ana M. 1995. "Our Welcomed Guests: Telenovelas in Latin America." In *To Be Continued... Soap Opera around the World*, edited by Robert C. Allen, 256–275. London: Routledge.

López de la Roche, Fabio. 2003. "Debate público, guerra y desregulación informativa en Colombia." *Íconos: Revista de FLACSO-Ecuador*, no. 16: 54–64.

López-Castaño, Carlos E., and Martha C. Cano-Echeverri. 2011. "En torno a los primeros poblamientos en el noroccidente de Sudamérica: Acercamientos desde el valle internandino del Magdalena, Colombia." *Boletín de Arqueología* 15: 43–79.

López-Quintero, Catalina, and Yehuda Neumark. 2012. "Membresía a barras bravas y su influencia en el uso de drogas." *Revista Peruana de Medicina Experimental y Salud Publica* 29, no. 1: 21–27.

Lukács, György. 1972. *History and Class Consciousness: Studies in Marxist Dialectics*. Translated by Rodney Livingstone. Cambridge, MA: MIT Press.

Luna Geller, Alfonso José. 2016. "¿Armada Nacional al servicio de intereses de Ardila Lülle en la Copa América?" *Las 2 Orillas*, June 3, 2016. http://www.las2orillas.co/armada-nacional-al-servicio-de-intereses-de-ardila-lulle-en-la-copa-america/.

Luna-Galván, Mauricio, Iván Vargas-Chaves, and Anna Franco-Gantiva. 2017. "Towards an Inclusive Approach for Climate Change Adaptation Strategies: The Case of the Plan 4C in the City of Cartagena de Indias." *European Journal of Sustainable Development* 6, no. 3: 457–472.

Luxemburg, Rosa. 1970. *Rosa Luxemburg Speaks*. Edited by Mary-Alice Waters. New York: Pathfinder Press.

———. 2004. *The Rosa Luxemburg Reader*. Edited by Peter Hudis and Kevin B. Anderson. New York: Monthly Review Press.

Lynch, Michael J., Michael A. Long, Kimberly L. Barrett, and Paul B. Stretesky. 2013. "Is It a Crime to Produce Ecological Disorganization? Why Green Criminology and Political Economy Matter in the Analysis of Global Ecological Harms." *British Journal of Criminology* 53, no. 6: 997–1016.

MacCabe, Janet, and Kim Akass, eds. 2013. *TV's Betty Goes Global: From Telenovela to International Brand*. London: IB Tauris.

MacKenna, Ewan. 2016. "Narco-Football Is Dead: Celebrating a Colombia Reborn." *Bleacher Report*, June 1, 2016. http://bleacherreport.com/articles/2642116-narco-football-is-dead-celebrating-a-colombia-reborn.

Mackie, Vera. 2012. "The 'Afghan Girls': Media Representations and Frames of War." *Continuum: Journal of Media & Cultural Studies* 26, no. 1: 115–131.

Macon, Alexandra. 2017. "A Four-Day Wedding Extravaganza in Cartagena." *Vogue*, April 11, 2017. https://www.vogue.com/article/andrea-mosquera-swain-brian-laks-four-day-wedding-cartagena-colombia.

Magallón, Carmen. 2016. "La paz en Colombia: Decepción, controversia y esperanza." *Cultura de Paz*, no. 70: 4–10.

Malem Seña, Jorge F. 2014. "La corrupción en el deporte." *Fair Play: Revista de Filosofía, Ética y Derecho del Deporte* 2, no. 2: 105–121.

Manrique Rueda, Gabriela, and Samuel Tanner. 2016. "To Prevent the Existence of People Dedicated to 'Causing Trouble': Dirty Work, Social Control and Paramilitaries in Colombia." *British Journal of Criminology* 56, no. 1: 87–104.

Marcos, Ana. 2016. "El voto evangélico, clave en la victoria del 'no' en el plebiscite de Colombia." *El País*, October 12, 2016. https://elpais.com/internacional/2016/10/12/colombia/1476237985_601462.html.

———. 2018. "Why Pablo Escobar Is Anything but Cool." *El País*, September 3, 2018. https://elpais.com/elpais/2018/08/31/inenglish/1535708632_118999.html.

Marcuse, Herbert. 1972. "Ecology and Revolution." *Liberation* 16: 10–12.

———. 2009. *Negations: Essays in Critical Theory*. Translated and edited by Jeremy J. Shapiro. London: MayFlyBooks.

Marinetto, Mike. 2015. "Off the Pitch and Off the Books: Professional Football's Money Laundering Problem." The Conversation, March 27, 2015. https://theconversation.com/off-the-pitch-and-off-the-books-professional-footballs-money-laundering-problem-39222.

Mariscal, Jorge. 2006. "The Making of an American Soldier: Why Young People Join the Military." *National Network Opposing the Militarization of Youth*. https://nnomy.org/en/content_page/item/649-the-making-of-an-american-soldier-why-young-people-join-the-military.html.

Marks, Shula, and Dagmar Engels, eds. 1994. *Contesting Colonial Hegemony: State and Society in Africa and India*. New York: IB Tauris.

Marlon, Jennifer, Peter Howe, Matto Mildenberger, Anthony Leiserowitz, and Xinran Wang. 2018. "Estimated % of Adults Who Think Global Warming Is Happening, 2018." Yale Climate Opinion Maps 2018, August 7, 2018. http://climatecommunication.yale.edu/visualizations-data/ycom-us-2018/?est=happening&type=value&geo=county.

Marshall, T. H. 1950. *Citizenship and Social Class and Other Essays*. Cambridge: Cambridge University Press.

Martín-Barbero, Jesús. 1993. *Communication, Culture and Hegemony: From Media to Mediations*. Translated by Elizabeth Fox and Robert A. White. Newbury Park: Sage.

———. 2003. "Proyectos de modernidad en América Latina." *Metapolítica*, no. 29: 35–51.

———. 2004. "Nuestra excéntrica y heterogénea modernidad." *Estudios Políticos* 25: 115–134.

———. 2006. "Between Technology and Culture: Communication and Modernity in Latin America." In *Cultural Agency in the Americas*, edited by Doris Sommer, 37–51. Durham, NC: Duke University Press.

Martín-Barbero, Jesús, and Sonia Muñoz, eds. 1992. *Televisión y melodrama: Géneros y lecturas de la telenovela en Colombia*. Bogotá: Tercer Mundo Ediciones.

Martínez, Helda. 2010. "COLOMBIA: Drug Trade's Hold on Football Persists." Inter Press Service, June 22, 2010. http://www.ipsnews.net/2010/06/colombia-drug-trades-hold-on-football-persists/.

Martínez, Manuel. 2008. "Imágenes de ciudad: Cartagena de Indias y La Habana en *El amor en los tiempos del cólera* y *La novela de mi vida*." *Co-Herencia* 9, no. 5: 63–79.

Martínez Colorado, Marcos. 2013. "1989: Olimpia versus Narcotráfico." *ABC Color*, August 21, 2013. http://www.abc.com.py/lectores-opinan/1989-olimpia-versus-narcotrafico-609158.html.

Martínez Miranda, Luis Gerardo. 2011. "La champeta: Una forma de resistencia palenquera a las dinámicas de exclusión de las elites "blancas" de Cartagena y Barranquilla entre 1960 y 2000." *Boletín de Antropología* 25, no. 42: 150–174.

Martínez-Alier, Joan. 2012. "Environmental Justice and Economic Degrowth: An Alliance between Two Movements." *Capitalism Nature Socialism* 23, no. 1: 51–73.

Marx, Karl. 1987. *Capital: Vol. 1: A Critical Analysis of Capitalist Production*, 3rd ed. Translated by Samuel Moore and Edward Aveling. Edited by Frederick Engels. New York: International Publishers.

Marx, Leo. 2008. "The Idea of Nature in America." *Daedalus* 137, no. 2: 8–21.

Maslen, Richard. 2014. "Avianca to Return to London Market in July 2014." Routes, February 4, 2014. http://www.routesonline.com/news/29/breaking-news/238576/avianca-to-return-to-london-market-in-july-2014/.

Massardo, Jaime. 1999. "La recepción de Gramsci en America Latina: Cuestiones de orden teórico y político." *International Gramsci Society Newsletter* 9: electronic supplement 3. http://www.internationalgramscisociety.org/igsn/articles/a09_s3.shtml.

Mattelart, Armand. 1980. *Mass Media, Ideologies and the Revolutionary Movement*. Translated by Malcolm Joad. Brighton: Harvester Press/Atlantic Highlands: Humanities Press.

Maxwell, Richard, and Toby Miller. 2016. "The Propaganda Machine behind the Controversy over Climate Science: Can You Spot the Lie in This Title?" *American Behavioral Scientist* 60, no. 3: 288–304.

Maya Restrepo, Luz Adriana. 2001. "Memorias en conflicto y paz en Colombia: la discriminación hacia lo(s) 'negro(s).'" *Estudios Latinoamericanos sobre cultura y transformaciones sociales en tiempos de globalización* 2: 179–195.

———. 2009. "Racismo institucional, violencia y políticas culturales: Legados coloniales y políticas de la diferencia en Colombia." *Historia Crítica Revista Edición Especial* 39, no. 1: 218–245.

Mayora Ronsini, Veneza. 2014. "'Many People Are Just Dreamers': Telenovelas and the Ideology of Meritocracy." *Television & New Media* 15, no. 6: 551–561.

Mazziotti, Nora. 1996. *La industria de la telenovela: La producción de ficción en América Latina*. Buenos Aires: Paidós.

Mazzotti, José Antonio. 2016. "Criollismo, Creole, and Créolité." In *Critical Terms in Caribbean and Latin American Thought*, 87–99. London: Palgrave Macmillan.

Mbembe, Achille. 2003. "Necropolitics." Translated by Libby Meintjes. *Public Culture* 15, no. 1: 11–40.

McCausland Sojo, Ernesto. 2012. "El partido que no distrajo ni a los hinchas." *El Heraldo*, January 31, 2012. http://www.elheraldo.co/galeria-fotos/55303/noticias/nacional/el-partido-que-no-distrajo-ni-a-los-hinchas-55303.

McEvoy, Kevin John. 2018. "Britain's Secret War in Colombia." *Jacobin*, November 2018. https://www.jacobinmag.com/2018/11/uk-colombia-political-violence-bp-drug-war-counterinsurgency.

McGraw, Jason. 2014. *The Work of Recognition: Caribbean Colombia and the Postemancipation Struggle for Citizenship*. Chapel Hill: University of North Carolina Press.

McIlwaine, Cathy. 2014. "Everyday Urban Violence and Transnational Displacement of Colombian Urban Migrants to London, UK." *Environment and Urbanization* 26, no. 2: 1–10.

McKay, Jim. 2018. *Transnational Tourism Experiences at Gallipoli*. Singapore: Springer.

McKenzie, Sheena. 2015. "England vs. France: How Singing 'La Marseillaise' Became a Different War Chant." CNN, November 17, 2015. http://edition.cnn.com/2015/11/17/sport/paris-attacks-french-national-anthem-football-wembley/.

McMichael, Philip. 2017. *Development and Social Change: A Global Perspective*. Los Angeles: Sage.

McNeill, John R. 2010. *Mosquito Empires: Ecology and War in the Greater Caribbean, 1620–1914*. New York: Cambridge University Press.

McPherson, Alan. 2016. *A Short History of U.S. Interventions in Latin America and the Caribbean*. Malven: Wiley-Blackwell.

Meadwell, Hudson. 2016. "The Rationalist Puzzle of War." *Quality & Quantity* 50, no. 4: 1415–1427.

Medialdea, S. 2014. "Madrid no retirará la estatua a Blas de Lezo y afea a Barcelona la «reedición interesada de la Historia»." *ABC*, November 20, 2014. http://www.abc.es/madrid/20141120/abci-madrid-blas-lezo-barcelona-201411201433.html.

Medina, Oscar. 2016. "Caribbean Beaches Help Rescue Colombia from Commodities Slump." *Bloomberg*, February 5, 2016. https://www.bloomberg.com/news/articles/2016-02-05/caribbean-beaches-help-rescue-colombia-from-commodities-slump.

Meisel Roca, Adolfo. 1999. "Cartagena 1900–1950: A remolque de la economía nacional." *Cuadernos de Historia Económica y Empresarial* 4. http://www.banrep.gov.co/sites/default/files/publicaciones/archivos/4.pdf.

Mejia, E. 2007. *Colombia es Pasión—Creación campaña marca*. December 16, 2007. https://www.youtube.com/watch?v=hbiYwys-vs4.

Mekhail, Natasha. 2018. "In Colombia's Cartagena, a Trendy Tourist Destination Emerges." *Globe and Mail*, April 5, 2018. https://www.theglobeandmail.com/life/travel/destinations/in-colombias-cartagena-a-trendy-tourist-destinationemerges/article38143544/.

Mele, Christopher, and Sandra E. Garcia. 2016. "The Colombian Hit Man Who Became a YouTube Star." *New York Times*, June 12, 2016. https://www.nytimes.com/2016/06/13/world/americas/john-jairo-velasquez-colombia-youtube-pablo-escobar.html.

"Me les adelanté a los políticos." 2014. *El Tiempo*, November 5, 2014. http://www.eltiempo.com/colombia/otras-ciudades/un-hombre-rompen-placa-de-cartagena/14796760.

Melián González, Santiago, Jacques Bulchand Gidumal, and Beatriz González López-Valcárcel. 2010. "La participación de los clientes en sitios web de valoración de servicios turísticos: El caso de Tripadvisor." *Análisis Turístico* 10: 17–22.

Meltzer, Judy and Cristina Rojas. 2005. "Elusive Peace: International, National, and Local Dimensions of Conflict in Colombia." In *Elusive Peace: International, National, and Local*

Dimensions of Conflict in Colombia, edited by Cristina Rojas and Judy Meltzer, 1–18. London: Palgrave Macmillan.

Menchero Sánchez, Miriam. 2017. "Las fortificaciones de Cartagena de Indias y su función turística en el turismo cultural de la ciudad." *Methaodos: Revista de Ciencias Sociales* 5, no. 1: 100–118.

———. 2018. "Colombia en posconflicto: ¿Turismo para la paz o paz para el turismo?" *Araucaria: Revista Iberoamericana de Filosofía, Política y Humanidades* 20, no. 39: 415–438.

Mendal, Monica. 2018. "These Private Islands Off the Coast of Cartagena Are Practically Made for Instagram." *Vogue*, April 28, 2018. https://www.vogue.com/article/islas-del-rosario-private-islands-off-the-coast-of-cartegena-colombia.

Meneses, Guillermo Alonso, and Juan Manuel Avalos González. 2013. "La investigación del fútbol y sus nexus con los estudios de comunicación: Aproximaciones y ejemplos." *Comunicación y Sociedad nueva época* 20: 33–64.

Merritt, Russell. 1983. "Melodrama: Postmortem for a Phantom Genre." *Wide Angle* 5, no. 3: 24–31.

Michels, Robert. 2001. *Political Parties: A Sociological Study of the Oligarchical Tendencies of Modern Democracy*. Translated by Eden and Cedar Paul. Kitchener, ON: Batoche Books.

"Miembros de la FARC se relajan y juegan fútbol al acercarse la paz." 2016. *El Caribe*, August 24, 2016. http://www.elcaribe.com.do/2016/08/24/miembros-farc-relajan-juegan-soccer.

Miguel, Edward, Sebastian M. Saiegh, and Shanker Satyanath. 2011. "Civil War Exposure and Violence." *Economics and Politics* 23, no. 1: 59–73.

Mill, John Stuart. 1859. *On Liberty*, http://www.econlib.org/library/Mill/mlLbty3.html.

Miller, Jade L. 2010. "*Ugly Betty* Goes Global: Global Networks of Localized Content in the *Telenovela* Industry." *Global Media and Communication* 6, no. 2: 198–217.

Miller, Toby. 2001. *SportSex*. Philadelphia: Temple University Press.

———. 2012. "Política cultural/industrias creativas." Translated by Laura Victoria Navas. *Cuadernos de Literatura* 31: 17–38.

———. 2018a. "Social Identities from Leicester to Latin London." *Social Identities: Journal for the Study of Race, Nation and Culture* 24, no. 1: 7–15.

———. 2018b. *Él trabajo cultural*. Barcelona: Editorial Gedisa.

Milton, John. 1909-14. *Areopagitica: A Speech for the Liberty of Unlicensed Printing*. Cambridge, MA: Harvard University Press.

Ministerio de Cultura. 2014. *Caracterización metodológica para una valoración económica del patrimonio cultural en Colombia*. http://convenioandresbello.org/documentos/Caracterizacion_Metodologica_Valoracion_Economica_Patrimonio.pdf.

"Miss Colombia to Sue Letterman." 2001. *BBC News*, May 16, 2001. http://news.bbc.co.uk/1/hi/entertainment/1334464.stm.

Modak, Sebastian. 2017. "How Colombia, Once Consumed by Violence, Became Your Next Destination." *Condé Nast Traveler*, November 9, 2017. https://www.cntraveler.com/story/how-colombia-once-consumed-by-violence-became-your-next-destination.

Molano, Alfredo. 2001. *Desterrados: Crónicas del desarraigo*. Bogotá: El Áncora Editores.

Moloney, Anastasia. 2015. "Colombia Approves Femicide Law to Tackle Violence against Women." Reuters, June 4, 2015. https://www.reuters.com/article/us-colombia-femicide-idUSKBN0OK22C20150604.

———. 2018. "Colombia Failing to Fight Child Sexual Exploitation, Officials Admit." Reuters, September 12, 2018. https://www.reuters.com/article/us-colombia-humantrafficking-youth/colombia-failing-to-fight-child-sexual-exploitation-officials-admit-idUSKCN1LS0I6.

Montaña, Silvia. 2014. "*Case 2*: Colombia—an Ethnographic Study of Digital Journalistic Practices." In *Global Journalism Practice and New Media Performance*, edited by Yusuf Kalyango Jr. and David H. Mould, 146–160. London: Palgrave.

Montaño, John. 2018. "Las relaciones de 'Madame' con proxenetas israelíes." *El Tiempo*, August 1, 2018. https://www.eltiempo.com/colombia/otras-ciudades/quien-es-liliana-del-carmen-campos-puello-alias-madame-249974.

More, Thomas. 2012. *Utopia*. Edited by Stephen Duncombe. London: Minor Compositions.

Moreno, Carolina. 2014. "Netflix's 'Narcos' Series on Pablo Escobar 'Will Be Like Nothing Ever Seen Before.'" Huffington Post, April 3, 2014. http://www.huffingtonpost.com/2014/04/03/netflix-narcos-_n_5087063.html.

Morgan, Nick. 2013. "Sex, Soap, and Society: Telenovela Noir in Álvaro Uribe's Colombia." *Journal of Iberian and Latin American Studies* 19, no. 1: 53–76.

Morgenthau, Hans J. 1969. *A New Foreign Policy for the United States*. New York: Frederick A. Praeger.

Morris, William. 1884. "Art and the Beauty of the Earth." Marxist.org. http://www.marxists.org/archive/morris/works/1881/earth.htm.

Moser, Caroline, and Cathy McIlwaine. 2000. *Urban Poor Perceptions of Violence and Exclusion in Colombia: Conflict Prevention and Post-Conflict Reconstruction*. Washington: World Bank.

Mosquera, Mabel Valencia, and Carlos Ospina Bozzi. 2005. "El abordaje de la problemática de explotación sexual infantil en Cartagena." *Palabra* 6: 137–153.

Mowlana, Hamid. 2000. "The Renewal of the Global Media Debate: Implications for the Relationship between the West and the Islamic World." In *Islam and the West in the Mass Media: Fragmented Images in a Globalizing World*, edited by Kai Hafez, 105–118. Cresskill: Hampton Press.

Muecke, Stephen. 2008. *Joe in the Andamans and Other Fictocritical Stories*. Sydney: Local Consumption Publications.

Muñoz Rodríguez, Luisa Fernanda. 2016. "Violencia simbólica y dominación masculina en el discurso cinematográfico colombiano." *Revista Colombiana de Sociología* 39, no. 1: 103–122.

Myers, Teresa A., Edward W. Maibach, Connie Roser-Renouf, Karen Akerlof, and Anthony A. Leiserowitz. 2013. "The Relationship between Personal Experience and Belief in the Reality of Global Warming." *Nature Climate Change* 3: 343–347.

Naciones Unidas Oficina del Alto Comisionado en Colombia. 2018. *Comunicado conjunto: Frente a la situación de seguridad de los y las periodistas en Colombia*. http://www.hchr.org.co/index.php/informacion-publica/comunicados-de-prensa/427-ano-2018/8939-frente-a-la-situacion-de-seguridad-de-los-y-las-periodistas-en-colombia.

Naess, Arne. 1995. "The Deep Ecological Movement." In *Deep Ecology for the Twenty-First Century*, edited by George Sessions, 64–84. Boston: Shambhala Publications.

Narvaez Montoya, Ancizar, and Ana Carmenza Romero Peña. 2017. "La nación en la televisión informativa Colombiana: 1960 y 2015. Del infractor inexistente al enemigo omnipresente." *Revista Folios*, no. 46: 55–65.

Nasser De La Torre, Michelle Rocío. 2012. "Feminized Topographies: Women, Nature, and Tourism in *Colombia es Pasión*." *Revista de Estudios Colombianos* 40: 15–25.

———. 2013. "Bellas por naturaleza: Mapping National Identity on US Colombian Beauty Queens." *Latino Studies* 11, no. 3: 293–312.

Nelson, Julie A. 2009. "Between a Rock and a Soft Place: Ecological and Feminist Economics in Policy Debates." *Ecological Economics* 69, no. 1: 1–8.

Nemogá, Gabriel Ricardo. 2014. "Biodiversity Research and Conservation in Colombia (1990–2010): The Marginalization of Indigenous Peoples' Rights." *Canadian Journal of*

Latin American and Caribbean Studies/Revue canadienne des études latino-américaines et caraïbes 39, no. 1: 93–111.

Neville, Steve. 2018. "The Sun Newspaper Issues 'Apology'—of Sorts—for Controversial Colombia Headline." *Irish Examiner*, July 4, 2018. https://www.irishexaminer.com/breakingnews/sport/soccer/the-sun-newspaper-issues-apology—of-sorts—for-controversial-colombia-headline-853035.html.

New York Times. 2014. *Innovation. New York Times*, March 24, 2014. https://www.presscouncil.org.au/uploads/52321/ufiles/The_New_York_Times_Innovation_Report_-_March_2014.pdf.

Nielsen, Rasmus Kleis. 2010. "Participation through Letters to the Editor: Circulation, Considerations, and Genres in the Letters Institution." *Journalism* 11, no. 1: 21–35.

Niesing, Eva. 2013. *Latin America's Potential in Nation Branding: A Closer Look at Brazil's, Chile's and Colombia's Practices*. New York: Anchor Books.

Nietzsche, Friedrich. 2002. *Beyond Good and Evil: Prelude to a Philosophy of the Future*. Translated by Judith Norman. Edited by Rolf-Peter Horstmann and Judith Norman. Cambridge: Cambridge University Press.

"Noemí Sanín: Renuncia la embajadora de Los Millonarios." 2013. *Semana*, September 3, 2013. http://www.semana.com/nacion/articulo/noemi-sanin-renuncia-embajadora-los-millonarios/336309-3.

"Nomination of John F. Kerry to Be Secretary of State." 2013. *Hearing Before the Committee on Foreign Relations, United States Senate, One Hundred Thirteenth Congress, First Session*, January 24, 2013. https://www.foreign.senate.gov/imo/media/doc/012413_Transcript_Nomination%20of%20John%20F%20Kerry%20to%20be%20Secretary%20of%20State.pdf.

"Not the Kind of Press They Were After." 2012. *Economist*, April 21, 2012. https://www.economist.com/americas-view/2012/04/21/not-the-kind-of-press-they-were-after.

NULLVALUE. 1994. "Fútbol y violencia, una larga historia." *El Tiempo*, July 3, 1994. http://www.eltiempo.com/archivo/documento/MAM-164658.

NULLVALUE. 1999. "Juan José Bellini, otra vez en prisión." *El Tiempo*, February 2, 1999. http://www.eltiempo.com/archivo/documento/MAM-876909.

Nussbaum, Martha C. 1999. *Sex and Social Justice*. New York: Oxford University Press.

———. 2013. *Political Emotions. Why Love Matters for Justice*. Cambridge, MA: Harvard University Press.

Nye, David E. 1994. *American Technological Sublime*. Cambridge, MA: MIT Press.

———. 2006. "Technology and the Production of Difference." *American Quarterly* 58, no. 3: 597–618.

O'Brien, Erin, Sharon Hayes, and Belinda Carpenter. 2013. *The Politics of Sex Trafficking: A Moral Geography*. New York: Palgrave Macmillan.

Observatorio Iberoamericano de Ficción Televisiva. 2014. *Transmedia Production Strategies in Television Fiction*. Rio de Janeiro: Globo Universidade.

Ocampo, José Antonio, and Camilo Tovar. 2000. "Colombia in the Classical Era of 'Inward-Looking Development', 1930–74." In *An Economic History of Twentieth-Century Latin America. Volume 3. Industrialization and the State in Latin America: The Postwar Years*, edited by Enrique Cárdenas, José Antonio Ocampo, and Rosemary Thorp, 239–281. London: Palgrave.

Ochoa Gautier, Ana María. 2014. *Aurality: Listening and Knowledge in Nineteenth-Century Colombia*. Durham, NC: Duke University Press.

O'Connor James. 1998. *Natural Causes: Essays in Ecological Marxism*. New York: Guilford.

Oficina de Estudio Económicos. 2017. *Boletín Mensual Turismo: Junio 2017*. http://www.mincit.gov.co/loader.php?lServicio=Documentos&lFuncion=verPdf&id=81627&name=OEE_LL_Turismo_Junio_18-07-2017.pdf&prefijo=file.

O'Hanlon, Michael E., and David Petraeus. 2013. "The Success Story in Colombia." Brookings, September 24, 2013. https://www.brookings.edu/opinions/the-success-story-in-colombia/.

Ojeda, Diana. 2013. "War and Tourism: The Banal Geographies of Security in Colombia's 'Retaking.'" *Geopolitics* 18, no. 4: 759–778.

"Orange Economy Already Accounts for Almost 3% of GDP in Colombia." 2018. PR Newswire, October 15, 2018. https://finance.yahoo.com/news/orange-economy-already-accounts-almost-060000802.html.

Organisation for Economic Co-operation and Development. 2009. *Armed Violence Reduction: Enabling Development.* https://www.oecd-ilibrary.org/development/armed-violence-reduction_9789264060173-en.

———. 2014. *Environmental Performance Review: Colombia.* http://www.keepeek.com/Digital-Asset-Management/oecd/environment/oecd-environmental-performance-reviews-colombia-2014_9789264208292-en#page1.

———. 2016. *States of Fragility 2016: Understanding Violence.* http://dx.doi.org/10.1787/9789264267213-en.

———. 2017. *OECD Integrity Review of Colombia: Investing in Integrity for Peace and Prosperity.* https://read.oecd-ilibrary.org/governance/oecd-integrity-review-of-colombia_9789264278325-en.

———. 2018. *Latin American Economic Outlook 2018: Rethinking Institutions for Development.* https://www.oecd-ilibrary.org/development/latin-american-economic-outlook-2018_leo-2018-en.

———. Working Group on Bribery. 2019. *Implementing the OECD Anti-Bribery Convention: Phase 3 Report: Colombia.* http://www.oecd.org/corruption/Colombia-Phase-3-Report-ENG.pdf.

Organización Internacional para las Migraciones. 2015. *Justicia y violencia sexual: Cartilla explicativa de los contenidos de la Ley 1719 de 2014.* https://repository.oim.org.co/bitstream/handle/20.500.11788/1292/COL-OIM0508.pdf;jsessionid=B33BB9D1498A9D4123917CAD6786B71C?sequence=1.

Organización para la Cooperación y el Desarrollo Económico. 2015. *Estudios económicos de la OCDE: Colombia.* http://www.oecd.org/eco/surveys/Overview_Colombia_ESP.pdf.

Orlando Melo, Jorge. 1998. "The Drug Trade, Politics and the Economy: The Colombian Experience." Translated by Pam Decho. In *Latin America and the Multinational Drug Trade,* edited by Elizabeth Joyce and Carlos Malamud, 63–96. New York: St. Martin's Press.

Orozco, Guillermo. 2014. "Mexican Research on TV: A Tradition Framed by a Powerful Quasi-Monopolistic TV System." In *The Sage Handbook of Television Studies,* edited by Manuel Alvarado, Milly Buonanno, Herman Gray, and Toby Miller, 105–114. Thousand Oaks, CA: Sage.

Orozco-Triana, Jairo, Carlos Gabriel Vargas-Arrieta, and José David Florez-Reyes. 2015. "Análisis de la actividad de los sectores de la transformación y servicios industriales en Cartagena de Indias—Colombia." *Revista Panorama Económico,* no. 23: 71–90.

Oquendo, Catalina. 2019. "Hay cinco conflictos armados hoy en Colombia." *El País,* July 21, 2019. https://elpais.com/internacional/2019/07/20/colombia/1563649226_997490.html.

Orrego Ramírez, Lina Maria, Jorge Iván Velásquez Restrepo, and Lucas Uribe Lopera. 2010. "Caracterización psicosocial del futbolista perteneciente a la categoría primera "A" del Fútbol Professional Colombiano." *Pensando Psicología* 6, no. 10: 11–21.

Orser, Charles E., Jr. 2019. "Archaeological Research and the British in Latin America." In *Archaeologies of the British in Latin America,* edited by Charles E. Orser Jr., 1–11. New York: Springer.

Ortega y Gasset, José. 1994. *The Revolt of the Masses*. New York: W. W. Norton.
Orwell, George. 1937. *The Road to Wigan Pier*. London: Victor Gollancz.
———. 1945. "The Sporting Spirit." *Tribune*, December 1945. http://www.orwell.ru/library/articles/spirit/english/e_spirit.
———. 1949. *Nineteen Eighty-Four: A Novel*. London: Secker & Warburg.
Oslender, Ulrich. 2004. "Fleshing Out the Geographies of Social Movements: Colombia's Pacific Coast Black Communities and the "Aquatic Space." *Political Geography* 23, no. 8: 957–985.
———. 2008. "Another History of Violence: The Production of 'Geographies of Terror' in Colombia's Pacific Coast Region." *Latin American Perspectives* 35, no. 5: 77–102.
Ostrom, Elinor. 2000. "Reformulating the Commons." *Swiss Political Science Review* 6, no. 1: 29–52.
Ottosen, Rune. 2010. "The War in Afghanistan and Peace Journalism in Practice." *Media, War & Conflict* 3, no. 3: 261–278.
———. 2017. "To Deal with Impunity, We Must Address Both Political and Criminal Motivated Violence." *Journalism & Communication Monographs* 19, no. 2: 159–162.
Oxfam. 2009. *La violencia sexual en Colombia: Una arma de guerra*. https://www.oxfam.org/sites/www.oxfam.org/files/file_attachments/bp-sexual-violence-colombia-sp 3.pdf.
———. 2016. *Unearthed: Land, Power, and Inequality in Latin America*. https://www.oxfam.org/sites/www.oxfam.org/files/file_attachments/unearthed-executive-en-29nov-web.pdf.
Oxford, Sarah. 2019. "'You Look Like a Machito!': A Decolonial Analysis of the Social In/Exclusion of Female Participants in a Colombian Sport for Development and Peace Organization." *Sport in Society* 22, no. 6: 1025–1042.
Oxford, Sarah, and Ramón Spaaij. 2019. "Gender Relations and Sport for Development in Colombia: A Decolonial Feminist Analysis." *Leisure Sciences* 41, nos. 1–2: 54–71.
Padilla, Rebecca, Jerónimo Repoli, David González, Gabriel Moreno, Hugo García, Darwin Franco, and Guillermo Orozco. 2011. "México: la investigación de la recepción y sus audiencias: Hallazgos recientes y perspectivas." In *Análisis de recepción en América Latina: Un recuento histórico con perspectivas al futuro*, edited by Nilda Jacks, 227–266. Quito: Ciespal.
Pahwa, Sonali, and Jessica Winegar. 2012. "Culture, State, and Revolution." *Middle East Report* 42: 263.
"Palabras del Presidente Juan Manuel Santos en la entrega del Pabellón Nacional a la Selección Colombia y el lanzamiento de la emisión filatélica conmemorativa del Mundial de Fútbol Brasil 2014." May 23, 2014. http://wsp.presidencia.gov.co/prensa/2014/mayo/paginas/20140523_02-palabras-del-presidente-santos-entrega-pabellon-nacional-seleccion-colombia-emision-filatelica-mundial-futbol-b.aspx.
Palacios, Marco. 2003. *Entre la legitimidad y la violencia: Colombia, 1875–1994*, 2nd ed. Bogotá: Editorial Norma.
Pan, Bing, Zhen Xiang, Rob Law, and Daniel R. Fesenmaier. 2011. "The Dynamics of Search Engine Marketing for Tourist Destinations." *Journal of Travel Research* 50, no. 4: 365–377.
Pantti, Mervi, Karin Wahl-Jorgensen, and Simon Cottle, eds. 2012. *Disasters and the Media*. New York: Peter Lang.
Parekh, Bhikhu. 2000. *Rethinking Multiculturalism: Cultural Diversity and Political Theory*. Basingstoke: Palgrave.
Parker-Magyar, Katherine. 2019. "American Tourists No Longer Need Visas to Visit Brazil—Here's Where to Celebrate." *Forbes*, June 30, 2019. https://www.forbes.com/sites/katherineparkermagyar/2019/06/30/us-tourists-no-longer-need-visas-to-visit-brazil-heres-how-to-celebrate/#3fbdd8c65775.

Parsons, Talcott, and Robert F. Bales, in collaboration with James Olds, Morris Zelditch Jr., and Philip E. Slater. 1955. *Family, Socialization and Interaction Process.* Glencoe, IL: Free Press.

Paschel, Tianna S. 2010. "The Right to Difference: Explaining Colombia's Shift from Color Blindness to the Law of Black Communities." *American Journal of Sociology* 116, no. 3: 729–769.

———. 2016. *Becoming Black Political Subjects: Movements and Ethno-Racial Rights in Colombia and Brazil.* Princeton, NJ: Princeton University Press.

Passy, Florence, and Gian-Andrea Monsch. 2014. "Do Social Networks Really Matter in Contentious Politics?" *Social Movement Studies* 13, no. 1: 22–47.

Patnaik, Arun Kumar. 2004. "Gramsci Today." *Economic and Political Weekly* (March 13–19): 1120–1123.

PCNT. 1952. *Anales del Primer Congreso Nacional de Turismo: Colombia.* Bogotá: Ministerio de Fomento, Departamento Nacional de Turismo.

Pécaut, Daniel. 1987. "Acerca de La Violencia de los años cincuenta." *Boletín Socioeconómico,* no. 17: 33–48.

Pécaut, Daniel. 2001. "La tragedia colombiana: Guerra, violencia, tráfico de droga." *Revista Sociedad y Economía,* no. 1: 133–148.

Peláez Sierra, María José. 2019. "¿Por qué están matando a los líderes de Córdoba?" *Semana,* July 9, 2019. https-//semanarural.com/web/articulo/por-que-estan-matando-a-los-lideres-de-cordoba/1021?utm_source=semana.com&utm_medium=referral&utm_campaign=otras-publicaciones-footer.

Peña, Yussy Arteta, Mayra Rosario Moreno Pino, and Ingrid Steffanell De León. 2015. "La gestión ambiental de la cuenca del Río Magdalena desde un enfoque socialmente responsable." *Revista Amauta* 13, no. 26: 193–218.

Perazzi, Josefa Ramoni, and Giampaolo Orlandoni Merli. 2017. "Análisis de la estructura del mercado laboral en Colombia: Un estudio por género mediante correspondencias multiples." *Cuadernos de Economía* 40, no. 113: 100–114.

Pérez Carrascal, Airlin, and Davide Riccardi. 2019. "La mujer afrodescendiente frente al fascismo del apartheid social en Cartagena de Indias: ¿esperanzas para el cambio en un contexto de histórica discriminación?" *Memorias: Revista Digital de Historia y Arqueología desde el Caribe colombiano* 15, no. 38: 162–185.

Perkins, Ellie, and Edith Kuiper. 2005. "Introduction: Exploring Feminist Ecological Economics." *Feminist Economics* 11, no. 3: 107–110.

Pew Research Center. 2014. *Religion in Latin America: Widespread Change in a Historically Catholic Region.* http://assets.pewresearch.org/wp-content/uploads/sites/11/2014/11/Religion-in-Latin-America-11-12-PM-full-PDF.pdf.

Piketty, Thomas. 2014. *Capital in the Twenty-First Century.* Translated by Arthur Goldhammer. Cambridge, MA: Belknap Press of Harvard University Press.

Pineda Duque, Javier Armando. 2003. *Masculinidades, género y desarrollo: Sociedad civil, machismo y microempresa en Colombia.* Bogotá: Universidad de Los Andes.

Pinker, Steve. 2011. *The Better Angels of Our Nature: Why Violence Has Declined.* New York: Viking.

Pino Uribe, Juan Federico. 2017. "¿Un matrimonio infeliz? Democracia y violencia política en Colombia: Entre la restricción, cooptación y construcción." *Papel Político* 22, no. 2: 369–393.

Piñon, Juan. 2019. "Disruption and Continuity on [*sic*] *Telenovela* with the Surge of a New Hybrid Prime-Time Fictional Serial: The Super Series." *Critical Studies in Television: The International Journal of Television Studies* 14, no. 2: 204–221.

Pinto, Juliet, Paola Prado, and J. Alejandro Tirado-Alzaraz. 2017. *Environmental News in South America: Conflict, Crisis and Contestation*. London: Palgrave Macmillan.

"¡Pitalito sin censura!, Proyecto por la libertad de prensa." 2015. *La Crónica*, November 10, 2015. http://www.cronicadelquindio.com/noticia-completa-titulo-pitalito_sin_censura_proyecto_por_la_libertad_de_prensa-seccion-la_nacin-nota-93596.

Plato. 1972. *The Laws*. Translated by Trevor J. Saunders. Harmondsworth: Penguin.

Plumb, J. H. 1964. "Introduction." In *Crisis in the Humanities*, edited by J. H. Plumb, 7–10. Harmondsworth: Penguin.

Pointdujour, Danielle. 2019. "Black Travel Vibes: Get Into the Colorful City of Cartagena." *Essence*, May 3, 2019. https://www.essence.com/lifestyle/travel/black-travel-vibes-get-into-the-colorful-city-of-cartagena/.

"Political Will to Fight Climate Change is Fading, Warns UN Chief." 2019. *BBC News*, May 12, 2019. https://www.bbc.com/news/av/world-asia-48244315/political-will-to-fight-climate-change-is-fading-warns-un-chief.

Poniatowska, Elena. 1995. *Nothing, Nobody: The Voices of the Mexico City Earthquake*. Translated by Aurora Camacho de Schmidt and Arthur Schmidt. Philadelphia: Temple University Press.

"Popeye estará recluido en cárcel de máxima seguridad de Valledupar." 2018. *Semana*, May 28, 2018. https://www.semana.com/nacion/articulo/popeye-estara-recluido-en-carcel-de-maxima-seguridad-de-valledupar/569153.

Popovski, Vesselin, Gregory M. Reichberg, and Nicholas Turner, eds. 2009. *World Religions and Norms of War*. Tokyo: United Nations University Press.

"¿Por qué algunas estrellas del fútbol caen en el mundo del narcotráfico?" 2019. *Semana*, March 23, 2019. https://www.semana.com/deportes/articulo/futbolistas-y-narcotrafico-una-historia-de-tiempo-extra/606714.

Prager, Alicia, and Michael Hameleers. 2018. "Disseminating Information or Advocating Peace? Journalists' Role Perceptions in the Face of Conflict." *Journalism*. http://journals.sagepub.com/doi/10.1177/1464884918791788.

Pratt, Stephen, and Anyu Liu. 2016. "Does Tourism Really Lead to Peace? A Global View." *International Journal of Tourism Research*, no. 18: 82–90.

Prebisch, Raúl. 1982. *The Crisis of Capitalism and the Periphery: 1st Raúl Prebisch Lecture*. Geneva: United Nations Conference on Trade and Development.

"Presentadora Vanessa De la Torre denuncia amenazas. ¿Por qué?" 2018. *Publimetro*, July 26, 2018. https://www.publimetro.co/co/noticias/2018/07/26/vanessa-de-la-torre-denuncia-amenazas-de-muerte.html.

Preston, Tori. 2019. "'The Grand Tour' Finds Cocaine Hippos in Colombia." *Pajiba*, January 31, 2019. http://www.pajiba.com/tv_reviews/the-grand-tour-goes-to-colombia-for-cocaine-hippos.php.

Preston, William Jr., Edward S. Herman, and Herbert I. Schiller. 1989. *Hope and Folly: The United States and UNESCO 1945–1985*. Minneapolis: University of Minnesota Press.

Procolombia. 2015. "About Cali." Procolombia, July 31, 2015. http://www.procolombia.co/en/pacific-alliance/about-cali (site discontinued).

Programa de las Naciones Unidas para el Desarrollo. 2015. *Informe sobre desarrollo humano 2015*. New York: United Nations.

Pruitt, Deborah, and Suzanne LaFont. 1995. "For Love and Money: Romance Tourism in Jamaica." *Annals of Tourism Research* 22, no. 2: 422–440.

Puello Sarabia, Cielo Patricia. 2017. "Narrativas de la memoria, conflicto y organizaciones territoriales en Los Montes de María." *Economía & Región* 11, no. 2: 81–113.

Puello Sarabia, Cielo Patricia, and Erika Paola Ardila Palacio. 2019. "La ciudad erotizada: Análisis discursivo de un blog turístico sobre Cartagena de Indias." *Actas ICONO* 14: 166–181.

Puentes Sánchez, Diego Felipe. 2015. "La reconfiguración de la Seguridad Ciudadana: El caso de la seguridad y la convivencia del fútbol en Colombia." *Revista de Paz y Conflictos* 8, no. 1: 241–268.

Pufendorf, Samuel. 2000. *On the Duty of Man and Citizen According to Natural Law*. Translated by Michael Silverthorne. Edited by James Tully. Cambridge: Cambridge University Press.

Puig-i-Abril, Eulàlia, and Hernando Rojas. 2018. "Silencing Political Opinions: An Assessment of the Influence of Geopolitical Contexts in Colombia." *Communication Research* 45, no. 1: 55–82.

Puyosa, Iria. 2015. "Los movimientos sociales en red: Del arranque emocional a la propagación e ideas de cambio político." *Chasqui: Revista Latinoamericana de Comunicación* 128: 197–214.

"Queman bandera de las Farc en Cartagena en víspera de firma de acuerdo." 2016. *Pulzo*, February 25, 2016. https://www.pulzo.com/nacion/queman-bandera-farc-union-sovietica-cartagena-PP128957.

Quevedo H., Norbey. 2012. "Los secretos del Envigado Fútbol Club." *El Espectador*, June 30, 2012. http://www.elespectador.com/noticias/investigacion/los-secretos-del-envigado-futbol-club-articulo-356383.

Quintero, Paola, and Camila Bernal. 2007. "Diversificación y cultura: Qué ofrece y cómo se promociona Cartagena de Indias (Colombia)." *Paso: Revista de turismo y Patrimonio Cultural* 5, no. 3: 307–322.

Quitián Roldán, David Leonardo. 2007. "El narcotráfico en área de penal: Reflexiones sobre goles y cárteles de la droga en Colombia." *Caravelle* 89: 157–182.

———. 2013. "La economía del fútbol colombiano: De la ilegalidad y el crimen al glamur globalizado." *Polémika* 10, no. 1: 60–65.

Quitián Roldán, David Leonardo, and Olga Lucia Urrea Beltrán. 2016a. "Fútbol, desarrollo social y patria: La violencia como factor de *lo nacional* en clave de gol." *Revista San Gregorio* especial no. 2: 162–170.

———. 2016b. "Fútbol, radio y nación (1946–1974): Una visión antropológica de la violencia en Colombia." *Espacio Abierto: Cuaderno Venezolano de Sociología* 25, no. 2: 51–66.

Raeymaeckers, Karin. 2005. "Letters to the Editor: A Feedback Opportunity Turned into a Marketing Tool." *European Journal of Communication* 20, no. 1: 199–221.

Raine, Adrian. 2013. *The Anatomy of Violence: The Biological Roots of Crime*. New York: Pantheon.

Ramírez, Lucia, and Aldo Santiago. 2015. "El río de la vida: defensa comunitaria contra hidroeléctrica El Quimbo." SubVersiones, July 8, 2015. https://subversiones.org/archivos/117064.

Ramírez Botero, Isabel Cristina. 2010. *El arte en Cartagena a través de la colección del Banco de la República*. Cartagena: Banco de la República.

Ramírez Murcia, Armando. 2016. "Telenovela y género en Colombia." *Nóesis*: 46–64.

Rathbone. John Paul. 2013. "The History and Politics of Colombian Media." *Financial Times*, June 3, 2013. https://www.ft.com/content/621bcdfc-9de5-11e2-9ccc-00144feabdc0.

Rathbone, John Paul, and Gideon Long. 2018. "Colombia and Corruption: The Problem of Extreme Legalism." *Financial Times*, August 14, 2018. https://www.ft.com/content/0b833ef8-9c81-11e8-9702-5946bae86e6d.

Rawls, John. 1999. *The Law of Peoples with "The Idea of Public Reason Revisited."* Cambridge, MA: Harvard University Press.

Rayas Velasco, Lucía 2009. *Armadas: Un análisis de género desde el cuerpo de las mujeres combatientes*. Mexico City: Colegio de México.

Rec.Sport.Soccer Statistics Foundation. 2015. "Argentines in the Italian National Team." http://www.rsssf.com/miscellaneous/argital-recintlp.html.

Redacción Deportes. 2012. "Narcos y fútbol colombiano, conexión de más de treinta años." *El Tiempo*, September 26, 2012. http://www.eltiempo.com/archivo/documento/CMS-12253785.

Reis, Giuliano, and Wolff-Michael Roth. 2009. "A Feeling for the Environment: Emotion Talk in/for the Pedagogy of Public Environmental Education." *Journal of Environmental Education* 41, no. 2: 71–87.

Relly, Jeannine E., and Celeste González de Bustamante. 2017. "Global and Domestic Networks Advancing Prospects for Institutional and Social Change: The Collective Action Response to Violence Against Journalists." *Journalism and Communication Monographs* 19, no. 2: 84–152.

Rentoul, John. 2011. "Threatened, Isolated, Under Siege: The UK's Working Class Today." *Independent*, June 25, 2011. http://www.independent.co.uk/news/uk/home-news/threatened-isolated-under-siege-the-uks-working-class-today-2302850.html.

Renwick, Douglas W. S., Tom Redman, and Stuart Maguire. 2013. "Green Human Resource Management: A Review and Research Agenda." *International Journal of Management Reviews* 15, no. 1: 1–14.

Reporters Without Borders. 2018. *Day of the Journalist: Colombia's Journalists Need More Protection*. Reporters Without Borders, August 3, 2018. https://rsf.org/en/news/day-journalist-colombias-journalists-need-more-protection.

Restrepo, Eduardo, Ernesto Schwartz-Martín, and Roosbelinda Cárdenas. 2014. "Nation and Difference in the Genetic Imagination of Colombia." In *Mestizo Genomics: Race Mixture, Nation, and Science in Latin America*, edited by Peter Wade, Carlos López Beltrán, Eduardo Restrepo, and Ricardo Ventura Santos, 55–84. Durham, NC: Duke University Press.

Restrepo, Juan Camilo, Kerstin Schrottke, Camille Traini, Alexander Bartholomae, Silvio Ospino, Juan Carlos Ortíz, Luís Otero, and Andrés Orejarena. 2018. "Estuarine and Sediment Dynamics in a Microtidal Tropical Estuary of High Fluvial Discharge: Magdalena River (Colombia, South America)." *Marine Geology*, no. 398: 86–98.

Restrepo, Juan D. 2015. "El impacto de la deforestación en la erosion de la cuenca del río Magdalena (1980–2010)." *Revista Academia Colombiana de Ciencias Exactas, Físicas y Naturales* 39, no. 151: 250–267.

Restrepo, Juan D., Bjöorn Kjerfve, Michel Hermelin, and Juan C. Restrepo. 2006. "Factors Controlling Sediment Yield in a Major South American Drainage Basin: The Magdalena River, Colombia." *Journal of Hydrology* 316, no. 1: 213–232.

Restrepo, Juan D., Albert J. Kettner, and James P. M. Syvitski. 2015. "Recent Deforestation Causes Rapid Increase in River Sediment Load in the Colombian Andes." *Anthropocene* 10, no. 1: 13–28.

Restrepo Escobar, Sandra Milena. 2015. "Violencia en el fútbol, asociada a consume de sustancias psicoactivas." In *Prevención y tratamiento de las adicciones desde lo psicosocial*, edited by Ángela Marita Lopera Jaramillo, César Augusto Jaramillo Jaramillo, Wilson Armando Montaño Pardo, and Sandra Lorena Botina Narvaéz, 35–44. Medellín: Fundación Universitaria Luis Amigó.

"Reunion de acolfutpro y dimayor que pasó en ministerio de trabajo." 2019. *Futbolred*, November 1, 2019. https://www.futbolred.com/futbol-colombiano/liga-aguila/reunion-de-acolfutpro-y-dimayor-que-paso-en-ministerio-de-trabajo-2019-108934.

Rich, Adrienne. 1997. "The Springboard." In *A Whole Other Ball Game: Women's Literature on Women's Sport*, edited by Joli Sandoz, 1. New York: Noonday Press.

Richani, Nazih. 2013. *Systems of Violence: The Political Economy of War and Peace in Colombia*, 2nd ed. Albany: State University of New York Press.

Richardson, James D., comp. 2004. *A Compilation of the Messages and Papers of the Presidents, Volume 2: James Monroe*. Project Gutenberg. https://www.gutenberg.org/ebooks/10919.

Richford, Rhonda. 2018. "John Krasinski Talks Playing a "Superhero" in 'Jack Ryan.'" *Hollywood Reporter*, June 17, 2018. https://www.hollywoodreporter.com/news/john-krasinski-talks-playing-a-superhero-jack-ryan-1120761.

Riley, Robin L., Chandra Talpade Mohanty, and Minnie Bruce Pratt, eds. 2008. *Feminism and War: Confronting U.S. Imperialism*. London: Zed Books.

Rincón, Omar. 2015. "Amamos a Pablo, odiamos a los políticos: Las repercusiones de *Escobar, el patrón del mal*." *Nueva Sociedad*, no. 255: 94–105.

———. 2018. "La narcoficción/El otro lado." *El Tiempo*, July 22, 2018. https://www.eltiempo.com/cultura/cine-y-tv/la-narcoficcion-en-mexico-y-colombia-el-otro-lado-de-omar-rincon-246578.

———. 2019. "TV-violencias: Mejor contados en la ficción que en la información." *Revista de Estudios Hispánicos* 53, no. 1: 187–209.

Rincón, Sebastián. 2019. "La industria naranja colombiana, ¿pierde color?" *Forbes México*, December 20, 2019. https://www.forbes.com.mx/la-industria-naranja-colombiana-pierde-color/.

Rincón-Escobar, Erika Andrea, Sara Sofía Escobar-González, Juan Esteban Gómez-Mesa, and Juan Pablo Martínez-Cano. 2018. "Relación entre eventos cardiovasculares y un mundial de fútbol." *Revista Colombiana de Cardiología* 25, no. 1: 19–25.

Rivera, José Eustasio. 1985. *La Vorágine*. Caracas: Fundación Biblioteca Ayacucho.

Rivero, Yeidy M. 2003. "The Performance and Reception of Televisual "Ugliness" in *Yo soy Betty la fea*." *Feminist Media Studies* 3, no. 1: 65–81.

Robertson, James Alexander. 1919. "The English Attack on Cartagena in 1741; And Plans for an Attack on Panama." *Hispanic American Historical Review* 2, no. 1: 62–71.

Rocha, Carolina. 2018. "La productora colombiana Dynamo: Del cine nacional al transnacional?" *Studies in Spanish and Latin American Cinemas* 15, no. 3: 349–367.

Rochlin, James. 2015. "Boom, Bust and Human Security in the Extractive Sector: The Case of Colombia." *The Extractive Industries and Society* 2, no. 4: 734–745.

Rodríguez Romero, Carlos, and Edison Jair Duque Oliva. 2007. "Seguimiento a la dinámica competitiva de dos grupos económicos colombianos." *Innovar* 17, no. 29: 137–154.

Rodrik, Dani. 2007. *One Economics, Many Recipes: Globalization, Institutions, and Economic Growth*. Princeton, NJ: Princeton University Press.

Rojas, Cristina. 2002. *Civilization and Violence: Regimes of Representation in Nineteenth-Century Colombia*. Minneapolis: University of Minnesota Press.

Roldán, Mary. 2002. *Blood and Fire: La Violencia in Antioquia, Colombia, 1946–1953*. Durham, NC: Duke University Press.

Rolston, Bill, and Sofi Ospina. 2017. "Picturing Peace: Murals and Memory in Colombia." *Race and Class* 58, no. 3: 23–45.

Romero, César. 2018. "262.197 muertos dejó el conflicto armado." Centro Nacional de Memoria Histórica, August 9, 2018. http://www.centrodememoriahistorica.gov.co/noticias/noticias-cmh/262-197-muertos-dejo-el-conflicto-armado.

Romero, Mauricio, ed. 2007. *Parapolítica: La ruta de expansión paramilitar y los acuerdos políticos*. Bogotá: Corporación Nuevo Arcoiris.

Rosen, Jonathan D., and Bruce M. Bagley. 2015. "Introduction." In *Colombia's Political Economy at the Outset of the Twenty-First Century: From Uribe to Santos and Beyond*, edited by Bruce M. Bagley and Jonathan D. Rosen, ix–xvii. Lanham: Lexington Books.

Rosen, Jonathan D., and Hanna Samir Kassab. 2019. *Drugs, Gangs, and Violence*. New York: Springer.

Rouch, Jean. 2003. *Ciné-Ethnography*. Edited and translated by Steve Feld. Minneapolis: University of Minnesota Press.

Roxborough, Ian. 2015. "The Future of War." *Sociological Forum* 30, no. 2: 459–474.

Rubio, Mauricio. 2000. "El desbordamiento de la violencia en Colombia." In *Violencia en América Latina*, edited by Juan Luis Londoño, Alejandro Gaviria, and Rodrigo Guerrero, 103–170. Washington: Banco Internacional de Desarrollo.

Rueda De la Hoz, Linda. 2018. "'Los colombianos viven convencidos de que su país está condenado al fracaso': Daniel Pécaut." *El Espectador*, April 1, 2018. https://www.elespectador.com/noticias/nacional/los-colombianos-viven-convencidos-de-que-su-pais-esta-condenado-al-fracaso-daniel-pecaut-articulo-747138.

Rueda de Vivero, Fabio, and Aarón Espinosa Espinosa. 2008. *¿Los pobres de hoy serán los pobres del mañana? Determinantes de la pobreza y magnitud de la vulnerabilidad de Cartagena de Indias*. https://papers.ssrn.com/sol3/papers.cfm?abstract_id=1411775.

Ruiz, Daniel, Douglas G. Martinson, and Walter Vergara. 2012. "Trends, Stability and Stress in the Colombian Central Andes." *Climate Change* 112, nos. 3–4: 717–732.

Ruiz Bonilla, Guillermo. 2008. *Historia del fútbol profesional colombiano*. Bogotá: Dayscript.

Ruiz Patiño, Jorge Humberto. 2017. "Balance sobre la historiografía del deporte en Colombia: Un panorama de su desarrollo." *Materiales para la Historia del Deporte*, no. 15: 24–44.

Ryan, Erin Gloria. 2012. "Colombian Prostitutes More Addictive Than Colombian Cocaine for U.S. Officials." *Jezebel* (blog), May 22, 2012. http://jezebel.com/5912278/colombian-prostitutes-more-addictive-than-colombian-cocaine-for-us-officials.

Ryan, Gery W., and H. Russell Bernard. 2003. "Techniques to Identify Themes in Qualitative Data." *Field Methods* 15, no. 1: 85–109.

Saavedra, Glory. 2018. "Colombian Resistance against the Odebrecht-Nurtured Mafia." Democracia Abierta, December 6, 2018. https://www.opendemocracy.net/democracia abierta/glory-saavedra/colombian-resistance-against-odebrecht-nurtured-mafia.

Sacipa-Rodriguez, Stella, and Maritza Montero, eds. 2014. *Psychosocial Approaches to Peace-Building in Colombia*. New York: Springer.

Safford, Frank, and Marco Palacios. 2002. *Colombia: Fragmented Land, Divided Society*. New York: Oxford University Press.

Salazar, Miguel. 2018. "Soccer and Domestic Violence: When the Beautiful Game Turns Ugly." *Nation*, September 26, 2018. https://www.thenation.com/article/soccer-and-domestic-violence-when-the-beautiful-game-turns-ugly/.

Salazar, Alejandro, Adriana Sanchez, Juan Camilo Villegas, Juan F. Salazar, Daniel Ruiz Carrascal, Stephen Sitch, Juan Darío Restrepo, Germán Poveda, Kenneth J. Feeley, Lina M. Mercado, Paola A. Arias, Carlos A. Sierra, Maria del Rosario Uribe, Angela M. Rendón, Juan Carlos Pérez, Guillermo Murray Tortarolo, Daniel Mercado-Bettin, José A. Posada, Qianlai Zhuang, and Jeffrey S. Dukes. 2018. "The Ecology of Peace: Preparing Colombia for New Political and Planetary Climates." *Frontiers in Ecology and the Environment* 16, no. 9: 525–531.

Salcedo, Edwin. 2016. Interview with Anamaria Tamayo-Duque, December 2016.

Salcedo Ramos, Alberto. 2014. "El alcalde de Cartagena es, tristemente, de esos cartageneros que presumen de virreinales y tienen nostalgia del látigo." Twitter. November 2, 2014. https://twitter.com/SalcedoRamos/status/529081837818482688.

Saldaña, Magdalena, and Rachel R. Mourão. 2018. "Reporting in Latin America: Issues and Perspectives on Investigative Journalism in the Region." *International Journal of Press/Politics* 23, no. 3: 299–323.

Salinas Arango, Natalia Andrea. 2018. "Encrucijada de la violencia asociada al fútbol: Entre el desagrado y la complacencia." *Trabajo Social* 20, no. 1: 49–68.

Sanchez Taylor, Jacqueline. 2006. "Female Sex Tourism: A Contradiction in Terms?" *Feminist Review*, no. 83: 42–59.

Sánchez-Garzoli, Gimena. 2018. "December Update: At Least 120 Activists Killed in Colombia So Far This Year." WOLA (Washington Office on Latin America), December 18, 2018. https://www.wola.org/2018/12/december-update-least-120-activists-killed-colombia-far-year/.

Sancho Gómez, Miguel Pablo. 2003. "Blaz de Lezo y Cartagena de Indias: Una perspectiva desde el siglo XXI." *Revista de Comunicación de la Sociedad Española de Estudios de la Comunicación Iberoamericana* 10: 75–94.

Sandel, Michael J. 2007. *The Case against Perfection: Ethics in the Age of Genetic Engineering.* Cambridge, MA: Harvard University Press.

Sandilands, Catriona. 1999. *The Good-Natured Feminist: Ecofeminism and the Quest for Democracy.* Minneapolis: University of Minnesota Press.

Sanín, Juan. 2016. "Colombia Was Passion: Commercial Nationalism and the Reinvention of Colombianness." In *Commercial Nationalism: Selling the Nation and Nationalizing the Sell,* edited by Zala Volcic and Mark Andrejevic, 46–64. London: Palgrave Macmillan.

Santofimio-Ortiz, Rodrigo. 2018. "El pensamiento de Antonio Gramsci en América Latina y Colombia." *Revista de Antropología y Sociología: VIRAJES* 20, no. 1: 177–196.

Santos Gómez, David. 2018. "La política a la mesa." *El Colombiano,* February 27, 2018. http://www.elcolombiano.com/opinion/columnistas/la-politica-a-la-mesa-DE8262234.

Santos Molano, Enrique. 2016. "Fútbol: Una pasión incontenible." *Credencial Historia,* September 2016. http://www.revistacredencial.com/credencial/historia/temas/futbol-una-pasion-incontenible.

Sartre, Jean-Paul. 2004. "Preface." In *The Wretched of the Earth,* edited by Frantz Fanon, 99–158. Translated by Richard Philcox. New York: Grove Press.

Schelling, F. E. 1914. "New Humanities for Old." *Classical Weekly* 7, no. 23: 179–184.

Schiffrin, Anya. 2017a. *Same Beds, Different Dreams? Charitable Foundations and Newsroom Independence in the Global South.* https://www.cima.ned.org/wp-content/uploads/2017/02/CIMA-Media-Philanthropy_Schiffrin.pdf.

———, ed. 2017b. *In the Service of Power: Media Capture and the Threat to Democracy.* Washington: Center for International Media Assistance.

Schiller, Herbert I. 1976. *Communication and Cultural Domination.* New York: International Arts and Sciences Press.

———. 1989. *Culture Inc.: The Corporate Takeover of Public Expression.* Oxford: Oxford University Press.

———. 1991. "Not Yet the Post-Imperialist Era." *Critical Studies in Mass Communication* 8, no. 1: 13–28.

Schimmel, Kimberly S., C. Lee Harrington, and Denise D. Bielby. 2007. "Keep Your Fans to Yourself: The Disjuncture between Sport Studies' and Pop Culture Studies' Perspectives on Fandom." *Sport in Society* 10, no. 4: 580–600.

Schmitt, Casey S. 2015. "Virtue in Corruption: Privateers, Smugglers, and the Shape of Empire in the Eighteenth-Century Caribbean." *Early American Studies: An Interdisciplinary Journal* 13, no. 1: 80–110.

Schopenhauer, Arthur. 2015. *Panerga and Paralipomena: Short Philosophical Essays*. Volume 2. Translated and edited by Adrian Del Caro and Christopher Janaway. Cambridge: Cambridge University Press.

Schreiber, Darren, Greg Fonzo, Alan N. Simmons, Christopher T. Dawes, Taru Flagan, James H. Fowler, and Martin P. Paulus. 2013. "Red Brain, Blue Brain: Evaluative Processes Differ in Democrats and Republicans." *PLoS ONE* 8, no. 2. http://journals.plos.org/plosone/article?id=10.1371/journal.pone.0052970.

Schwaller, John Frederick. 2011. *The History of the Catholic Church in Latin America: From Conquest to Revolution and Beyond*. New York: New York University Press.

Segoviana García, Jenny. 2011. "Dialéctica de la ilustración y sus aportaciones al estudio de los medios masivos." *Razón y Palabra* 75 (February–April). http://www.razonypalabra.org.mx/N/N75/monotematico_75/34_Segoviano_M75.pdf.

"Se investiga relación de préstamo de exalcalde Vélez con los 'Papeles de Panamá.'" 2016. *El Universal*, June 17, 2016. http://www.eluniversal.com.co/politica/se-investiga-relacion-de-prestamo-de-exalcalde-velez-con-los-papeles-de-panama-228487.

"Selección Colombia dice 'no' a la violencia contra mujeres." 2014. *El Universal*, April 16, 2014. https://www.eluniversal.com.co/deportes/seleccion-colombia-dice-no-la-violencia-contra-las-mujeres-157227-IWEU249364.

Sen, Amartya. 2000. *Development as Freedom*. New York: Alfred A. Knopf.

———. 2009. *The Idea of Justice*. Cambridge, MA: Belknap Press of Harvard University Press.

Serrano-Amaya, José Fernando. 2018. *Homophobic Violence in Armed Conflict and Political Transition*. London: Palgrave Macmillan.

Shanley, Patrick. 2018. "'Hitman 2's' Colombia Map Shows Off Another Massive, Lethal Sandbox." *Hollywood Reporter*, October 8, 2018. https://www.hollywoodreporter.com/heat-vision/hitman-2-colombia-map-hands-details-1150039.

Shapiro, Jacob, Abbey Steele, and Juan Vargas. 2014. "Endogenous Taxation in Ongoing Internal Conflict: The Case of Colombia." Development Bank of Latin America Corporación Andina de Fomento Working Paper 2014/07. http://scioteca.caf.com/bitstream/handle/123456789/763/Shapiro_Steele_Vargas_VF.pdf?sequence=1&isAllowed=y.

Sharma, Devinder. 2005. "Tsunamis, manglares y economía de mercado." Translated by Felisa Sastre. Rebelión, January 14, 2005. http://www.rebelion.org/noticia.php?id=10010.

Sharma, Vivek Swaroop. 2015. "A Social Theory of War: Clausewitz and War Reconsidered." *Cambridge Review of International Affairs* 28, no. 3: 327–347.

Sheinin, David M. K. 2015. "Boxing in the Making of a Colombian *Costeño* Identity." In *Sports Culture in Latin American History*, edited by David M. K. Sheinin, 139–160. Pittsburgh: University of Pittsburgh Press.

Sherriff, Lucy. 2018. "#MyColombia: 13 of the Best Things to Do in Colombia." CNN, July 9, 2018. https://edition.cnn.com/travel/article/things-to-do-colombia/index.html.

Shils, Edward. 1966. "Mass Society and Its Culture." In *Reader in Public Opinion and Communication*, 2nd ed., edited by Bernard Berelson and Morris Janowitz, 505–528. New York: Free Press.

Shiva, Vandana. 2005. "Lecciones del tsunami para quienes menosprecian a la madre tierra." Rebelión, January 15, 2005. http://www.rebelion.org/noticia.php?id=10045.

Sierra Becerra, Diana Carolina. 2017. "The First Black Miss Colombia and the Limits of Multiculturalism." *Latin American and Caribbean Studies* 12, no. 1: 71–90.

Sifuentes, Lírian. 2014. "Being a Woman, Young and Poor." *Feminist Media Studies* 14, no. 6: 976–992.

Silva, Eric Orion, and Clayton Cory Lowe. 2015. "Evolutionary Theory in Letters to the Editor." *Public Understanding of Science* 24, no. 4: 440–449.

Silva, Mauricio. 2013. *El 5-0*. Bogotá: Géminis.

Simmel, Georg. 1949. "The Sociology of Sociability." Translated by Everett C. Hughes. *American Journal of Sociology* 55, no. 3: 254–261.

Simon, Joel. 2015. *The New Censorship: Inside the Global Battle for Media Freedom*. New York: Columbia University Press.

Singhal, Arvind, Rafael Obregon, and Everett M. Rogers. 1994. "Reconstructing the Story of *Simplemente María*, the Most Popular *Telenovela* in Latin America of All Time." *Gazette* 54, no. 1: 1–15.

Sjoberg, Laura. 2013. *Gendering Global Conflict: Toward a Feminist Theory of War*. New York: Columbia University Press.

Sklar, Robert. 1992. *City Boys: Cagney, Bogart, Garfield*. Princeton, NJ: Princeton University Press.

Slavtcheva-Petkova, Vera. 2016. "Are Newspapers' Online Discussion Boards Democratic Tools or Conspiracy Theories' Engines? A Case Study on an Eastern European 'Media War.'" *Journalism and Mass Communication Quarterly* 93, no. 4: 1115–1134.

Small Arms Survey. 2016. "A Gendered Analysis of Violent Deaths." Small Arms Survey Research Notes 63, November 2016. http://www.smallarmssurvey.org/fileadmin/docs/H-Research_Notes/SAS-Research-Note-63.pdf.

Smith, Anthony D. 2000. *The Nation in History: Historiographical Debates about Ethnicity and Nationalism*. Oxford: Polity Press.

Smith, Chad L., Gregory Hooks, and Michael Lengefeld. 2014. "The War on Drugs in Colombia: The Environment, the Treadmill of Destruction and Risk-Transfer Militarism." *Journal of World-Systems Research* 20, no. 2: 185–206.

Smith, Dorothy E. 1987. *The Everyday World as Problematic: A Feminist Sociology*. Boston: Northeastern University Press.

Smith, Kimberly K. 2007. *African American Environmental Thought: Foundations*. Lawrence: University of Kansas Press.

Soderlund, Gretchen. 2005. "Running from the Rescuers: New U.S. Crusades Against Sex Trafficking and the Rhetoric of Abolition." *Feminist Formations* 17, no. 3: 64–87.

———. 2011. "The Rhetoric of Revelation: Sex Trafficking and the Journalistic Exposé." *Humanity: An International Journal of Human Rights, Humanitarianism, and Development* 2, no. 2: 193–211.

Soja, Edward W. 2010. *Seeking Spatial Justice*. Minneapolis: University of Minnesota Press.

Solano, Yusmidia. 2003. "Entramado actual del movimiento de mujeres en Colombia." In *Cartografía de mujeres, para pensar los derechos*, edited by María Eugenia Martínez, 98–111. Bogotá: Red Nacional de Mujeres/Corporación Humanizar.

Solidarity. 2001. "Paris May 1968." In *Beneath the Paving Stones: Situationists and the Beach, May 1968*, compiled by Dark Star. Edinburgh: AK Press/Dark Star.

Soloudre-La France, Renée. 2015. "Sailing Through the Sacraments: Ethnic and Cultural Geographies of a Port and its Churches—Cartagena de Indias." *Slavery and Abolition: A Journal of Slave and Post-Slave Studies* 36, no. 3: 460–477.

Sonneland, Holly K. 2018. "Explainer: What Is Colombia's Orange Economy?" Americas Society/Council of the Americas, December 4, 2018. https://www.as-coa.org/articles/explainer-what-colombias-orange-economy.

Sontag, Deborah. 2016. "The Secret History of Colombia's Paramilitaries and the U.S. War on Drugs." *New York Times*, September 11, 2016, A1.

Soper, Kate. 1995. *What Is Nature? Culture, Politics and the Nonhuman*. Oxford: Blackwell.

Sorel, George. 2004. *Reflections on Violence*. Edited by Jeremy Jennings. Translated by Thomas Ernest Hulme, rev. Jeremy Jennings. Cambridge: Cambridge University Press.

Soto, Martha. 2017. *Los goles de la cocaína*. Bogotá: Intermedio.

Spurrell, Megan. 2019. "Inside the Women Who Travel Trips: Our Inaugural Trip to Colombia." *Condé Nast Traveler*, March 8, 2019. https://www.cntraveler.com/gallery/inside-the-women-who-travel-trips-our-inaugural-trip-to-colombia.

Stanfield, Michael Edward. 2013. *Of Beasts and Beauty: Gender, Race, and Identity in Colombia*. Austin: University of Texas Press.

Stavenhagen, Rodolfo. 2002. "Indigenous Peoples and the State in Latin America: An Ongoing Debate." In *Multiculturalism in Latin America: Indigenous Rights, Diversity and Democracy*, edited by Rachel Sieder, 24–44. New York: Palgrave Macmillan.

Steele, Abbey, and Livia I. Schubiger. 2018. "Democracy and Civil War: The Case of Colombia." *Conflict Management and Peace Science* 35, no. 6: 587–600.

Stein, Alfredo, and Caroline Moser. 2014. "Asset Planning for Climate Change Adaptation: Lessons from Cartagena, Colombia." *Environment and Urbanization* 26, no. 1: 166–183.

Stevens, Evelyn P. 1973. "Marianismo: The Other Face of *Machismo* in Latin America." In *Female and Male in Latin America: Essays*, edited by Ann Pescatello, 89–101. Pittsburgh: University of Pittsburgh Press.

Stewart, Frances 2002. "Root Causes of Violent Conflict in Developing Countries." *British Medical Journal* 324, no. 7333: 342–345.

Stott, Robin, Richard Smith, Rowan Williams, and Fiona Godlee. 2019. "Schoolchildren's Activism is a Lesson for Health Professionals." *British Medical Journal*, no. 365: 1–2.

Strasser, Ulrike, and Heidi Tisman. 2010. "It's a Man's World? World History Meets the History of Masculinity, Latin American Studies, for Instance." *Journal of World History* 21, no. 1: 75–96.

Straubhar, Joseph. 2007. *World Television: From Local to Global*. London: Sage.

Strause, Jackie. 2016. "The Real DEA Agents of 'Narcos' Break Down What Season 2 Got Right." *Hollywood Reporter*, September 15, 2016. http://www.hollywoodreporter.com/lists/narcos-real-dea-agents-murphy-928933/item/murphy-pena-escobar-narcos-season-929031.

Streicker, Joel. 1995. "Policing Boundaries: Race, Class, and Gender in Cartagena, Colombia." *American Ethnologist* 22, no. 1: 54–74.

———. 1997. "Spatial Reconfigurations, Imagined Geographies, and Social Conflicts in Cartagena, Colombia." *Cultural Anthropology* 12, no. 1: 109–128.

Sturges, Fiona. 2019. "Lazy Homophobia Signals the End of the Road for Clarkson and Co." *Guardian*, January 31, 2019. https://www.theguardian.com/commentisfree/2019/jan/31/lazy-homophobia-the-grand-tour-jeremy-clarkson-amazon?utm_term=RWRpdG9yaWFsXod1YXJkaWFuVG9kYXlVS19XZWVrZGF5cyoxOTAyMDE%3D&utm_source=esp&utm_medium=Email&utm_campaign=GuardianTodayUK&CMP=GTUK_email.

Suárez Pinzón, Ivonne. 2015. "Violencia de género y violencia sexual del conflicto armado colombiano." *Cambios y Permanencias* 6: 173–203.

Suárez Serrano, Chema. 2016. "El periodismo en los conflictos armados del siglo XXI: Entre las nuevas tecnologías y las amenazas de siempre." *Revista del Instituto Español de Estudios Estratégicos* 8. http://revista.ieee.es/index.php/ieee/article/view/307.

Subcommission on Quaternary Stratigraphy, Working Group on the "Anthropocene." 2016. *What Is the "Anthropocene?" Current Definition and Status*. http://quaternary.stratigraphy.org/workinggroups/anthropocene/.

Taborda Herrera, Ernesto. 2015. "Hombre que rompió placa a los ingleses es aspirante a la Alcaldía de Cartagena." *El Universal*, March 6, 2015. https://www.eluniversal.com.co/politica/hombre-que-rompio-placa-los-ingleses-es-aspirante-la-alcaldia-de-cartagena-186801-LBEU285259.

Tao, Rongrong, Baojian Zhou, Feng Chen, Naifeng Liu, David Mares, Patrick Butler, and Naren Ramakrishnan. 2017. "Can Self-Censorship in News Media be Detected Algorithmically? A Case Study in Latin America." arXiv:1611.06947v2, March 17, 2017. https://arxiv.org/abs/1611.06947.

Tate, Julee Anne. 2007. "The Good and Bad Women of *Telenovelas*: How to Tell Them Apart Using a Simple Maternity Test." *Studies in Latin American Popular Culture*, no. 26: 97–111.

Tate, Winifred. 2007. *Counting the Dead: The Culture and Politics of Human Rights Activism in Colombia*. Berkeley: University of California Press.

Tatis Guerra, Gustavo. 2017. "Atabaques, una danza ancestral." *El Universal*, June 18, 2017. https://www.eluniversal.com.co/suplementos/facetas/atabaques-una-danza-ancestral-255736-FVEU367064.

Taussig, Michael. 2010. *The Devil and Commodity Fetishism*, rev. ed. Chicago: The University of Chicago Press.

Taylor, Luke. 2018. "Colombians Angry and Bemused by *The Sun's* Controversial Harry Kane 'Cocaine' Front Page." *Independent*, July 3, 2018. https://www.independent.co.uk/news/world/americas/harry-kane-england-colombia-the-sun-cocaine-front-page-newspaper-three-lions-a8429756.html.

"13 Wounded in Colombian Nightclub Explosion." 2018. AZERTAC, December 17, 2018. https://azertag.az/en/xeber/13_Wounded_in_Colombia_Nightclub_Explosion-1225053.

Thompson, Charis. 2006. "Back to Nature? Resurrecting Ecofeminism after Poststructuralist and Third-Wave Feminisms." *Isis* 97, no. 3: 505–512.

Thompson, E. P. 1971. "The Moral Economy of the English Crowd in the Eighteenth Century." *Past and Present*, no. 50: 76–136.

———. 1979. "The Secret State." *Race and Class* 20, no. 3: 219–242.

Thorne, Will. 2019. "TV Ratings: 'Jack Ryan' Season 2 Averaging 4.6 Million Viewers, Per Nielsen." *Variety*, December 3, 2019. https://variety.com/2019/tv/news/tv-ratings-jack-ryan-season-2-averaging-4-6-million-viewers-nielsen-1203422886/.

Tokatlian, Juan Gabriel. 1997. "Drogas psicoactivas ilícitas y política mundial: La indudable e inestable internacionalización de Colombia." In *Colombia entre la inserción y el aislamiento: la política exterior colombiana en los años noventa*, edited by S. Ramírez, S. and L. A. Restrepo. Bogotá: Siglo del Hombre Editores/IEPRI, Universidad Nacional.

Tolstoy, Leo. 1990. *Government Is Violence: Essays on Anarchism and Pacifism*. Edited by David Stephens. London: Phoenix Press.

Toro, Gustavo. 2013. "La política pública de turismo en Colombia." *Turismo y Sociedad* 2, no. 2: 9–15.

Torrado, Santiago. 2019. "Más de cien exguerrilleros que firmaron la paz han sido asesinados en Colombia desde 2016." *El País*, July 1, 2019. https://elpais.com/internacional/2019/06/29/colombia/1561827002_421510.html.

Torres, Jennifer Florez. 2011. "La Diplomacia Pública en una perspectiva comparada: Una estrategia de la política exterior y su implementación en la política colombiana." *Pensamiento Jurídico*, no. 30: 263–293.

Torres Velasco, Javier. 2019. "Civilization and Sport in Colombia's Drive to Modernization." *Journal of Mediterranean Knowledge* 4, no. 1: 55–77.

Transparency International. 2017. *Las Personas y la Corrupción: América Latina y el Caribe—Barómetro Global De la Corrupción*. https://www.transparency.org/whatwedo/publication/las_personas_y_la_corrupcion_america_latina_y_el_caribe.

Transparency International and Chr. Michelsen Institute. 2013. *Colombia: Overview of Corruption and Anti-Corruption*. Anti-Corruption Resource Centre. https://knowledgehub

.transparency.org/assets/uploads/helpdesk/373_Colombia_Overview_of_corruption_and_anti-corruption.pdf.

"Treasury Designates the Financial Core and Support Network of Colombian Criminal Group La Oficina de Envigado." 2014. U.S. Department of the Treasury, November 19, 2014. https://www.treasury.gov/press-center/press-releases/Pages/jl9705.aspx.

Trotsky, Leon. 1925. *Where Is Britain Going?* https://www.marxists.org/archive/trotsky/britain/wibg/ch08.htm.

———. 1970. *Leon Trotsky on Literature and Art.* Edited by Paul N. Siegel. New York: Pathfinder Press.

Tyor, Anna. 2013. "Cartagena's Gentrification, but for Whom?" *Colombia Politics*, December 20, 2013. http://www.colombia-politics.com/cartagena-gentrification/.

United Nations. 1993. *Declaration on the Elimination of Violence against Women.* http://www.un.org/documents/ga/res/48/a48r104.htm.

———. 2010. *The World's Women 2010: Trends and Statistics.* http://unstats.un.org/unsd/demographic/products/Worldswomen/WW_full%20report_color.pdf.

United Nations Conference on Trade and Development. 2013. "Trade in Creative Products Reached New Peak in 2011, UNCTAD Figures Show." UNCTAD, May 15, 2013. https://unctad.org/en/pages/newsdetails.aspx?OriginalVersionID=498.

———. 2015. *Creative Economy Outlook and Country Profiles: Trends in International Trade in Creative Industries.* https://unctad.org/en/PublicationsLibrary/webditcted2016d5_en.pdf.

United Nations Economic Commission for Latin America and the Caribbean. 2018. *Economic Survey of Latin America and the Caribbean 2018: Evolution of Investment in Latin America and the Caribbean: Stylized Facts, Determinants and Policy Challenges.* https://doi.org/10.18356/3b44d4a2-en.

United Nations Office on Drugs and Crime. 2013. *Global Study on Homicide 2013: Trends, Contexts, Data.* https://www.unodc.org/documents/data-and-analysis/statistics/GSH2013/2014_GLOBAL_HOMICIDE_BOOK_web.pdf.

———. 2014. *Global Study on Homicide 2013.* https://www.unodc.org/documents/data-and-analysis/statistics/GSH2013/2014_GLOBAL_HOMICIDE_BOOK_web.pdf.

———. 2018a. *Analysis of Drug Markets: Opiates, Cocaine, Cannabis, Synthetic Drugs.* https://www.unodc.org/wdr2018/prelaunch/WDR18_Booklet_3_DRUG_MARKETS.pdf.

———. 2018b. *Colombia: Monitoreo de territorios afectados por cultivos ilícitos 2017* https://www.unodc.org/documents/crop-monitoring/Colombia/Colombia_Monitoreo_territorios_afectados_cultivos_ilicitos_2017_Resumen.pdf.

——— 2018c. *Global Report on Trafficking in Persons 2018.* https://www.unodc.org/documents/data-and-analysis/glotip/2018/GLOTiP_2018_BOOK_web_small.pdf.

United Nations Verification Mission in Colombia. 2019. *Report of the Secretary-General S/2019/988.* https://reliefweb.int/sites/reliefweb.int/files/resources/S_2019_988_E.pdf.

UN Women. n.d. *Prevalence Data on Different Forms of Violence against Women.* https://evaw-global-database.unwomen.org/en/countries/americas/colombia.

United States of America against various. 2015. DSS: EMN/AH/DAL/SPN/MKM/PT/KDE/TH/BDM F. #2015R00747. United States District Court. Eastern District of New York, November 25, 2015.

United States Department of the Treasury, Office of Foreign Assets Control. 2019. *Specially Designated Nationals and Blocked Persons List.* https://www.treasury.gov/ofac/downloads/sdnlist.pdf.

United States Global Change Research Program. 2018. *Climate Change Impacts in the United States.* U.S. National Climate Assessment. https://nca2014.globalchange.gov/downloads.

Urbina Joiro, Hernán. 2006. *Entre las huellas de la India Catalina*. Sevilla: Academia de la Historia de Cartagena de Indias.

Uribe, Ana Berta. 2009. *Mi México imaginado: Televisión, telenovelas y migrantes*. Colima: Editorial Porrúa/El Colegio de la Frontera Norte/Universidad de Colima.

Uribe, María Victoria. 2018. "Phantasmatic Entities and Identities: Criminals without Guilt in Colombia." *Journal of Latin American Cultural Studies* 27, no. 4: 451–462.

Uribe Alarcón, María Victoria. 2011. "Against Violence and Oblivion: The Case of Colombia's Disappeared." Translated by Joseph Pierce. In *Meanings of Violence in Contemporary Latin America*, edited by Gabriela Polit Dueñas and María Helena Rueda, 37–52. New York: Palgrave Macmillan.

Uribe Aramburo, Nicolás Ignacio. 2018. "Violencia, psicología de masas y barras de fútbol." *Revista Criminalidad* 61, no. 1: 85–96.

Uribe Aramburo, Nicolás Ignacio, and Guillermo Alonso Castaño Pérez. 2014. "Barras de fútbol, consumo de drogas y violencia." *Psicología desde el Caribe* 31, no. 2: 243–279.

Uribe-Jongbloed, Enrique and Manuel A. Corredor-Aristizábal. 2020. "Creative Industries Policies and Conditions of Cinema Labor in Colombia in the 21st Century." *Creative Industries Journal*. https://doi.org/10.1080/17510694.2019.1709016.

Valdés, Carlos. 2017. "En Colombia la violencia no desaprece, se transforma." *Semana*, July 1, 2017. https://www.semana.com/nacion/articulo/carlos-valdes-director-del-instituto-de-medicina-legal-violencia-en-colombia/511538.

Valle, Melissa M. 2018. "The Discursive Detachment of Race from Gentrification in Cartagena de Indias, Colombia." *Ethnic and Racial Studies* 41, no. 7: 1235–1254.

Van Ausdal, Shawn. 2008. "When Beef Was King. Or Why Do Colombians Eat So Little Pork?" *Revista de Estudios Sociales* 29 (January/April). http://www.scielo.org.co/scielo.php?script=sci_arttext&pid=S0123-885X2008000100006.

van Manen, Max. 1990. *Researching Lived Experience: Human Science for an Action Sensitive Pedagogy*. Albany: SUNY Press.

Vargas, Ricardo Motta. 2009. "Prioridades ambientales en la region central de Colombia y su problemática en el recurso hídrico." *Revista Republicana* 6: 99–110.

Varoufakis, Yanis. 1998. *Foundations of Economics: A Beginner's Companion*. New York: Routledge.

Vásquez, Juan Gabriel. 2013. *The Sound of Things Falling*. New York: Riverhead.

Vaughn, Abigail. 2019. "Colombia, 1990–2010: Cooperation in the War on Drugs." In *Proxy Wars: Suppressing Violence through Local Agents*, edited by Eli Berman and David A. Lake, 80–109. Ithaca, NY: Cornell University Press.

Vázquez Montalbán, Manuel. 1987. "Barça, el ejército de un país desarmado." *Catalonia*, no. 1: 45.

Velandia-Morales, Andrea, and Juan Carlos Rincón. 2014. "Estereotipos y roles de género utilizados en la publicidad transmitida a través de la television." *Universitas Psychologica* 13, no. 2: 517–527.

Velasco, Marcela. 2016. "Injustice and Organisation in Anchicayá, Colombia: An Environmental Legal Case in a Hydropower Watershed." *Local Environment: The International Journal of Justice and Sustainability* 21, no. 6: 707–729.

Velásquez Forero, Augusto. 2010. "El fútbol como mercancía simbólica." *Ensayos de Economía* 37: 45–65.

Vélez, Beatriz. 2001. "La puesta en escena del género en el juego de fútbol." *Revista Educación Física y Deporte* 21, no. 2: 39–49.

Vélez-Maya, Margarita María, and Juan Carlos Arboleda-Ariza. 2016. "Memoria social y violencia en fútbol: Recuerdos institucionalizados en la prensa de Medellín, Colombia." *Pensando Psicología* 12, no. 20: 53–63.

Vergara-Figueroa, Aurora. 2018. *Afrodescendant Resistance to Deracination in Colombia: Massacre at Bellavista-Bojayá-Chocó.*New York: Palgrave Macmillan.

Vergara, Sintana E., Anders Damgaard, and Daniel Gomez. 2016. "The Efficiency of Informality: Quantifying Greenhouse Gas Reductions from Informal Recycling in Bogotá, Colombia." *Journal of Industrial Ecology* 20, no. 1: 107–119.

Villanueva Bustos, Alejandro. 2013. "Hinchas del fútbol, academia y nuevas emergencias urbanas." *Revista Colombiana de Sociología* 36, no. 1: 93–108.

Villarreal Méndez, Norma. 1994. "El camino de la utopía feminista en Colombia, 1975–1991." In *Mujer y participación política: Avances y desafíos en América Latina,* edited by Magdalena León, 181–204. Bogotá: Tercer Mundo.

Villasmil Faría, Liseth Alexandra. 2015. "Narconovelas: Retratos de la ambigüedad en la construcción de valores sociales." *Revista Ontosemiótica* 2, no. 4: 61–74.

Villota Galeano, Fabián Felipe. 2017. "Identidad nacional colombiana: Discursos, recurrencias y desafíos en contextos de globalización." *Textos y Sentidos,* no. 15: 47–70.

"Visita real: Detalles de la llegada del Príncipe Carlos a Colombia." 2014. *El País,* October 27, 2014. http://www.elpais.com.co/elpais/entretenimiento/noticias/visita-real-detalles-llegada-principe-carlos-colombia.

Visitcolombia. 2008. *Colombia, el riesgo es que te quieras quedar/Colombia, the only risk is wanting to stay*. March 17, 2008. https://www.youtube.com/watch?v=8kUU-DWOqmI.

Viveros, Mara. 2013. "Género, raza y nación: Los réditos políticos de la masculinidad blanca en Colombia." *Maguaré* 27, no. 1: 71–104.

Von Clausewitz, Carl. 1989. *On War.* Edited and translated by Michael Howard and Peter Paret. Princeton, NJ: Princeton University Press.

von der Lippe, Berit, and Rune Ottosen, eds. 2016. *Gendering War and Peace Reporting: Some Insights—Some Missing Links.* Göteborg: Nordicom.

von Germeten, Nicole. 2013. *Violent Delights: Sex, Race, and Honor in Colonial Cartagena de Indias.* Albuquerque: University of New Mexico Press.

von Humboldt, Alexander. 2009. *Letters of Alexander von Humboldt: Written between the Years 1827 and 1858, to Varnhagen von Ense; Together with Extracts from Varnhagen's Diaries, and Letters from Varnhagen and Others to Humboldt.* Cambridge: Cambridge University Press.

Wade, Peter. 2013. "Blackness, Indigeneity, Multiculturalism and Genomics in Brazil, Colombia and Mexico." *Journal of Latin American Studies,* no. 45: 205–33.

Wahl-Jorgensen, Karin. 2002. "The Construction of the Public in Letters to the Editor: Deliberative Democracy and the Idiom of Insanity." *Journalism* 3, no. 2: 183–204.

Waisbord, Silvio. 2000. *Watchdog Journalism in South America: News, Accountability, and Democracy.* New York: Columbia University Press.

Wallerstein, Immanuel. 1989. "Culture as the Ideological Battleground of the Modern World-System." *Hitotsubashi Journal of Social Studies* 21, no. 1: 5–22.

Watson, Peter J. 2018. "Colombia's Political Football: President Santos' National Unity Project and the 2014 Football World Cup." *Bulletin of Latin American Research* 37, no. 5: 598–612.

Watts, Jonathan. 2018. "We Have 12 Years to Limit Climate Change Catastrophe, Warns UN." *Guardian,* October 8, 2018. https://www.theguardian.com/environment/2018/oct/08/global-warming-must-not-exceed-15c-warns-landmark-un-report.

Wearden, Graeme, and Damian Carrington. 2019. "Teenage Activist Takes School Strikes 4 Climate Action to Davos." *Guardian,* January 24, 2019. https://www.theguardian.com/environment/2019/jan/24/school-strikes-over-climate-change-continue-to-snowball.

Weber, Max. 1946. *From Max Weber: Essays in Sociology.* Translated by and edited by H. H. Gerth and C. Wright Mills. New York: Free Press.

———. 1981. "Some Categories of Interpretive Sociology." Translated by E. E. Graber. *Sociological Quarterly* 22, no. 2: 151–180.

———. 1992. *The Protestant Ethic and the Spirit of Capitalism.* Translated by Talcott Parsons. London: Routledge.

Weber, Samuel. 2000. "The Future of the Humanities: Experimenting." *Culture Machine* 2. http://www.culturemachine.net/index.php/cm/article/viewArticle/311 (site discontinued).

Wells, H. G. 1902. *Anticipations of the Reaction of Mechanical and Scientific Progress upon Human Life and Thought*, 2nd ed. London: Chapman & Hall.

Wentz, Laurel. 2009. "Univision: YouTube's Most Pirated Broadcast TV Network." *AdvertisingAge*, February 12, 2009. http://adage.com/article/hispanic-marketing/univision-youtube-s-pirated-broadcast-tv-network/134572/.

Whitehouse, Harvey, and Brian McQuinn. 2013. "Divergent Modes of Religiosity and Armed Struggle." In *The Oxford Handbook of Religion and Violence*, edited by Michael Jerryson, Mark Juergensmeyer, and Margo Kitts, 701–730. Oxford: Oxford University Press.

Whitten-Woodring, Jenifer. 2009. "Watchdog or Lapdog? Media Freedom, Regime Type, and Government Respect for Human Rights." *International Studies Quarterly* 53, no. 3: 595–625.

Wickcreativo. 2012. *Nuevo logo, nueva imagen, marca país Colombia.* YouTube, September 7, 2012. https://www.youtube.com/watch?v=PvVGDHmMbYg.

Williams, Raymond. 1963. *The Long Revolution.* Harmondsworth: Penguin.

———. 1977. *Marxism and Literature.* London: Oxford University Press.

———. 1983. *Keywords: A Vocabulary of Culture and Society*, rev. ed. New York: Oxford University Press.

Williams, Raymond L. 2013. "Rural and Urban Rivers: Displacements and Replacements in the Modern Latin American Novel." *Hispanic Issues Online* 12: 195–211.

Wills, Maria E. 2011. *La memoria histórica desde la perspectiva de género: Conceptos y herramientas.* Bogotá: Grupo de Memoria Histórica.

"WiN sports dimayor censuran protesta futbolistas acolfutpro." 2019. *Pulzo*, October 6, 2019. https://www.pulzo.com/deportes/win-sports-dimayor-censuran-protesta-futbolistas-acolfutpro-PP779513.

Wittgenstein, Ludwig. 1965. "I: A Lecture on Ethics." *Philosophical Review* 74, no. 1: 3–12.

"Wonder Women and Macho Men." 2015. *Economist*, August 22, 2015. http://www.economist.com/news/americas/21661800-latin-american-women-are-making-great-strides-culture-not-keeping-up-wonder-women-and.

Woo, Chungwon, Yanghon Chung, Dongphil Chun, Seunghun Han, and Dukhee Lee. 2014. "Impact of Green Innovation on Labor Productivity and Its Determinants: An Analysis of the Korean Manufacturing Industry." *Business Strategy and the Environment* 23, no. 8: 567–576.

Woodward, Nicholas. 2018. "No a la sociedad enferma." *El Universal*, August 10, 2018. https://www.eluniversal.com.co/opinion/columna/no-la-sociedad-enferma-14941-GUEU401465.

World Bank. 1972. *Economic Growth of Colombia: Problems and Prospects: Report of a Mission Sent to Colombia in 1970 by the World Bank.* Chief of mission and coordinating author Dragoslav Avramovic. Baltimore, MD: Johns Hopkins University Press.

World Bank. 2018. *Afro-Descendants in Latin America: Toward a Framework of Inclusion.* https://openknowledge.worldbank.org/handle/10986/30201.

"World Cup Made of Cocaine Seized in Colombia." 2010. *Telegraph*, July 4, 2010. http://www.telegraph.co.uk/sport/football/world-cup/7870901/World-Cup-made-of-cocaine-seized-in-Colombia.html.

World Economic Forum. 2015. *Global Gender Gap Report 2015.* https://www.weforum.org/reports/global-gender-gap-report-2015.

World Health Organization (WHO). 2002. *World Report on Violence and Health*. www.who.int/.violence_injury_prevention/violence/world_report/en.

———. 2017. *Violence against Women*. http://www.who.int/news-room/fact-sheets/detail/violence-against-women.

World Travel and Tourism Council. 2018. *Travel and Tourism Economic Impact 2018: Colombia*. https://www.wttc.org/economic-impact/country-analysis/country-reports/.

Wu, Wenyuan. 2019. *Chinese Oil Enterprises in Latin America: Corporate Social Responsibility*. London: Palgrave Macmillan.

Xiang, Zheng, and Ulrike Gretzel. 2010. "Role of Social Media in Online Travel Information Search." *Tourism Management* 31, no. 2: 179–188.

Yang, Guobin. 2009. *The Power of the Internet in China: Citizen Activism*. New York: Columbia University Press.

Yang, Raina. 2018. "5 Reasons Why Colombia Should Be on Your Travel List." *The Daily Californian*, June 29, 2018. http://www.dailycal.org/2018/06/29/5-reasons-colombia-travel-list/.

Yardi, Sarita, and Danah Boyd. 2010. "Dynamic Debates: An Analysis of Group Polarization Over Time on Twitter." *Bulletin of Science, Technology and Society* 30, no. 5: 316–327.

Young, Iris Marion. 2000. *Inclusion and Democracy*. New York: Oxford University Press.

Yúdice, George. 2002. *El recurso de la cultura: Usos de la cultura en la era global*. Barcelona: Editorial Gedisa.

———. 2016. "Músicas plebeyas." In *Memorias, saberes y redes de las culturas populares en América Latina*, edited by Graciela Maglia and Leonor Hernández Fox, 94–139. Bogotá: Universidad Externado de Colombia, Facultad de Ciencias Sociales y Humanas.

———. 2018. "Innovations in Cultural Policy and Development in Latin America." *International Journal of Cultural Policy* 24, no. 5: 647–663.

Zavall, Lisa, Ezra M. Markowitz, and Elke U. Weber. 2015. "How Will I Be Remembered? Conserving the Environment for the Sake of One's Legacy." *Psychological Science* 26, no. 2: 231–236.

Zuleta, Estanislao. 2015. *Colombia: Violencia, democracia y derechos humanos*. Bogotá: Ariel.

INDEX

ABOUT THE AUTHORS

TOBY MILLER is Stuart Hall Professor of Cultural Studies, Universidad Autónoma Metropolitana—Cuajimalpa. The author and editor of over forty books, his most recent volumes are *How Green Is Your Smartphone?* (co-authored, 2020), *El Trabajo Cultural* (2018), *Greenwashing Culture* (2018), *Greenwashing Sport* (2018), and *The Routledge Companion to Global Cultural Policy* (co-edited, 2018).

ALFREDO SABBAGH FAJARDO is in the department of social communication at the Universidad del Norte in Barranquilla, Colombia, where he has served as director of the School of Social Communication and Journalism and director of the Media Production Center. He currently combines teaching with media production, broadcast journalism, and his newspaper column.

OLGA LUCIA SORZANO is an economist with a PhD in cultural policy and management from City, University of London. She worked at the Colombian National Planning Department and the Ministry of Foreign Affairs for over ten years and is currently a postdoctoral researcher at the Royal Holloway, London, and an independent researcher on various art projects.

ANAMARIA TAMAYO-DUQUE is an assistant professor in the performing arts department of the Universidad de Antioquia, Colombia. She has a BA in anthropology from the Universidad de Antioquia, Colombia, and a PhD in critical dance studies from University of California, Riverside. Her current research interrogates the role of embodied practices in processes of memory construction and reconciliation during the Colombian conflict in the Pacific coast.

MARTA MILENA BARRIOS is an associate professor in the School of Communication and Journalism at the Universidad del Norte, Barranquilla, Colombia. Her research focuses on journalism, social media analysis, conflict, and disaster and risk management. Her articles have been published in *Feminist Media Studies, Journalism, Journalism Studies,* and the *Catalan Journal of Communication & Cultural Studies,* among others.

JESÚS ARROYAVE is a full professor in the School of Communication and Journalism at the Universidad del Norte, Barranquilla, Colombia. His areas of interest include journalism and media studies, health communication, and communication for social change. His research has been published in journals such as *Journalism, Journalism Studies, Feminist Media Studies, Palabra Clave,* and *Signo y Pensamiento.*